Relationship Counselling for Children, Young People and Families

Also by Kathryn Geldard and David Geldard

Counselling Children: A Practical Introduction (3rd edn, SAGE, 2008)

Counselling Adolescents: The Pro-active Approach (2nd edn, SAGE, 2004)

Basic Personal Counselling: A Training Manual for Counsellors (5th edn, Prentice-Hall/Pearson Education, 2005) (available in Australia and New Zealand)

Working with Children in Groups: A Handbook for Counsellors, Educators, and Community Workers (Palgrave Macmillan, 2001)

Counselling Skills in Everyday Life (Palgrave Macmillan, 2003)

Practical Counselling Skills: An Integrative Approach (Palgrave Macmillan, 2005) (available in UK and Europe)

Personal Counseling Skills: An Integrated Approach (C.C. Thomas, 2008) (available in the USA)

Relationship Counselling for Children, Young People and Families

**Kathryn Geldard and
David Geldard**

Los Angeles • London • New Delhi • Singapore • Washington DC

First published 2009

SAGE Publications Ltd
1 Oliver's Yard
55 City Road
London EC1Y 1SP

SAGE Publications Inc.
2455 Teller Road
Thousand Oaks, California 91320

SAGE Publications India Pvt Ltd
B 1/I 1 Mohan Cooperative Industrial Area
Mathura Road
New Delhi 110 044

SAGE Publications Asia-Pacific Pte Ltd
33 Pekin Street #02-01
Far East Square
Singapore 048763

Library of Congress Control Number: 2008931885

British Library Cataloguing in Publication data

A catalogue record for this book is available from the British Library

ISBN 978-1-84787-550-1
ISBN 978-1-84787-551-8 (pbk)

Typeset by C&M Digitals (P) Ltd, Chennai, India
Printed and bound in Great Britain by TJ International Ltd, Padstow, Cornwall
Printed on paper from sustainable resources

Contents

List of Figures and Tables

Figures

Tables

Introduction

This book provides a practical introduction to relationship counselling for members of the family and the whole family. As counsellors in our private practice we have focused for many years on counselling children, young people, and their parents. This work has encompassed whole family therapy together with individual and subgroup counselling. As a consequence of our counselling work, we saw the need for an introductory textbook which would be useful for new counsellors who were inexperienced in relationship counselling. Our hope is that this book will also be useful for experienced counsellors who wish to use it as a reference and source of practical ideas.

We believe that this book is different from other textbooks in the area as its focus is not only on family therapy, and is not limited to couple relationship counselling, but describes an integrative practical relationship counselling approach. The approach described in this book stresses the importance of Communication, Awareness, Choice, and Outcomes, hence the acronym CACHO. The CACHO model, is useful when working with individuals, subgroups within a family, and the family as a whole. Additionally, we believe there is a need for a text describing the practical application of those skills which are most suitable for producing relationship change. In this book, we have placed considerable emphasis on describing specific practical counselling strategies and techniques for addressing relationship issues.

Throughout the book we stress the importance of a clearly defined theory of change as being central to any integrative model of counselling. Consequently, we have explained the basis for the theory of change which underpins the CACHO model and which, we believe, best suits an integrative approach to relationship counselling.

By using an integrative approach based on a single, well-defined theory of change, we are able to take advantage of using a number of strategies taken from a variety of counselling approaches in order to promote change over a short period of time. As explained by Street (2006), it has been found that positive results from all types of interactive and systemically based therapies typically occur in treatments of short duration, that is less than 20 sessions. In our experience, the practical strategies described in this book are generally effective in producing change within a limited period of time.

The book is divided into five parts. The first of these gives an overview of relationship counselling, describing established models and explaining the integrative CACHO model. Also in Part One, we describe the use of co-therapists and reflecting teams as part of the counselling process and discuss the counselling skills useful when practising relationship counselling. Subsequent parts of the book address relationship counselling issues specifically for different members of the family.

Theory and practice are sequentially described as the reader progresses through the book. However, we have also made each chapter complete and useful in itself, so that the book is user-friendly as a reference. In order to do this, we have cross-referenced from one chapter to other chapters where necessary so that when reading a particular chapter the reader can easily access relevant material which may have been discussed elsewhere in the book.

As counsellors, we are interested in people's perceptions of the differences between counselling and therapy, and counsellors and therapists. Cynthia Reynolds (2005), when discussing Gestalt therapy with children, writes about her training with regard to differentiating between counselling and therapy. Counselling was viewed as a more short-term, educational approach and therapy as a long-term remedial approach. However, Reynolds goes on to say that in working with children in schools she has found the boundary to be blurred and indistinct. We recognize that there are many different points of view with regard to the issue. We take the view that counselling is therapeutic, it may be short-term and educational, or it may be long-term and involve psychotherapeutic processes. Consequently, in this book we do not differentiate between counselling and therapy or counsellors and therapists; we use these words interchangeably.

We hope that you enjoy reading this book and will find it useful as an introduction to relationship counselling and a source of practical ideas for counselling a family and its members.

Kathryn and David Geldard

Part 1

Overview of Relationship Counselling

In this part of the book we will begin by discussing a number of well-known, established models of relationship counselling which generally come under the umbrella of family therapy. We will explain why we believe that family therapy is most effective if integrated with individual counselling and/or subgroup counselling. In particular, we will describe our own integrative relationship counselling model, called the CACHO model. We will also discuss the advantages of using a co-therapist and/or reflecting team, and those counselling skills which are particularly suitable for relationship counselling.

1

Established Models of Relationship Counselling

Relationship counselling wasn't considered as an option for working with clients until the 1950s. Before that time all counselling work was carried out with individuals and relationships were only considered in terms of their past impact on the individual (Street, 2006). Interest in relationship counselling began with the work of Gregory Bateson in Palo Alto, California. He investigated communication processes in families and, in collaboration with others, examined the effect of the family system on family members diagnosed with schizophrenia (Bateson et al., 1956). Following on from this work, some British psychodynamic counsellors began to see clients conjointly rather than individually (Nichols and Schwartz, 2007). Since then a number of different approaches to relationship counselling have been developed.

In this book, we will promote the use of a particular integrative approach to relationship counselling that we have called the CACHO model. Before discussing this model (in Chapter 2), we will review a number of significant relationship counselling models that have been developed and which contribute to the CACHO model.

The majority of family therapy approaches have as their foundation the notion that families operate as systems. Notable exceptions to the systemic approaches to family therapy are those approaches that are based on constructivist theory. Consequently, before describing a number of significant relationship counselling models, we will discuss systems theory and constructivist theory.

Systems Theory

System theory describes a family as a system which includes both the individuals in the family and the way these individuals function together (Dattilio, 1998). Further, the family system is made up of smaller systems called subsystems. Typically, subsystems within the family include the parental subsystem, the spousal subsystem, and the sibling subsystem. In any family, there are likely to be other subsystems as a result of factors such as gender, attachments, alliances, and coalitions. Additionally, a family as a group can be seen as a subsystem of a number of larger systems. For example, the family is a subsystem of the community in which the family lives. Also, the family will relate to a number of other systems, such as the school system, the work system, and the health system.

> **Families are systems comprising interactive subsystems**

There are boundaries surrounding every system and subsystem and the properties of these boundaries are important in understanding how the system functions. Most of these boundaries are semi-permeable; that is to say some things can pass through them while others cannot. In families, boundaries are invisible barriers which perform a number of functions, including regulating the amount of contact with others. Generally speaking, boundaries are useful in safeguarding the separateness and autonomy of the family and its subsystems.

Homoeostasis

Homoeostasis is an important concept related to family systems theory. Homoeostasis is a process that enables a system to maintain itself in a state of dynamic balance. However, the way balance within a family system is maintained can sometimes be problematic even though homoeostasis has a stabilizing influence on the family. For example, imagine that a family has come to counselling believing that an emotionally disturbed child is always causing tension between the parents. It may emerge that in order to avoid focusing on tension in their own relationship the parents are focusing their attention on the child who draws attention to herself by acting out. As a consequence, homoeostasis in the system enables the parents to maintain a stable but stressful relationship with each other but in this instance at the cost of the child's emotional well-being.

The effect of change on a system

The one central principle agreed upon by family therapy practitioners regardless of their particular approach is that change in one part of a family system is likely to cause responses from other parts of the system. These responses can sometimes be in the form of resistance to change, as the family will naturally tend to seek homoeostasis rather than allow the system to temporarily go out of balance before seeking a new homoeostasis.

Homoeostasis can be a restraint to change

Constructivist Theory

As discussed previously, not all family therapy approaches are grounded in systemic theory. The constructivist family therapy approaches, such as narrative therapy and solution oriented therapy, believe that focusing on systemic issues is unimportant. They contend that it is more important to take account of each individual family member's perceptions of the family and to discover how the family as a whole makes meaning of their family's experience of the problem. However, Lowe (2004) does suggest that in practice a considerable degree of overlap exists between counsellors trained in systemic approaches and constructive family therapists.

Whereas systems theory contributes to family counselling by enabling us to see how people's lives are shaped by the interchanges with those around them, constructivism emphasizes that individuals have their own subjective experience of reality which gives meaning to the way their families function. Constructivism invites us to look beyond behaviour to the ways each individual family member perceives, interprets, and constructs their experience of living in the family.

Established Models of Family Therapy

We have selected for discussion those models of relationship counselling that provide concepts and strategies which can readily be incorporated into an integrated model of counselling, such as the CACHO model described in Chapter 2.

The following approaches will be discussed:

- Multigenerational family therapy
- Strategic family therapy
- Experiential family therapy
- Structural family therapy
- Constructive family therapy

Multigenerational Family Therapy

Murray Bowen was one of the early pioneers in family therapy although he was more concerned with theory than developing techniques. This was evident in his work with families, where he focused on helping the family to develop insights (Bowen, 1978). His theory evolved from psychoanalytic principles and practices and is sometimes referred to as multigenerational, transgenerational, or intergenerational family therapy.

A brief outline of Bowen's theory and concepts follows.

Differentiation of self

Central to Bowen's theory was the emphasis he placed on the importance of each family member differentiating. He described differentiation as both an intrapsychic and interpersonal concept.

The intrapsychic concept of differentiation of self involved the psychological separation of the individual's intellect from their emotions, so that they were able to respond in a reasoned way without automatically responding in an emotionally reactive way. The interpersonal concept of differentiation of self refers to the ability of an individual to separate emotionally from others and become independent as an individual.

Multigenerational transmission processes

Bowen believed that unhelpful family dynamics from a previous generation are transmitted from one generation to the next. He suggested that individuals tend to repeat in their marital choices and other significant relationships patterns of relating learnt in their families of origin and that they pass similar patterns on to their children. Consequently, he believed that the only effective way to resolve current family problems was to change the individual's interactions with their family of origin.

An example of a multigenerational transmission process is the suggestion that people who are enmeshed with their family of origin tend to marry others with whom they can become enmeshed, resulting in two undifferentiated individuals seeking and finding each other and becoming a couple. This is a situation that Bowen perceived as undesirable.

Emotional cut-off

Bowen insisted that adults must resolve their emotional attachment to their families of origin. However, he did not believe that a satisfactory solution was to attempt to differentiate themselves from their family of origin by seeking geographic separation or by the use of psychological barriers such as not talking to their parents. Even though this might resemble a differentiation process and freedom in the form of emotional cut-off, according to Bowen such behaviour did not indicate true differentiation and emancipation, but was a flight of extreme emotional distancing in an attempt to break emotional ties (Nichols and Schwartz, 2007).

Triangulation

Bowen recognized that anxiety can easily develop within intimate relationships. He suggested that two people in such a situation might recruit a third person into the relationship, thereby reducing their anxiety and gaining stability in the relationship. This is called triangulation and will be discussed further in Chapter 6. He believed that the more poorly people within the family were differentiated, the more intense and insistent triangulation efforts would be. Further, he suggested that the least well differentiated person in the family was particularly vulnerable to being drawn into a triangle to reduce the tension between others.

Using genograms with families

Bowen developed a graphic way of investigating the beginnings of the presenting problem. Called genograms, he used diagrams to map out the family over at least three generations (genograms will be discussed more fully in Chapter 7). When using genograms in Bowenian family therapy, the intention was to modify the influence of historical and predisposing factors arising from the family of origin. Genograms are a relatively emotion-free way of collecting information that makes sense to the family and connects them to the therapeutic exploratory process.

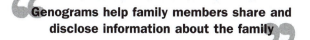

Genograms help family members share and disclose information about the family

Strategic Family Therapy

Strategic family therapy was developed in the USA by a number of contributors, including Bateson, Watzlawick, Haley, and Madanes, who were associated with the Mental Research Institute, Palo Alto, California, and in Milan, Italy, by Selvini Palazzoli, Boscolo, Cecchin, and others (Nichols and Schwartz, 2007). In this model of relationship counselling emphasis is placed on cybernetic and structural explanations of family dynamics.

Cybernetic explanations of family dynamics

The cybernetic concepts of *circular causality* and *feedback loops* provide an explanation of the way problems escalate in a family when family members continue to respond to a problem by applying more of the same attempted solutions (see Chapter 6 for a discussion of circular causality).

Structural explanations of family dynamics

Structural explanations of how problems develop rely on the recognition that families have *unspoken rules* that govern behaviour. In strategic family therapy it is assumed that problems result when family members try to protect or control one another covertly by using the unspoken rules. These rules do serve a purpose, and this is to preserve family homoeostasis. They help the family to continue in a stable equilibrium when confronted by behaviours, events, or situations which threaten to alter the family dynamic. Because the unspoken rules inevitably constrain change, strategic therapists attempt to change the rules. They do this through the use of a number of strategies, including reframing behaviour or changing the interpretation of particular behaviours.

The counsellor is the expert

In strategic therapy, the counsellor is considered to be an *expert* consultant who is in charge of the session and has the responsibility for initiating change. The counsellor gives family members specific directives on what they are to do with the aim of changing the manner in which the individual members behave in their relationships with other family members. The directives given may be straightforward or paradoxical.

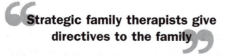

Strategic family therapists give directives to the family

Straightforward directives

Straightforward directives include giving advice, making suggestions, coaching, and giving assignments. For example, if a father was indirectly siding with his daughter (who was wetting her bed) against his wife, the strategic therapist might direct the father to wash the sheets when the daughter wet the bed. This directive would be designed to disengage the daughter and father.

Paradoxical interventions

Paradoxical interventions are intended to circumvent the clients' natural resistance to change. In using such interventions, clients may be asked to exaggerate or even perfect problematic behaviour. For example, a mother who is overly involved with her daughter, watching everything she does, may be asked to increase her behaviour and 'hover' over her daughter every waking minute. This intervention would be intended to entice the mother to protest that the daughter is not taking enough responsibility for herself.

Use of a co-therapist and/or therapeutic team

Strategic therapists from the Milan group stress the importance of working with co-therapists and of the counselling session being observed by other members of the therapy team (Selvini Palazzoli et al., 1980). This has the advantage of providing different perspectives of the family and its interactions.

Use of circular questions

The Milan group placed considerable emphasis on the use of circular questions, as described in Chapters 4 and 8. Additionally, they believed that it was important that the clients should not view the therapist as being aligned with, or forming a judgement about, any member of the group.

> **"The Milan group introduced the use of circular questions and an observing team"**

Use of positive connotation

Another important strategy employed by the Milan group, was that of positive connotation. Positive connotation was achieved by using a reframing technique which positively connotes the problem and the behaviours of all members of the system, and in particular that of the symptomatic member. For example, the therapist might say, 'We think we understand why you are all behaving in this way, and believe your behaviour is motivated by good intentions and the desire to alleviate your anxiety about …'.

Hypothesizing

The Milan group also believed in hypothesizing about the family's interactions and in particular about the function the symptoms served in the family. The counsellor would then explore the hypothesis with the family. When a hypothesis was rejected by the family, it was not considered a failure but was seen as promoting greater understanding.

Experiential Family Therapy

Major contributors to experiential family therapy included Carl Whittaker, Virginia Satir, August Napier, David Keith, and Leslie Greenberg (Nichols and Schwartz, 2007). Experiential family therapy is existential, humanistic, and phenomenological.

An *existentialist* perspective suggests that the only way human beings can make sense of their existence is through their personal experiences. Thus, existentialist counselling requires the clients to have a personal experience which will bring them in touch with their emotions during the therapeutic process.

A *humanistic* perspective requires a belief in the natural wisdom of honest communication and emotion, and that people are naturally resourceful and, if left to their own devices, will be energetic, creative, loving and productive.

Phenomenology is concerned with how we try to make sense of the world. The phenomenological perspective involves forming constructs which encapsulate an individual's concepts but these constructs can be revised and replaced by new constructs as new information becomes available.

According to this model, healthy families allow for individuality as well as togetherness, and individual family members feel safe enough to be honest about their feelings and free enough to be themselves. In contrast, families who experience problems are seen to be locked into self-protection and avoidance. In seeking security they restrict their emotions and desires.

Experiential family therapists focus on the subjectivity of the individual. They believe that all members of a family have the right to be themselves and the needs of the family sometimes suppress this individuation. Experiential family therapists help individuals to get in touch with their honest emotions, disclose them, and then forge more genuine family ties from this enhanced authenticity. They believe that these encounters must be reciprocal, which requires the therapist to be genuine instead of hiding behind a professional role.

Role of the therapist

The therapist is seen as a catalyst for change, using their personal impact on the family. Thus, Carl Whitaker, an experiential family therapist, insisted on sharing his own feelings with the family. Clearly, this raised transference and counter-transference issues. However, he believed that to minimize counter-transference it was essential to share his own feelings openly (Whitaker, 1976).

As an experiential therapist Virginia Satir's goal was to help clarify communication in the family and move people away from complaining towards finding solutions. She supported the self-esteem of family members by pointing out their positive intentions (Satir and Baldwin, 1983).

> ❝Experiential family therapists see themselves as a catalyst for change❞

Experiential therapists are usually active and personally involved in the counselling process, making use of expressive techniques such as strategies from Gestalt therapy and psychodrama. In using these techniques, the experiential counsellor focuses on the immediate here-and-now experience, and expression of feelings. The goal in using these techniques is to give the family an experience which enables them to get in touch with their emotions and increases their awareness of how they function. The experiential techniques provide an opportunity for experimentation with alternative ways of functioning. A good example of an experiential technique is the use of family sculpture. This strategy and a number of other experiential strategies are described in Chapter 9.

Structural Family Therapy

Salvador Minuchin was the originator of structural family therapy. Minuchin (1974) placed emphasis on:

1. Family structure.
2. Subsystems.
3. Boundaries.

Family structure

In any family, the family members will interact with each other in particular sequences or organized patterns. These define the family structure. For example, most families have some kind of hierarchical structure with adults and children having different amounts of authority. Even though most family structures have some common features, each family will have its own idiosyncratic ways of relating which are particular to the family. Thus, in a particular family, we may find that one parent assumes a powerful role as an organizer while the other parent takes a low-key role. In another family, the two parents may work collaboratively, sharing their responsibilities.

Subsystems

A family system contains subsystems of members who join together for various purposes. According to structural family therapy, a subsystem may consist of only one family member, or of a dyad, or of a larger group of family members. In most families, there is a parental subsystem and a sibling subsystem. However, there are likely to be other subsystems. For example, there may be a subsystem consisting of a mother and son who are acting in partnership or coalition for a specific purpose, such as mutual support against a perceived aggressor in the family. It is important to recognize that an individual family member may belong to more than one subsystem; if a mother and son are in a subsystem, it is also possible that the mother will be in a subsystem with her spouse and that the son will be in a subsystem with other siblings.

Boundaries

The family system and the subsystems within the family will all have boundaries around them. These boundaries protect the separateness and autonomy of each system or subsystem. While some boundaries will be rigid, others will be more diffuse. Rigid boundaries limit contact with outside systems with the advantage that a subsystem protected by a rigid boundary can operate very independently. A disadvantage of a rigid boundary is disengagement from other systems, with the result that contact, warmth, affection, and nurturing from those outside the boundary is restricted. Diffuse boundaries permit a higher degree of contact with other subsystems, which may result in feelings of mutual support at the expense of independence and autonomy. Whereas rigid boundaries may result in disengagement, diffuse boundaries may result in enmeshment. Members of a family where there is a high degree of enmeshment are likely to be supportive of each other and emotionally close but at the cost of their independence and autonomy.

Adaptive family functioning

Structural family therapists emphasize the need for a parental hierarchy where the parents work together in managing the family, but believe that what is required is for a family to be able to vary their family structure on an ongoing basis in order to adapt to changing family circumstances and developmental stages. For example, as children grow into adolescence it is usually appropriate for the style of parenting to change to meet the needs of the emerging adult. In particular, as an adolescent seeks to individuate their relationship with the family and the subsystems within the family are likely to need to change.

> **Family structures need to change to adapt to circumstances and developmental stages**

Unfortunately, in response to situational and developmental changes, some families respond by trying to increase the rigidity of structures that are no longer functional. This often leads to disturbance and unhappiness in the family.

Therapeutic processes

Structural family therapists attempt to bring about change to a family's structure with the expectation that doing this will result in solving the family's problems. Frequently, the goal will be to create an effective hierarchical structure where the parents are in charge and functioning together as a cohesive subsystem.

The structural family therapist makes hypotheses with regard to the family structure and invites family members to communicate directly in an attempt to modify unhelpful patterns. During this process the therapist will intervene forcefully at appropriate times in order to directly confront the family with what the therapist considers are unhelpful elements of the family structure.

Constructive Family Therapy

Constructive family therapy relies on understanding families rather than focusing on theories about how families 'normally' function. Thus, constructive therapists view each family as unique, with its own preferred way of functioning. Instead of focusing on pathology, or what is wrong with the family, they focus their attention on the experiences and hopes of family members. They view the family as being made up of different members, each with their own individual stories about the family (Parry and Doan, 1994). Family therapy is then seen as counselling, where the focus is on helping individual family members to get along better with each other by coordinating their differing stories (O'Hanlon and Wilk, 1987).

Gergen (2000) identified four characteristics underpinning constructive therapy practice:

1. A focus on meaning.
2. Therapy as co-construction.
3. A focus on relationship.
4. Value sensitivity.

A focus on meaning

Rather than focusing on what is 'really there', constructivist therapists seek to find out through the language of conversation, narrative, and consultation, the way the family makes sense of their experience through the 'story' they have created about the family. The 'story' of the family is not derived directly from the facts, but is negotiated and co-constructed through social conversations within the family.

Therapy as co-construction

Therapy as co-construction suggests that from a constructionist perspective meaning is not communicated from the therapist to the client but is generated collaboratively. The therapist's role is in structuring the conversation using a consultative approach and this structuring is continually guided by client feedback.

A focus on relationship

The constructivist approach believes that meaning is not made from one individual mind but is derived from the relationship between people and involves an ongoing process of negotiation and coordination with others. Constructive family therapy uses the therapeutic session as a space in which clients can discover and expand their 'stories'.

Value sensitivity

Constructive therapists are sensitive to the values held by them and those held within a family. Constructive therapy practice encourages a process of reflexivity so that assumptions which are taken for granted can be suspended. Consequently, there is a shift in emphasis from the objective application of professional knowledge to a consideration of the values inherent in the therapist's practice.

Constructivist approaches

Under the umbrella of constructive family therapy there are a number of distinct approaches, with solution-oriented family therapy and narrative family therapy being the two most commonly practised.

Solution-oriented family therapy is derived from brief solution-focused counselling pioneered by Steve de Shazer (1985). The emphasis is on what clients want to be different, how making the required changes will make a difference to their lives, how they will identify that these changes are occurring, whether these changes have occurred already and how this was achieved.

Narrative family therapy was developed by Michael White and David Epston (1990). Narrative therapists spend time discussing the problem in a way that avoids blame and invalidation, and encourages the possibility of an alternative picture. Narrative therapists use a process of externalizing and encourage family members to take a position with regard to this externalized story of their lives. By separating the problem from the people in the family, family members are invited to reflect on the effects of the problem, to adopt a preferred stance towards the problem, and to discover the choices that are available.

Summary

Table 1.1 summarizes the models of family therapy which have been described in this chapter. These are not the only models of relationship counselling available, but they are models which provide concepts, strategies, and techniques that we have found to be useful when developing the integrative relationship counselling CACHO model. The CACHO model, which guides our family counselling practice, is described in the next chapter.

TABLE 1.1   *Established models of family therapy*

	Multigenerational family therapy	Strategic family therapy	Experiential family therapy	Structural family therapy	Constructive family therapy
Key figures	Bowen	Bateson, Madanes, Selvini Palazzoli	Satir, Whitaker	Minuchin	de Shazer White
Goals	To block triangulation and encourage members of the family to move towards differentiation	Identify interactional sequences that maintain a problem	Attempt to reduce defensiveness and facilitate open and honest expression of feelings and thoughts	Realign psychological boundaries and strengthen hierarchical organization	Identify resources for overcoming the problem. Deconstruct the problem and co-construct a new life story
Function of counsellor	To guide objective research, teach	Active director of change, problem-solving	Active facilitator, challenger	Promoter of change in family structure	Listener and questioner, collaborator to find solutions
Process of change	Cognitive processes lead to an understanding of family of origin	Change occurs through action-oriented directives and paradoxical interventions	Awareness-raising and seeds of change are planted in therapy confrontations. Family moves to new possibilities and new integration	Therapist joins the family in a leadership role to change structures and sets boundaries	Focus on solutions. Life stories are reauthored
Techniques	Genograms and de-triangulation of relationships	Hypothesizing, reframing, amplifying	Empathy, sculpting, role-playing, self-disclosure, confrontation	Boundary-making techniques, unbalancing and tracking	Adopting a not-knowing position, questions of curiosity, externalizing the problem

KEY POINTS

- Systems theory involves the notion that families are systems that interact with other systems and have subsystems within them.
- Families naturally seek homoeostasis, but for change to occur the system needs to temporarily destabilize before seeking a new position of homoeostasis.

- Multigenerational family therapy places emphasis on the way patterns of behaviour are passed from generation to generation.
- Strategic family therapy is based on cybernetic, structural, and functional explanations of family functioning.
- Strategic family therapists offer straightforward and paradoxical directives to the family.
- Experiential family therapists use expressive techniques to help the family experience their emotions and enhance their awareness of how the family functions.
- Structural family therapists intervene in an attempt to change the family structure with the expectation that this will solve the family's problem.
- Constructive family therapy relies on understanding families rather than on focusing on theories about how families 'normally' function.
- Constructive family therapy focuses on meaning, relationship, and value sensitivity. It focuses on helping family members to improve their relationships by coordinating their differing stories.

QUESTIONS FOR GROUP DISCUSSION OR STUDENT ASSIGNMENTS

1. Describe your own family or another family you know in terms of family systems theory.
2. Describe a family, either real or invented, where there is a problem within the family. Briefly describe how two different approaches to family therapy might try to address this problem.
3. Compare differences between strategic family therapy, structural family therapy, and experiential family therapy, in the therapist's style of working and understanding of their role.
4. How might systems theory and constructive family therapy overlap in practice?

2

The CACHO Model of Integrative Relationship Counselling

As discussed in the previous chapter, each of the single-model approaches to relationship counselling tends to emphasize a particular way of conceptualizing the family, or couple relationship, and to rely on the use of specific strategies or techniques in promoting change. As a consequence, each of the single models has limitations when working with particular families (or couples) as each family has their own idiosyncratic ways of functioning, of perceiving their relationships, and of responding to processes intended to produce change. We would strongly suggest that, as with individual counselling models, no one relationship counselling approach can meet the emotional, psychological, behavioural and social needs of diverse families, couples, and individuals. It is not surprising, therefore, that for some years now many, if not most, relationship counsellors have tended to make use of concepts and strategies taken from several of the single-model approaches.

Nichols and Schwartz (2007) point out that there are three different ways in which counsellors can make use of concepts and strategies drawn from a variety of single-therapy approaches. These can be described as:

- eclecticism
- selective borrowing
- specially designed integrative models.

Eclecticism

Until recently, many relationship counsellors have described themselves as eclectic. They have been flexible in making use of concepts, strategies, and techniques from a variety of single-model approaches. They have done this in the belief that an eclectic approach enables them to choose those particular interventions, aimed at producing change, which are most appropriate for a particular family or couple. Although this approach may have some advantages when working with particular families, compared with a single-model approach, it does have some quite serious limitations. When using such an approach, the counsellor is unlikely to consistently rely on a single clearly defined theory of change and, consequently, there is likely to be a lack of clinical consistency throughout the counselling work. As a result, uncertainty and disillusionment in the clients due to a lack of a clear direction in the therapeutic process is likely to be experienced.

Selective Borrowing

In order to overcome the limitations of using an eclectic approach some counsellors have chosen to use what may be described as selective borrowing. In selective borrowing, the counsellor bases their therapeutic approach primarily on one particular relationship counselling model but then borrows techniques and strategies from other approaches to achieve particular goals at any point in the counselling session. When considering options, a counsellor may choose those techniques and strategies, together with their associated theories of change, which the counsellor believes will be particularly suited to the clients involved and which the counsellor assumes will be likely to help in producing change at a particular point in the counselling process.

Consider a practical example of selective borrowing. Imagine a counsellor who chooses to use narrative therapy as their primary relationship counselling model. The counsellor will naturally invite the family to tell their stories about living in their family, and may discover unique outcomes where the family has been able to live their preferred story at times. However, the family might find it difficult to describe how their family interacts as a result of the effects of the problem and, in particular, might have difficulty in explaining how 'power' and 'lack of intimacy' influence the family. To help the family explain more clearly, the counsellor could borrow strategies and techniques from experiential family counselling and use family sculpting to help the family tell their story about how 'power' affects the family and to discover a preferred way of being.

Unfortunately, the counselling process might be compromised as a result of this approach. Family sculpture is a strategy used in experiential family therapy and is designed to facilitate the experience and raised awareness of emotions and emotional relationships within the family. Using this strategy in the context of narrative therapy could distract the family from the narrative therapy task of discovering the effects of the problem, and instead invite them to connect with their emotions and with more problem-saturated stories. In experiential counselling, it is assumed that use of the strategy will produce change as a result of the experience. In contrast, using narrative therapy, change occurs through deconstructing problem stories and reconstructing alternative preferred stories, and not through experiencing emotions. Conflict in the therapeutic process will inevitably arise because the different theories of change related to narrative therapy and experiential therapy collide.

> **Selective borrowing leads to confusion related to theories of change**

From the above discussion, it is clear that a problem with selective borrowing is that the theoretical process of change associated with the primary relationship counselling model may be compromised by introducing strategies, with their associated theories of change, from different models in an *ad hoc* way.

Specially Designed Integrative Models

There are several types of integrative model but the two most common are:

1. Models which sequentially integrate a number of different approaches together with their theories of change.
2. Models based on one theory of change.

Models which sequentially integrate a number of different approaches together with their theories of change

A good example of an integrative counselling model which is based on sequentially using a number of different approaches with their theories of change is the Sequentially Planned Integrative Counselling for Children (SPICC) model (Geldard and Geldard, 2008a). In the SPICC model there are five phases which follow each other sequentially in the counselling process. In each phase a new counselling approach is used with its associated theory of change. In the first phase, client-centred counselling is used to join with the child and enable the child to tell their story. In the second phase, Gestalt therapy is used to help raise the child to awareness and enable them to get in touch with strong emotions. This allows for catharsis to occur. In the third phase, narrative therapy is used with the goal of helping the child to change their view of themselves. In the fourth phase, cognitive behavioural therapy is used to help the child deal with self-destructive beliefs and look at options and choices. In the final phase, behaviour therapy is used to help the child rehearse and experiment with new behaviours. Because the process is sequential, a number of different theories of change can be used to achieve the goals required at various stages in the counselling process.

Models based on one theory of change

Integrative models that are based on one theory of change from a particular counselling model usually combine strategies and techniques from a number of single-model approaches which are compatible with each other and can be incorporated into a comprehensive model. Using such an integrative model is different from selective borrowing because the integrative model is based on a single theory of change taken from a preferred single model. In achieving positive outcomes in accordance with this single theory of change, compatible strategies and techniques taken from other models can be intentionally introduced provided that they do not compromise the underlying single theory of change.

> **Single theory of change models only use strategies which will not compromise the theory of change**

Because these integrative models are based on a single theory of change, the counsellor is clear about the potential conflicts that might arise when choosing strategies and/or techniques taken from a variety of models of counselling. The advantage of such an integrative approach is that it increases the counsellor's repertoire in such a way that it is possible to address the needs and problems of particular clients more effectively by offering more options for intervention than a traditional single approach.

It is essential for an integrated model of this kind to have a clearly defined process of change and this process of change must be central to the integration process. An integrative approach to the practice of relationship counselling must include the development of a working model with guiding principles that help the therapist and family to organize goals, explore interactions, enhance communication, and discover ways to promote change. It is also essential to have a rationale for the techniques and strategies that are used, with some sense of the expected outcomes. We refer to this process as the counsellor's practice framework. It is described in detail in Chapter 10.

The CACHO Integrative Model of Relationship Counselling

As relationship counselling practitioners, we have developed and use an integrative model of relationship counselling which we call the CACHO model. This model is based on a single theory of change. The model relies on a systems approach to counselling families, focusing on change within the session, and also integrating change that occurs between sessions. The theory of change underlying the model is based on Gestalt therapy theory and practice (Resnick, 1995; Yontef, 2005). Extensive use is made of the Milan systemic family therapy practice of using circular questions and also Gestalt therapy experiments. At appropriate times during the therapeutic process strategies from a number of other therapeutic models, including experiential family therapy, multigenerational family therapy, structural family therapy, solution-focused counselling, and narrative therapy, are introduced without compromising the theory underlying the process of change.

It is important to remember that the CACHO integrated model of relationship counselling is grounded in the Gestalt therapy theory of change. CACHO is an acronym representing the following:

C – communication
A – awareness
CH – choice
O – outcome

C – communication

A basic tenet of Gestalt therapy is that change occurs as a result of raised awareness (Yontef, 2005). When we are working as counsellors with a couple or family system, we believe that the first step in raising awareness is to use strategies which will help the participants to communicate with each other so that they are able to begin to understand the pictures and/or discourses which each of them have with regard to their relational system. Hence the first stage in the therapeutic process using the CACHO model involves helping the members of the system to look at their family pictures through multiple lenses. Each member of the system will have their own lens through which they perceive the system. By looking through each other's lenses, each individual's awareness of the reality of the present system and its functioning is heightened (Resnick, 1995).

Throughout this book we will refer to *'what is'* and the way things are in the *'here and now'*. Raising awareness of 'what is' in the 'here and now' moves family members and the family as a whole to a position where decisions with regard to change can be made.

In the CACHO model, in order to encourage communication so that individuals start to look through multiple lenses use is made of circular questions. The use of circular questions is an integral part of the Milan systemic family therapy model (Selvini Palazzoli et al., 1980).

A – awareness

Once family members are able to share each other's pictures, their awareness is inevitably raised not only of their own perspective and story about the family, but also of other family members' perspectives and stories. The underlying Gestalt therapy theory of change used in the CACHO model relies on using strategies to intensify the raising of awareness.

In order to intensify the raising of awareness, the CACHO integrative model makes use of a variety of practical strategies and techniques which are particularly suitable for this task. These techniques are taken from a number of relationship counselling models, including experiential, multigenerational, and structural family therapy, together with practices from social constructionism. For example, techniques taken from Satir's experiential family therapy, such as the use of a family sculpture, might be included at an appropriate point in the counselling process in order to increase the family's awareness of family interactional patterns and dynamics. Similarly, awareness might be raised using a genogram, as in Bowenian family therapy.

> **"Strategies to raise AWARENESS are central to
> the CACHO model"**

Other strategies which are helpful in intensifying the raising of awareness involve the use of a reflecting team or feedback by a co-therapist. These will be described in Chapter 3.

CH – choice

At those points in the counselling process where awareness is raised sufficiently so that a Gestalt 'Ah-ha' experience occurs for an individual or individuals in the system, it is inevitable that choices with regard to possible change will emerge. The most basic option that frequently emerges is the choice to continue thinking and behaving as now with no change or to think and behave differently. Clearly, there will be consequences for any decision made with regard to either choice. It is here that the counsellor needs to once again raise awareness with regard to the outcomes of decisions which might be made. In raising awareness regarding decisions for the future, it may be helpful to use strategies from narrative therapy and solution-focused therapy. Both of these approaches invite the client to collaboratively work with the counsellor in order to explore future possibilities, solutions, and preferred ways of being.

O – outcome

When decisions have been made to change thinking and behaviour, there will be an outcome for the system. As a consequence of any changes by an individual in the system, there will be responses from other members of the system. In Gestalt terms, the system is undergoing an experiment through which changes in behaviours can be monitored with regard to the outcome or consequences resulting from the changes. Once again, using the CACHO model, it is appropriate to move back into the communication stage of the process so that individual members can share their pictures with regard to the outcome of decisions and subsequent changes that have occurred. Thus, to help in this communication process circular questions taken from the Milan model of family therapy might be used.

Promoting Change Using the CACHO Model

As has been explained, the promotion of change using the CACHO model is achieved through raising awareness of 'what is' in accordance with Gestalt therapy theory. Once members of a family system become fully aware of how the system functions, they will recognize that they have a choice – to keep doing as they are, or to do something different. Consequently, when using this model it is not essential for the counsellor to make hypotheses about what is happening, or to try to use strategies that are designed to deliberately promote a particular change. The method is respectful of the individual members and the family as a whole as it invites each member of the system to make their own decisions with regard to the choices available in order to improve relationships.

The paradoxical theory of change

Many relationship counsellors, and particularly strategic family therapists, believe that it is important for them to hypothesize with regard to how the system (family or couple) they are working with is operating. Once they have formulated a hypothesis, they will devise strategies to bring about change in the system in a particular way. However, according to Gestalt therapy theory, this practice is unhelpful. The Gestalt view (Yontef, 2005) is that pushing for change in a particular direction by the therapist will inevitably be resisted. Resisting the urge to push for change and instead focusing on raising awareness of what is in the 'here and now' is, paradoxically, likely to spontaneously precipitate change.

Our own practice as counsellors confirms the Gestalt paradoxical theory of change. We have found that it is generally not useful to try to push a family, couple, or individual to change. Human beings as a whole do not like being manipulated, directed, or told what to do; their natural response to such attempts to change their behaviour is almost always to resist. However, if as counsellors we use strategies which are aimed at enhancing the client's awareness of what is in the here and now, almost always the clients will decide for themselves how they want to change and will go ahead in trying to do this.

Continuing a circular process until counselling is concluded

Figure 2.1 summarizes in diagrammatic form the process used in the CACHO model. The process is circular and will generally keep repeating itself until the clients have achieved their goals through counselling. For example, after moving around the Communication, Awareness, Choice, and Outcome circle, the clients may need to return again to the communicating stage in order to share with each other their pictures of the outcomes of any changes that have been made. Once again, circular questions from the Milan method can be used to help individuals share their pictures with other members of the system. If members of the system are not satisfied with the outcomes that have been achieved, it may be helpful for the counsellor to assist the family once again by raising awareness of 'what is' through the use of suitable strategies taken from a variety of therapeutic models, as will be discussed in subsequent chapters. This might lead to new choices being made with further outcomes.

Using this relationship counselling model, the counsellor can facilitate movement around the CACHO circle several times if necessary until satisfactory outcomes for the

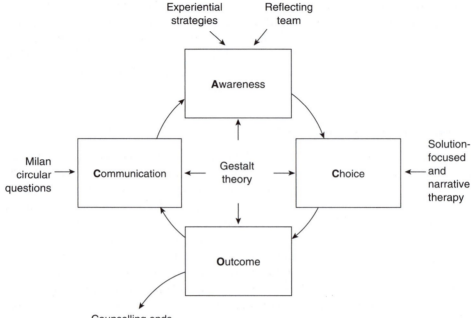

FIGURE 2.1   *CACHO integrative relationship counselling*

clients are achieved. Clearly, when this occurs it is appropriate for counselling to end, and in most cases the clients will decide to do this themselves.

KEY POINTS

- Eclecticism may lack clinical consistency as strategies and techniques are selected in an *ad hoc* fashion.
- In selective borrowing, one particular model is used and techniques and strategies are borrowed from other approaches. However, allegiance to a clearly defined theory of change may be compromised.
- Integrative models grounded in a clearly defined theory of change may incorporate strategies and techniques from a variety of models.
- The CACHO integrative model is grounded in Gestalt therapy theory of change and makes use of strategies and techniques from a variety of models at particular points in the therapeutic process.
- The paradoxical theory of change suggests that clients are likely to resist attempts to encourage them to change in a particular way and that change is more likely to occur by raising awareness of what is.

QUESTIONS FOR GROUP DISCUSSION OR STUDENT ASSIGNMENTS

1. Describe how you believe other members of your family would describe you and describe how you think people from outside your family would describe you. Explain whether or not these descriptions fit with your own description of yourself. Discuss what you would like to do in order to try to change any of these descriptions.
2. Think about a behaviour of yours, or of another member of your family, that concerns you in some way. Describe what you would do if you decided that you would like to change the troubling behaviour.
3. Choose the model of relationship counselling that most appeals to you. Explain how you could use this model as the basis for an integrative model. Describe how your model might be effective in helping a particular family, either imagined or real, which is experiencing problems.

3

Use of a Co-therapist and/or Reflecting Team

Gregory Bateson (1972) pointed out that for people to learn and change, new information is required. The CACHO model described in this book depends on a Gestalt therapy theory of change. As stated previously, this theory of change is based on the assumption that change is produced by raised awareness. One way of raising awareness is to provide new information, or to highlight information that has been available but has been undiscovered, hidden, discounted, or disregarded by the clients.

In Chapters 8 and 9 we will discuss a variety of ways in which to raise a family's awareness through helping them to share information with each other and by inviting them to engage in experiential exercises. In some situations it is possible for the counsellor to provide information directly to the family that can be helpful in raising awareness. Other useful ways of providing information are through the use of:

- a co-therapist
- a reflecting team.

Looking at a situation from one angle provides a limited view and perspective about that situation (Friedman, 1997). This is certainly the case in families where each member of the family will have their own perspective as though they were looking at the family through a single lens. By helping the members of the family to share their pictures with each other, they can begin to look through multiple lenses and, as a consequence, their own individual pictures are likely to change.

> **Looking through multiple lenses raises awareness and promotes change**

The use of a co-therapist or reflecting team offers an additional possibility that new and different pictures of the family can be shared with the family. A co-therapist's picture of a family, or the pictures provided by members of the reflecting team, enable family members to think about their own pictures and to modify them if they wish. In this process, the co-therapist's picture or a reflecting team member's picture is not an objective picture of the family, as these pictures come from the subjective observations of the people concerned. Even so, they are of value as they provide another perspective and give another point of view to expand the family's perceptions and raise the family's awareness of alternative pictures and possibilities for change.

The Observation Room

Generally, when a co-therapist or reflecting team are involved in the counselling process they will observe the family through a one-way mirror from an observation room which is adjacent to the counselling room. The observation room includes a sound system which enables the observers to hear what is being said in the counselling room as well as to observe visually through the one-way mirror. When using such an arrangement it is essential to attend to the ethical issues involved. Clients need to be fully informed about the arrangements that will be used and why, and to give their consent in writing for this to occur. In order for clients to feel comfortable before counselling begins, they can be introduced to the co-therapist or the members of the reflecting team.

Use of a Co-therapist

When a co-therapist is involved in the counselling process it is essential that an explanation is given to the family with regard to the role of the co-therapist and the possible actions that the co-therapist might take. There are a number of different ways in which a co-therapist can provide a family with additional information that might be helpful. These include:

- telephone interventions
- presentation of the co-therapist's picture
- open therapist/co-therapist discussion.

Telephone interventions

While actively counselling a family, the counsellor continually pays attention to individuals in the family, carefully listening to what they are saying, watching the processes and interactional patterns that are occurring between them, and observing their behaviour. The counsellor guides the conversation by inviting family members to speak and responding to them by giving feedback, and perhaps by drawing attention to information that has been minimized or by sharing curiosity about the family and the way the family functions. Consequently, a family counsellor is trying to attend to many different processes simultaneously. As a result, it is almost certain that they will miss some important interactional and behavioural processes as they are occurring. By contrast, a co-therapist watching and listening from an observation room, who is not involved in family interactions, can focus completely on the activity of observation. Where a co-therapist notices that information that might be useful for the family has not been brought to the attention of the family, it is appropriate at times for the co-therapist to share this information with the counsellor. If the counsellor also believes that sharing the information may be constructive, they can relay this information to the family. In this situation the co-therapist might phone through to the counsellor using an intercom phone connecting the counselling room with the observation room. Once the information from the co-therapist has been passed to the counsellor, the counsellor can decide whether or not to pass this information on to the family. If the counsellor decides to give this information to the family, it is important for the counsellor to preface such information by explaining to the family that the information comes from the co-therapist and not from the counsellor themselves. This makes it easier for the family to reject the information if they disagree with it, to discuss the information openly, and, if applicable, to use the information in developing their pictures.

> **The family consider and evaluate the co-therapist's information**

Typically, a co-therapist will intervene for the following purposes:

- to feedback processes
- to feedback interactional patterns
- to feedback observations of behaviour
- to draw attention to information that has been minimized
- to suggest a hypothesis to explain particular behaviours.

Feeding back processes

There are many different processes which occur when families are interacting together and sometimes they will not be noticed by the counsellor but will be recognized by the co-therapist. Consider an example where a teenage daughter tells her mother several times in a counselling session that she would like to have a better relationship with her. However, instead of responding to this request each time, the mother complains about the daughter's behaviour. If this process can be brought into the open, then it is possible that the mother can begin to consider changing her behaviour and respond directly to her daughter's request.

Feeding back interactional patterns

Because the counsellor is attending to their relationship with individual members in the family, they may not notice some important interactional patterns that are occurring between other members of the family. In this instance, it may be that the co-therapist notices these interactions and believes that the family may find the observation useful. For example, the co-therapist may notice that whenever tension starts to build between a father and daughter, a son intervenes with the goal of reducing that tension, but in doing so undermines the father and daughter's attempts to find a resolution to their conflict.

Feeding back observations of behaviour

A family can often benefit from information received from a co-therapist about both verbal and non-verbal behaviour that is occurring in the family. It might be noticed that a great deal of interrupting and not much listening occurs in a family, and that one person dominates the conversation, or that one person remains silent and hardly talks at all. Similarly, feedback about non-verbal behaviour, such as heightened activity when particular issues are being discussed, or a member of the family turning their back on another member of the family, may be important information which will help the family to better understand the way their family functions.

Drawing attention to information that has been minimized

It is important for the counsellor to maintain equality in their relationships with each family member and for family members to feel equally respected and validated with regard to their individual perspectives. However, a co-therapist might advocate on behalf of a family member. For example, a co-therapist might notice that whenever a son in the family complains about his lack of privacy and the way that his siblings treat his room as communal space the other members of the family either minimize or ignore what he is saying and move on to talk about other issues. It might be useful in this instance for a co-therapist to pass this observation on to the counsellor so that they can tell the family without compromising their own relationship with any family member.

Suggesting a hypothesis to explain particular behaviours

We would like to stress that we do not believe that as counsellors it is helpful for us to behave as experts who can give families reliable hypotheses in order to explain particular behaviours. Even so, we do think that it can be valuable for a co-therapist to tentatively put forward a suggestion which could possibly add other dimensions to the family's perspectives with regard to particular behaviours. For example, consider a family where the father has recently left and the mother has, by her own admission, become very depressed, withdrawn into herself, and given up trying to run the family. She has complained that her teenage son and daughter are continually fighting with each other and distressing their younger brother and sister. It may seem to the co-therapist watching the family counselling session that the teenage son and daughter are in conflict with each other because both of them are very concerned about the need for leadership in the family and are in a power struggle with each other to take over control of the family. This hypothesis of the co-therapist's could be quite wrong, but even so it could be useful for the co-therapist to let the counsellor know about this hypothesis so that the counsellor can, if they wish, share it with the family. In sharing the hypothesis, the counsellor would need to let the family know that this hypothesis may be quite wrong, and that the idea is simply that of the co-therapist. The family can then be invited to discuss the hypothesis with regard to how it fits for them in their current situation. This discussion is likely to lead to an increase in the family's awareness of what is actually happening in the family.

Guidelines regarding making telephone interventions

- Telephone interventions need to be given sparingly. Generally, there should not be more than one or two interventions in a counselling session.
- The message from the co-therapist should be short and direct with a minimum of discussion.
- Usually the message will be passed on to the family without amendment.
- The counsellor should make it clear that the message comes from the co-therapist and not from themselves.
- After a message has been given, the counsellor will generally ask the family if they agree or disagree with the message.
- The counsellor has the right to ignore a message.

Presentation of the co-therapist's picture

Often, when using the CACHO model, such a tentative hypothesis as described above, will be presented to the family by the co-therapist in the form of a feedback picture or metaphor at the end of the first counselling session, as will be explained in Chapter 8.

Open therapist/co-therapist discussion

As is explained throughout this book, the theory of change used in the CACHO model is a Gestalt therapy theory of change, which depends on raising awareness of what is in the 'here and now'.

We have already described the way that it can be useful for a co-therapist to intervene by phoning in to the counsellor with information which may be related to the family. Using such an intervention enables the counsellor to manage the counselling session in the way that they see as most appropriate. The counsellor can either immediately pass on the information relayed by the co-therapist, or retain the information until a suitable or appropriate window arises in the conversation. Alternatively, the counsellor can decide not to introduce the information from the co-therapist but instead to focus on the current issues being discussed as this may be more useful and helpful for the family at the time. Focusing on current issues is a way of raising the family's awareness of what is in the 'here and now'.

Another way of working with a co-therapist that can have a strong impact on the family is for the co-therapist to come into the counselling room and have an open discussion with the counsellor about the family. The idea of having an open discussion between the counsellor and co-therapist in the presence of the family was first promoted by Carl Whitaker (1976).

> **" Therapist/co-therapist discussion in the presence of the family helps make the counselling process transparent "**

Before undertaking this process it is important for the counsellor to talk with the family about the process and to check whether they would like to be involved by listening to the discussion between counsellor and co-therapist. Having a discussion in this way in the company of the family helps to make the counselling process transparent and enables the counsellor to become a direct contributor to the counselling process. After this discussion has been completed, the co-therapist withdraws to allow an opportunity for the family to comment on and respond to the discussion.

The Use of a Reflecting Team

The use of the reflecting team is a powerful way to raise a family's awareness of what is in the here and now. Additionally, reflecting teams can be very useful with regard to the training and ongoing supervision of relationship counsellors.

Change in families can often be inhibited by family members becoming 'fixed' on the idea that a particular type of solution is required. As a consequence, they may experience significant difficulty shifting to more effective and more economical alternatives, even when these are evident (Friedman, 1997). It is easy for 'tunnel vision' to develop, with the family looking towards a particular solution and ignoring other alternatives that may also be possible. We know that it is difficult for human beings to let go of one fixed point of view. A goal in relationship counselling must therefore be to help family members let go of their preconceived ideas and open themselves up to receiving and taking into account new information with regard to their preferred choices.

The reflecting team process

The reflecting team model was initially suggested and developed by Tom Anderson (Wetchler, 1996). Reflecting teams consist of a group of counsellors, or trainee counsellors, who are introduced to the family before counselling starts, and who observe the counselling process from an observation room through a one-way mirror with a sound system. Reflecting teams can vary in size from a minimum of two and a maximum of six members. Having more than six members in a reflecting team is usually unwieldy and leads to lengthy reflecting team discussions which may be tedious for the family.

After observing the counselling process during the main part of the counselling session, which may last typically from 30 to 40 minutes, the reflecting team exchange places with the client family and the counsellor, who now enter the observation room. The family and counsellor then observe the reflecting team as they discuss their individual perceptions of the client family, and the processes occurring within the family. The team members are encouraged to present their pictures of the family spontaneously and openly, without attempting to arrive at a consensus or a particular point of view. Instead, the focus is on expanding the family's perceptions so that they are made aware of a number of differing perspectives regarding their family.

Having listened to the reflecting team's discussion, the counsellor and family exchange places with the reflecting team and return to the counselling room. The family then have an opportunity to discuss the reflecting team's conversation. By doing this, their awareness is raised as they are now able to view their family from many different perspectives and may consequently be in a position to make helpful choices with regard to change.

"Reflecting team discussions can intensify the raising of awareness"

Using a reflecting team intentionally minimizes the possibility that the family will see the counsellor or the reflecting team as hierarchical experts who will find solutions for them. Instead, they are able to see their family through multiple lenses and, in collaboration with the counsellor, to explore possible solutions. The process is transparent because the reflecting team talk spontaneously and openly while the family listen, and the family then have the right to dispute, disagree, agree, or generally comment on the reflecting team's ideas and, as a consequence, discover their preferred solutions.

Characteristics of a reflecting team discussion

Members of a reflecting team need to ensure that their discussion proceeds in a manner which will be acceptable to the family, recognizing the family's strengths and positively connoting the family's behaviours and attitudes wherever possible. In order to achieve this, the team need to adopt an attitude which is respectful and demonstrates an interest and curiosity regarding the family. Statements need to be made tentatively rather than with authority, so that they are recognized as the speaker's point of view and not as a statement made by an all-knowing expert. 'I' statements are used so that remarks made by individual team members are seen as genuinely their own and made without judgement. The team do not give advice, but may raise questions about what might happen if a particular change occurred (Lowe and Guy, 1999).

During the reflecting team discussion members of the team discuss with each other rather than directing their remarks to either the counsellor or the family. Generally, they will include in their discussion:

- the way the family have demonstrated success, coping, and personal resources
- exceptions when the problem did not occur
- instances of success in overcoming the problem
- positively connoting action taken by individuals
- conjecturing about future possibilities for individuals and the family
- validating preferred ways of being family members
- externalizing the problem
- themes or metaphors that emerged during the counselling session
- family activity that continues regardless of the existence of the problem
- canvassing ideas for alternative action
- raising questions about other people's perspectives, including those who are not present
- identifying and building on values, beliefs, and sense of identity of family members.

Additionally, it is appropriate for reflecting team members to disclose relevant experience of their own which might be helpful provided that they are careful not to use the reflecting team for their own therapeutic purposes.

Lowe and Guy (1999) suggest some expressions that members of a reflecting team are likely to use, such as:

'What struck me most was…'

'I gained a strong impression of Frank's commitment. I am curious about how this was achieved.'

'I am curious about …'

'I wonder what would happen if …'

'I wonder if … might be an issue here?'

'One thing I am curious about…'

'I was interested to see…'

'I wonder if…'

'A question I had was…'

'I noticed a change when…'

'I was surprised when…'

'I thought it was significant that…'

'I was hoping that the counsellor might ask about…'

'I wondered what a different approach might have had on… such as…'

'I wondered what was happening for… when…'

'I noticed the theme of… seemed to emerge'

'I was curious about how… was able to do….'

Additionally, members of the reflecting team might speculate on what other people connected with the family might think. Thus a team member might say, 'I am curious about what Sarah's grandmother might say if she was here.'

Members of a reflecting team try to avoid being patronizing or trivializing issues. It is not helpful for them to introduce too many ideas, to focus on one particular solution, or try to persuade other members of the team to accept their opinion. Rather than being competitive with the ideas, it is important for the team to share their different ideas.

Theory underpinning the use of the reflecting team

Clearly, a reflecting team's discussion can be used as a strategy for achieving raised awareness – the central concept underlying the Gestalt therapy theory of change on which the CACHO model is based. While being useful in raising awareness, it should be recognized that the reflecting team concept, which is derived from social constructionist thinking, is based on a number of assumptions:

- Meanings of events are constructed through language and are constantly being co-constructed through dialogue.
- People have the resources and capacities to generate other meanings in their particular circumstances; they are an expert in the development of meanings that are useful for themselves.
- There is no such thing as privileged expert knowledge; there are just new meanings and possibilities.
- Meanings imposed by authority are oppressive and not conducive to growth.

The use of the reflecting team, with its emphasis on meaning and meaning-making, is consistent with Gestalt therapy theory regarding the concepts of phenomenology and dialogue where the focus is subjective. Yontef (1993) describes a phenomenological method of awareness as an approach which enables clients to become aware of what they are doing, how they are doing it, and how they can change and at the same time accept and value themselves. Similarly, the aim of a reflecting team is to discuss in an unrehearsed way ideas and observations in order to extend the dialogue between the counsellor and clients so that alternative possibilities of thought and action can be co-constructed.

Training and supervision of relationship counsellors

Street (2006) contends that training at the highest level of family therapy should occur where supervised observed practice is available. He suggests that for the beginner and experienced therapist alike, observation of ongoing counselling work leads to an enhancement of therapeutic skills and outcomes. We strongly support Street's view and, because of this, believe that the use of co-therapists and reflecting teams in counselling is essential in good family therapy practice to ensure that the highest standards of therapeutic help are provided. Acting in the role of co-therapist or as a member of a reflecting team, or as the counsellor being observed, provides trainees with the supervision required of their practice, and can contribute to positive counselling outcomes for clients.

KEY POINTS

- Providing new information assists in raising awareness.
- A co-therapist or reflecting team is useful in providing additional information.
- Telephone interventions from a co-therapist can be used to feedback processes, interactional patterns and observations of behaviour, and to draw attention to information that has been minimized, and to suggest possible hypotheses.
- Open therapist/co-therapist discussion helps make the counselling process transparent.

- The reflecting team provides the family with the opportunity to view their family through additional and alternative lenses.
- The use of co-therapists and reflecting teams are extremely valuable in promoting high-quality work through ongoing training and supervision.

QUESTIONS FOR GROUP DISCUSSION OR STUDENT ASSIGNMENTS

1. Imagine if you are a member of the reflecting team and have just observed a family. You realize that you strongly disapprove of the family's beliefs and values. Discuss how you could contribute to the reflecting team discussion while being congruent and respecting the family's right to have different beliefs and values. What would you do after this counselling process in order to address issues which had been raised for you by the situation?
2. Discuss the way in which issues related to hierarchy, the power of the counsellor, and respect for a client family's own expertise can be addressed through the use of counselling processes and attention to the counsellor's own issues.

4

Relationship Counselling Skills

Relationship counsellors need to be able to use the full range of traditional counselling micro-skills, as described in our books *Practical Counselling Skills* (Geldard and Geldard, 2005b, available in the UK), *Basic Personal Counselling* (Geldard and Geldard, 2005a, available in Australia and New Zealand), and *Personal Counseling Skills* (Geldard and Geldard, 2008b, available in the USA). These skills include:

- reflection of content and feelings
- summarizing
- the use of questions
- normalizing
- confrontation
- challenging self-destructive beliefs
- externalizing
- solution-focused counselling skills
- reframing
- exploring options and facilitating action.

These skills are particularly useful for counselling individuals and are certainly useful to the relationship counsellor. However, there are a number of other skills which generally need to take precedence when carrying out relationship counselling with two or more people. These skills include the use of circular questions, together with a number of other skills which are particularly useful in helping to raise awareness.

Circular Questions to Raise Awareness

In order to invite family members to describe their individual pictures of the family the counsellor needs to ask questions. While linear questioning is useful within an intra-psychic model for finding out more about an individual, circular questioning is useful for gaining more information about relationships (Selvini Palazzoli et al., 1980).

A variety of circular questions can be used to help family members share their individual perceptions of the family and to share what they believe are the perceptions of other family members. Circular questions can be used to elicit information about family members' thoughts, feelings, behaviours, beliefs, attitudes, and perceptions.

There are four types of circular question:

- other-oriented
- triadic
- general
- openly-directed.

To help in explaining the way these questions are used, we will consider a fictitious family as an example:

In this family, the parental couple, Alice and Mark, were previously married to other partners before entering into a relationship with each other. Alice has a 12-year-old son Sean and a 10-year-old daughter Jill from her earlier marriage. Additionally, Alice and

Mark are the parents of a 5-year-old son Zachary. Alice's mother, Mrs Biggs (grand mother to Sean and Jill) lives with the family. There is a conflictual relationship between Sean and his stepfather Mark.

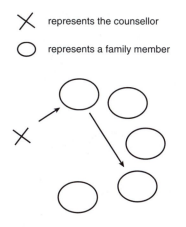

× represents the counsellor

○ represents a family member

FIGURE 4.1(a)   *The other-oriented circular question*

Other-oriented circular questions

When using questions of this type, the counsellor directs a question to one member of the family asking about the thoughts, feelings, behaviours, beliefs, attitudes, or perceptions of another member of the family. This is illustrated in Figure 4.1(a). For example, the counsellor might ask:

'Jill, if you had a guess, how do you think Sean feels in the current situation?'
'Mrs Biggs, what do you think Mark's attitude is to the family problem?'

The advantage of asking an other-oriented question is that it engages two people directly in the conversation as a result of the question. Mrs Biggs needs to answer the question and Mark is certain to want to hear her answer. Having heard it, he might agree with the answer or say that it is wrong. If he says it is wrong, this is likely to provoke discussion between Mark and Mrs Biggs and possibly other members of the family. This discussion will enable the family to start seeing each other's pictures of the family. While this discussion happens, the counsellor can observe the interactions and notice any processes which are occurring between family members.

Triadic circular questions

When using questions of this type the counsellor directs a question to one member of the family asking about the behaviours of, or relationship between, two other

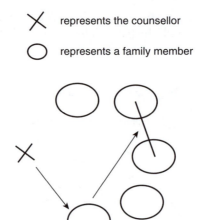

FIGURE 4.1(b)   *The triadic circular question*

members of the family. This is illustrated in Figure 4.1(b). For example, the counsellor might ask:

'Jill, what sort of relationship do Sean and Grandma have?'
'Alice, how does the conflict between Sean and Mark start?'

By asking triadic questions the counsellor directly involves three members of the family simultaneously. Additionally, a picture of the relationship between two members of the family is elicited from another family member. Questions like these generally promote discussion among the family members as they each present their point of view with regard to the relationship in question.

General circular questions

When asking a general circular question the counsellor directs a question to one member of the family, asking in general about relationships or behaviours of family members or enquires about the nature of the problem. Figure 4.1(c) illustrates the way this question is asked. For example, the counsellor might ask:

'Tell me, Sean, what is the biggest problem in this family?'
'Alice, do you think your family wants to change?'

The idea of asking a general circular question is to promote discussion between members of the family, as usually when one person replies other people will present different points of view and these will lead to discussion.

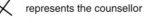

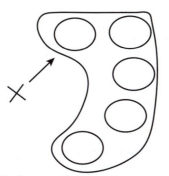

FIGURE 4.1(c)   *The general circular question*

Openly-directed circular questions

When asking an openly-directed circular question the counsellor does not direct the question to anyone in particular, but asks a question which anyone can answer concerning relationships or behaviours in the family. Figure 4.1(d) illustrates this type of question. For example, the counsellor might ask:

'What is the biggest problem in this family?'
'Why has this family come to counselling?'

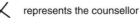

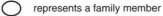

FIGURE 4.1(d)   *The openly-directed circular question*

Once again, this type of question is likely to lead to discussion between members of the family as it elicits different points of view.

Follow-up questions

After asking a circular question and receiving the answer, the counsellor can follow up by asking another person what they thought of the previous answer. For example, the counsellor might say:

'Sean, what do you think of what Jill said?'
'Mark, do you agree or disagree with what Alice said?'

There is also another type of follow-up question. Sometimes, in response to a circular question, the person responding will say that they don't know the answer to the question. For example, the counsellor might ask:

'Alice, how do you think Jill feels when this problem occurs?'

Alice might respond by saying that she doesn't know. In this case the counsellor can follow up by asking:

'If you had a guess, how do you think Jill feels when this problem occurs?'

Follow-up questions are extremely useful because they enable a counsellor to move from directly involving one person in the family in discussion to inviting a new person to become directly involved in the discussion. Hence, instead of one person dominating the conversation, by creative use of circular questions and follow-up questions the counsellor can ensure that each person in the family gets an opportunity to speak and present their point of view.

Particular advantages of using circular questions

As has been discussed, circular questions enable the counsellor to join with an individual while at the same time engaging other members of the family, who are included in the question. These other members of the family are likely to be drawn into discussion regarding their perceptions of the answers given. Additionally, other members of the family, who were not asked the question, or included in the question, may volunteer differing perceptions. Thus different perceptions are shared. Further, by addressing circular questions and follow-up questions to various members of the family the counsellor can move the discussion from one person to another so that all members of the family become involved in the counselling conversation.

> **Circular questions encourage communication between family members**

As members of the family share their pictures of the family by talking together, the counsellor can observe their interactional patterns and the relationships in the family.

Other Skills to Raise Awareness

Placing an emphasis on the use of circular questions, particularly in the first counselling session, enables the family members to begin to look through multiple lenses and see each other's perspectives of the family. There are a number of other skills which the counsellor can use in order to raise the family's awareness of what is happening in the family in the here and now. These skills include:

* listening and observation
* reflection and validation
* making information newsworthy
* feeding back observed family processes
* reframing
* relabelling
* externalizing the problem.

Listening and observation

Throughout the counselling process the counsellor's role is to attend continuously to what is being said, to observe the way that it is said, to observe the non-verbal behaviours of individual family members, and to observe the nature and processes of the interactions between family members.

It is also important for the counsellor to use appropriate skills to enable family members to communicate information in order to help the family to see each other's pictures. However, once the family have started to communicate with each other spontaneously, provided that the communications are of value, it is often best for the counsellor to remain silent and to focus on observing individual processes and the interactions between members of the family. Communication between family members is valuable and to be encouraged, because if they are to be able to solve problems outside the counselling environment, they will need to rely on their own communication processes and to have confidence that they can reach useful outcomes through talking with each other.

Reflection and validation

Reflecting back both content and feeling can be useful in a family counselling session in validating the experience of an individual member of the family. For example, the counsellor might say to Jill: *'You are saying that you feel frightened when Sean and Mark start to argue.'* At times such a reflection is useful in order to both validate what has been said and to emphasize the communication so that other members of the family pay attention to what has been said. However, we recommend that reflection be used sparingly in relationship counselling. In the example given, it might have been more useful for the counsellor to involve other members of the family in the conversation. This could be done in the following ways:

1. The counsellor might ask Jill an other-oriented circular question by asking, *'Jill, how do you think that Zachary feels when Sean and Mark start to argue?'* By using this question, the counsellor has acknowledged that Jill is troubled when Sean and Mark argue, but has moved the conversation towards Zachary, who might then respond.
2. The counsellor might ask Alice a general circular question by saying, *'Alice, how do you think other members of the family feel when Sean and Mark start to argue?'* Once again this question acknowledges what Jill has said about her own feelings, and additionally it invites Alice to respond and possibly make comments about other members of the family, which might then lead them to respond.

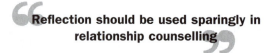

Reflection should be used sparingly in relationship counselling

Can you see that although at times it can be appropriate to use reflection in order to validate what a person has said or to highlight a comment so that the importance of what has been said is not missed by other members of the family, generally, in relationship counselling, it is more useful to rely on circular questions so that conversation between family members is generated and the focus does not stay with one person.

Making information newsworthy

In the previous section, we mentioned that reflection is useful in making sure that information disclosed by one member of the family has been heard by other members of the family. It frequently occurs in families where there is a problem that the family, or some family members, fail to hear what other members of the family say. Even in a counselling session members of a family may discount important information from individuals in the family because it is uncomfortable for them to acknowledge that it may be true. In the examples given, it is possible that either Mark or Sean are so intensely focused on their own conflict that they are not interested in hearing about the effect that it is having on other members of the family. Consequently, in a situation such as this the counsellor has an opportunity to make the information newsworthy so that it is heard and, as a consequence, hopefully receives a response which will have positive outcomes for the family.

One way to make information newsworthy is to repeat it clearly and loudly by reflecting what has already been said. Another way of making information newsworthy is to ask openly-directed questions, such as:

'Has anyone in the family noticed that Jill gets worried when Mark and Sean are in conflict?'
'Is there anyone else in the family who feels the same way that Jill does?'

Feeding back observed family processes

The simplest form of feedback involves feedback about the verbal or non-verbal behaviour of one member of the family. For example, the counsellor might say, *'Sean is a very good debater, and as a result he takes up a lot of air time.'* Notice, that instead of criticizing Sean for talking so much, the feedback is couched in ways which positively connote his behaviour while drawing attention to it. As a result of this feedback, it is likely that other members of the family will comment about Sean's behaviour and this may have an influence on his behaviour.

> **Feedback recognizes that the person is doing the best they can**

Feedback about non-verbal behaviour might include a statement such as: *'I noticed that Zachary runs to Jill whenever anyone in the family talks loudly.'* This feedback doesn't include an interpretation of Zachary's behaviour by saying 'runs to Jill for support'; it just states the facts as they are observed. Having received the feedback, the family are now in a position to make their own interpretations of Zachary's behaviour.

As well as giving feedback with regard to individual behaviours in the family it can be very useful for a relationship counsellor to give feedback about interactional patterns of behaviour between family members as it occurs during a counselling session.

Examples of typical feedback statements of interactional patterns are:

'I notice that you two have a lot of fun with each other.'
'Jill continually supports what her mother says.'
'Whenever Mrs Biggs says anything she gets interrupted.'
'Sean seems to be very isolated in this family except when he is arguing with someone.'

Each of these responses could be useful in helping the family look through another lens provided by the counsellor.

There are number of specific guidelines regarding the way in which feedback is given so that the family will find the process useful. These are discussed in Chapter 8.

Reframing

By reframing the family situation, or part of the situation, the counsellor presents a new perspective to the family for their consideration. As an example, consider the conflictual relationship between Sean and Mark in the example given previously. Members of the family are quite naturally perceiving this relationship negatively. It may be that both Mark and Sean would like to have a better relationship, similar to the relationship they had in earlier days. However, it could be that neither Mark nor Sean have discovered how to adjust their relationship so that it is relevant for the current developmental stage of the family. Sean is now in pre-adolescence. As a reframe, the counsellor might tentatively suggest the following:

'I'm not sure whether I am right or not because I'm not a member of your family, but I notice that Mark and Sean spend a lot of time arguing with each other. I have heard that in the past when Sean was younger that they had a very good relationship and did things together. I am wondering whether they both want to have a similar relationship with each other now that Sean is getting older and haven't discovered how to do this, except by arguing. I would be interested to hear what other members of the family think.'

The example above illustrates how a counsellor can tentatively suggest that maybe Sean and Mark would like to have a good relationship but don't know how to achieve this. This new perspective might have an influence on Sean and Mark's attitude to each other, and might also help other members of the family look at other explanations for their behaviour.

Relabelling

Relabelling refers to changing the label attached to a person or problem without necessarily moving from an individual to a systemic level. For instance, an undesirable behaviour may receive a positive label (Weeks and L'Abate, 1982). As an example, the previous reframe of Sean and Mark's attitude to each other includes relabelling each of their behaviours in terms of wanting to have a relationship with each other rather than wanting to fight with each other.

Externalizing the problem

Externalizing the problem involves separating the problem from the individual or family. It is easy for a family which is experiencing a problem to come to the conclusion that their family is a dysfunctional family. This description of the family in terms of pathology is unhelpful as it does not promote optimism about the possibility of change. Instead of describing the family as a dysfunctional family, externalizing the problem results in a new description. The family is now separated from the problem and is described not as a 'dysfunctional family' but as a family living with a problem. Once the problem has been separated from the family, the family is empowered to deal with the problem rather than believing that there is something wrong with them.

> "**Externalizing separates the problem from the person or family**"

In a similar way, when looking at individuals in the family, it can be useful to externalize the problem. In the example used previously, instead of describing Sean as a bad-tempered boy, by externalizing the problem we can describe Sean as someone who lives with anger. Sean can then be valued as a person who has the opportunity to discover ways to overcome the effects of a problem, instead of being seen as someone who is intrinsically bad-tempered.

KEY POINTS

- The relationship counsellor needs to be familiar with a full range of traditional counselling skills.
- Circular questions are particularly useful in relationship counselling as they enable family members to share their perspectives with each other and encourage communication.
- Listening and observation enables the counsellor to develop a picture of the nature and processes of interactions in the family.
- Validation confirms that the information has been heard and also increases the likelihood that other members of the family will pay attention to the information.
- Making information newsworthy amplifies information so that it can be brought to the attention of the family.
- Feeding back observations of family processes raises the family's awareness of these processes.
- Externalizing the problem removes negative connotations about a person or the family so that the problem can be addressed.

QUESTIONS FOR GROUP DISCUSSION OR STUDENT ASSIGNMENTS

1. Choose two different counselling skills that you believe would be particularly useful in relationship counselling. Describe a family situation where each of these skills could be used and explain what outcome you would hope might be achieved through using the skills.
2. Choose a problem of your own. For example, you may have problem concentrating when studying. Give the problem a name (the concentration problem could be called Mr Distractability). Write down an imaginary dialogue between yourself and the problem where the problem tries to convince you that it forms a useful function and you argue back. After writing down the dialogue, comment on the process you have used and any outcome for you.

Part 2

Relationship Counselling for the Family

This part of the book focuses on counselling for the whole family. We will begin by discussing the nature of the family and common interactions which occur in the family and which have an effect on family functioning. We will then discuss practical issues related to counselling families. These will include making an initial contact with the family before counselling begins, helping the family to communicate with each other and share their pictures of the family with each other in the first session, and promoting change through raising the family's awareness of the family dynamics. Finally, we will discuss the integration of counselling for individual family members or for subgroups of family members with counselling for the whole family.

5

The Family

When we began to write this chapter the first thing we did was to think about how to define a family with regard to its composition. You may wish to think about this yourself before reading on. After reflecting on the question, we decided that families usually fit the following descriptions:

- Generally, families consist of related children, young people, parents, and grandparents.
- Families may also include aunts, uncles, cousins, nieces and nephews.
- Families are often multigenerational.
- Some families include members who are not blood relatives but who are in close relationships with family members.

Family structure

When asked to define the structure of a family many people immediately think of the nuclear family; that is a family with a mother, father, and children. Clearly, in contemporary society there is a broad range of different types of family. These could include:

- the extended family (mother, father, children, grandmother, grandfather, aunts, uncles)
- a couple who don't have children, either because they have chosen not to, or because they are unable to have children (husband and wife/partners)
- the single-parent family (widows/widowers with children, divorced person with child, separated person with child, unmarried mother with child or adopted child)
- teenage mother with child living with parents or others who are not part of the family system
- a family where the child or children are adopted (parental couple with adopted child)
- the reconstituted/blended family (where one or both partners have been married before and bring children from a previous union into the family)
- the communal family (groups of families with children and some single adults)
- same-sex families (gay/lesbian couples with or without children).

> **The nuclear family is only one of many types of family**

Family function

One way of defining the family is in terms of its functions and not its composition or structure, as suggested by Reis and Lee (1988). They believed that it may be more useful to ask what family groups *do*, rather than defining families in terms of who belongs within it. In making this proposition, Reis and Lee suggest four central functions of family life: providing sexual intimacy, reproduction, economic cooperation, and socialization of children. It is clear that these are just some of the functions that families fulfil. There are many others that could be included. We suggest that it is most useful to think of families as fulfilling the primary functions of providing:

- a social system to meet the needs of its members
- an environment suitable for the reproduction and rearing of children
- an interaction with the wider community which promotes general social well-being.

The way a family is structured and functions will be influenced by the spiritual, ethnic, racial, cultural, societal and political ideas adopted by the family. Additionally, because a family holds within it, and is influenced by, the histories and experiences of each adult in the family, the values, beliefs, attitudes, introjects, prejudices, and other personal attributes of adult individual family members are also likely to influence the way the family behaves. Family composition, structure and function are also likely to be influenced as a result of stages in the family's development. In addition, we need to recognize that definitions of the family may change over time in response to social, cultural, religious, and economic transformations in a multicultural society.

The Family is a Social System for Meeting the Needs of its Members

Have you, the reader, noticed that most people choose family life as their preferred way of living rather than living alone. Also, we have noticed that it is common in contemporary society for some younger adults to live in communal houses with opposite gender and same-sex individuals who are friends but not partners rather than living alone. Perhaps this communal living is another type of family which should be included in our definition. While it does not meet the criteria for reproduction and the rearing of children, it is becoming an increasingly popular alternative social system which meets the needs of its members and can promote general well-being.

Why is it that most people select family life as their preferred way of living? This is not just a recent development but one that has passed from generation to generation over the years. Long ago human beings discovered that it was advantageous if they formed family groups. As a social system, family groups meet the needs of their members by providing for:

- security and safety
- economic and material well-being
- psychological, physical, and emotional well-being
- spiritual needs.

The family provides an environment suitable for the reproduction and rearing of children

It is obvious that children are not capable of rearing and looking after themselves; they need at least one parent, or carer. Family life can provide them with security, safety, nourishment, and generally look after their daily needs. The family provides an environment in which a child can move through the normal developmental stages of growth and learn from their parent/s or carer/s through modelling and through direct instruction.

The family interacts with the wider community to promote social well-being

It is important to remember that while providing for the individual needs of family members, a family makes a social contribution to the wider community. Etzioni (1993) suggests that strength in family life creates community strength. He suggests that if, as a consequence of family life, children perform better in school, are arrested less, are more responsible to civic law, and experience less violence, each individual in the wider community of families benefits. Social and economic standards increase for everyone and individuals are able to reach their desired life goals. Thus, the family is a fundamental unit of society that has influence on the wider society and can promote the well-being of the community. This is a circular process as well-being of the wider community in turn supports the well-being of individual family units.

> **The family is a social system which can promote social well-being**

Factors Affecting Family Function

The way that a family functions will be affected by a number of factors, including:

- the stage of the family's development
- culture/ethnicity
- processes and behaviours within the family.

The stages of family development

Families begin and develop in different ways. Until recently, two people of opposite sex would start a family by joining together as a couple without children. However, in contemporary society gay and lesbian couples also join in the same way to form families. Later, children may be produced, or join the couple, creating a larger family unit. Single-parent families are formed when a mother, who does not have a co-habiting partner, produces a child. Later, she may join with a partner, who may or may not have children, and form a larger family unit.

The arrival of a child is an important developmental stage in any family. Where a couple have joined together, either in partnership or marriage, this developmental stage will inevitably alter the nature of the couple relationship in some way. The attention which each partner gives to each other is certain to change with a significant amount of interest being given to the child. The arrival of a child adds a parental dimension to the system. Additionally, there is likely to be a change in the family's relationship with their extended family.

As children grow up they go to school and once again the family dynamic will change. In adolescence, young people seek individuation and again this will inevitably alter the way the family functions. During this stage there is likely to be a gradual but substantial change in parent–child relationships, as the young people in the family become increasingly independent. In many families, parents will begin to focus their attention more on marital and social activities as opposed to parental issues.

Later, young adults will leave home and may get married, or join with a partner, to start their own family. Parents now take on a new role as grandparents, and eventually their own parents may become frail and dependent on care as they age. Finally, children of the family may have to come to terms with the illness and/or death of their parents. At each of the described stages, if the family is to be fully functional, adjustment to these changes will be required.

The influence of culture/ethnicity

Most counsellors, regardless of ethnic background, will at times need to work with families from cultural groups which are different from their own. In order to do this successfully they need to consider those factors which will influence the family's emotional responses, thoughts, beliefs, attitudes, biases, relationships and behaviours. Of particular importance are attitudes related to:

- the individual and the community
- the way decisions are made
- who is perceived to be a natural helper?
- the extended family
- gender and gender role

- perceptions of time
- use of language
- spirituality
- physical and emotional issues
- experience of trauma.

The individual and the community

Whereas Western culture tends to place an emphasis on the individual and individuality, many other cultures place a much greater emphasis on the community and see an individual person as primarily a member of the community rather than as a separate autonomous entity. Also, there are cultural differences between communities with regard to the level of respect and obedience shown by children towards older people and their parents.

The way decisions are made

In some cultures, making decisions is most appropriately done in the company of other family members. In other cultures, when making decisions, a higher priority is placed on maintaining harmonious relationships than on expressing an individual point of view. In many Western families, decisions are made through democratic discussion and negotiation. However, in many Asian families communication patterns flow down from those of higher status (Lee and Richardson, 1991). Consequently, the father in the family may make major decisions with little input from others.

Who is perceived to be a natural helper?

Because some cultures place a high value on age and respect for elders, people belonging to these cultures tend to consult with elders when they need advice or counselling help. As a consequence, people from such cultures may prefer to work with older counsellors, and may find it difficult or impossible to work with young ones.

Attitudes of the extended family

In Australia, Aboriginal families generally include a wide network of people, many of whom are related in ways that could be considered distant in non-Aboriginal society. Relationships within the extended family are characterized by obligation and reciprocity. Also, strong restrictions are typically imposed on contact or the sharing of information between certain categories of relatives or strangers.

In many Asian families, child-rearing practices emphasize the importance of family ties and obligations. Praise is given for actions that are seen as benefiting the family and guilt-inducing techniques are sometimes used to maintain discipline. Children are expected to retain emotional ties with the mother, and a respectful attitude towards the father, even when they have become adults.

Gender and gender roles

The norms regarding relationships between members of the same sex and members of the opposite sex vary markedly across cultures. Additionally, gender-based norms regarding behaviour, roles and expectations vary, depending on culture.

In some Asian families, the mother is responsible for socializing the children. If they become rebellious, her parenting may be blamed. The mother is also expected to mediate between the dictates of her husband and the demands of the children. The greatest responsibility is placed on the eldest son, who is expected to help raise his younger siblings and be a role model for them. Daughters are expected to help in the house. However, generally, fewer demands are placed upon them because they become members of the husband's family when they marry (Lee and Richardson, 1991).

Latino culture is hierarchical and patriarchal, placing expectations on boys to be independent and perform outside the home. Girls, on the other hand, are taught to be selfless and to sacrifice. This passivity and deference to male authority is rewarded in that women may be seen as morally superior to, and spiritually stronger than, men. Machismo has been popularized as a desirable male characteristic (Lee and Richardson, 1991).

Perceptions of time

For most cultures, a linear view of time is appropriate. However, for several South American countries, and for Australian indigenous people, time is viewed in terms of 'being'. Previously agreed-upon times for meeting may not necessarily hold. This needs to be remembered and respected by counsellors who come from other cultural backgrounds where time-keeping is the expected norm and failure to keep time is considered to be inconsiderate and impolite.

Use of language

The way language is used will have a significant influence on the effectiveness of communication between a client and counsellor. Figures of speech, complex communication, proverbs and quotations may either be familiar or confusing, depending on the client's culture.

Spirituality

For many people throughout the world spiritual beliefs are very important. If these beliefs are challenged or questioned, the person concerned may be alienated. As counsellors, when working with people from other cultures, or with people who have different beliefs from ours, we need to learn how to put our own beliefs to one side so that we can join with and understand our clients more fully.

Physical or emotional issues

In some traditional Asian cultures emotional expression is restrained and displays of emotional reactions do not typically occur outside the family. Feelings are usually not openly expressed except by young children. If counsellors attempt to encourage some Asian clients to express emotions directly, they may be met with resistance and this is likely to be counter-productive.

Some Asian clients may express emotional and psychological disturbance indirectly by reference to somatic complaints. They may consider the symptoms of physical illness to cause psychological problems. For example, they may believe that having a headache may result in feelings of depression. This is also true for many South-East Asian families, such as the Vietnamese, because for them mental disturbance tends to be highly stigmatized so it is much easier for them to talk about physical complaints (Lee and Richardson, 1991). Consequently, when counselling such clients it can be a mistake to discount physical complaints.

Experience of trauma

The way in which individuals respond to traumatic experiences will differ depending on their cultural beliefs. Clients from some cultures hold the belief that individuals are responsible for their own misfortune. In contrast to this, clients from other cultures may view misfortune as being imposed on an individual by an outside agency, such as bad luck, or may view misfortune as the consequence of bad behaviour.

> **It is essential for counsellors to have an appreciation of cultural issues**

Processes and behaviours within the family

In all families there are distinct processes in operation which affect the functioning of the family. These processes have been described in a variety of ways by a number of different authors, including Epstein, Bishop and Levin (1978), Steinhauer, Santa-Barbara and Skinner (1984), Tseng and McDermott (1979) and Olson, Russell and Sprenkle (1983).

We have selected some important processes for discussion, including:

- power and intimacy processes
- role-structuring processes
- communication processes
- problem-solving processes
- change processes.

In order to promote the well-being of individual family members, and to preserve harmony in the family unit, negotiation will be required at times in order to make adjustments to these processes. It is important to recognize that the processes are not static but are dynamic aspects of family interaction, and the way they are negotiated will affect the way the family functions. Barnhill (1979) suggested that families can be distinguished from one another on the basis of how comfortably each family deals with these processes.

Power and intimacy processes

Many family counsellors would agree that the most common issues confronted in counselling families relate to power and intimacy (Melnick, 2000). The substantially modified and simplified version of Olson's circumplex model (Olson et al., 1983) shown in Figure 5.1 provides a map on which families can be placed with regard to the issues of power and intimacy. With regard to power, families range from those which are rigidly controlled, usually with the power being in the hands of one or both of the parents, to those laissez-faire families where there are few rules and family members do very much as they like. Using the model shown in Figure 5.1, power is mapped on the horizontal axis. With regard to intimacy, families vary from those where the family members are disengaged with each other and there is little warmth or emotional sharing, to those enmeshed families where there is a high level of connection between family members, intimacy, and emotional closeness.

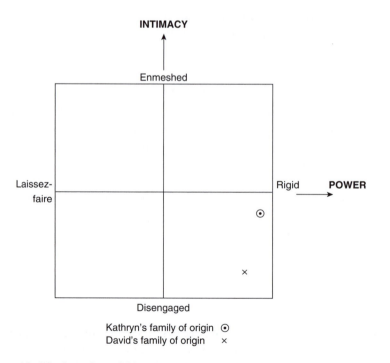

FIGURE 5.1   *Modified version of Olson's circumplex model*

"Family problems frequently involve power and intimacy"

It might be interesting for you, the reader, to think about your family of origin with regard to power and intimacy, and to place it somewhere on the map provided in Figure 5.1. We, the authors, have marked our perceptions of our families of origin on the map. Kathryn's family is marked by the circle with a dot on Figure 5.1 as her family was heavily controlled by her elderly grandmother and on the intimacy axis tended towards a level of disengagement. David's family is marked by a cross because he believed that his family of origin was fairly rigid and very disengaged. However, one of his sisters saw the family differently. Although she thought that the family was extremely rigid, she believed that the family was appropriately engaged while not being enmeshed. We think it's important to explain this because family members will each perceive their families differently from one another, as will be discussed more fully in Chapter 8.

You might ask the question: Where should the ideal family lie on the map shown in Figure 5.1? Our belief is that, as counsellors, we need to accept the way families choose to be. What suits members of one family in terms of power and intimacy may not suit another. For example, some people like to operate autonomously and independently so it might be uncomfortable for them living in an enmeshed family, whereas others prefer closeness and sharing and are not so concerned about operating independently of other members of the family. Similarly, some people are more comfortable in a fairly rigid system, where the rules are clear and they can feel secure because someone is in charge. Others prefer the freedom of the laissez-faire family. We are all different. Additionally, as has been discussed previously, it is important for families to be able to change when they identify difficulties that constrain their ability to function and live comfortably as a family group.

Role-structuring processes

In most families, many of the roles to be performed are not allocated in a formal way; rather, they become habitual patterns of behaviour carried out by particular family members (Barker, 1986). These patterns of behaviour fall into two categories: those which are essential and must be performed for healthy family functioning, and those which are non-essential but contribute to the way the family functions. Essential roles include:

- the provision of material resources, such as housing, food, and clothing
- the management of the family system
- attending to the essential needs of the children, such as looking after their health, providing schooling, and teaching them life skills.

Non-essential roles might include doing gardening, engaging in leisure activities, and cleaning the house. Even though these may affect the quality of life of members of the family, they are not roles that are absolutely essential.

The way that roles are structured in a family varies along a continuum. At one end of the continuum are families where the various functions which need to be performed are clearly assigned to specific members of the family and are consistently and effectively carried out. At the other end of the continuum are families where the functions are not clearly assigned to specific individuals and are not carried out consistently or effectively.

Communication processes

When considering communication processes it is important to take account of both verbal communication and meta-communication. Meta-communication includes non-verbal communication such as facial expression, tone of voice, body language, and also the types of words used.

Communication varies from family to family along a continuum. At one end of the continuum is communication which is clear, direct, open, and complete, so that the receiver is in no doubt about the message being communicated. Communication of this kind is best sent directly from one person to another rather than through an intermediary. At the other end of the continuum communication is not clear, and may be vague, confusing, or even ambiguous. Also messages may be sent indirectly through a third party.

Communications within families fall into a number of categories. Some communications involve the expression of feelings (affective communications) whereas others relate to the practical needs which arise in a family (these are known as instrumental communications). Additionally, there are those communications which occur in general discussion and are neither affective or instrumental in nature.

Problem-solving processes

The McMaster Model of Family Functioning developed by Epstein, Bishop and Levin (1978) describes family problems as those issues that threaten the integrity and functional capacity of the family. Problems related to everyday issues were described as instrumental problems, and problems related to feelings were described as affective problems. According to the McMaster model, problem-solving occurs in seven stages:

1. Identifying the problem.
2. Communicating the problem to the appropriate person.
3. Developing alternative action.
4. Deciding on one particular action.
5. Taking action.
6. Monitoring the action.
7. Evaluation of success of the action.

Family problem-solving processes can be seen as lying on a continuum with regard to the family's ability to problem-solve. According to the McMaster model, families who are able to proceed through all seven steps of the problem-solving process lie at one end of the continuum, whereas families who may not even be able to identify the problem lie at the other end.

Change processes

As described in this chapter, families progress through stages. Whenever a new stage is reached it is incumbent on the family to change in order to satisfy the needs of family members so that the family will continue to function adaptively. The changes require individual family members and the family as a whole to adjust to the new stage. For example, when a child reaches adolescence, while striving for individuation, the young person needs to adjust to the new tasks which they will face as an adolescent and to adjust to changing relationships with their parents, siblings, and significant others in their lives. Similarly, changes will need to be made by the parents in their parenting style and their relationship with the young person, and by siblings in their relationships with the young person.

There are considerable differences in the ways that families are able to successfully deal with the processes of change required as a family develops. Families' ability to deal with change lie on a continuum. At one end of this continuum are those families that are highly adaptive and stable in their responses to change. At the other end of the continuum are families that have great difficulty in adjusting to a new stage of development and respond by either becoming destabilized and chaotic or actively resisting change, with negative consequences for the family and its members.

KEY POINTS

- In contemporary society there is a broad range of different types of family.
- A healthily functioning family is a social system which can:
  - meet the needs of its members
  - provide an environment for raising children
  - promote social well-being in the community.

- Fully functioning families can provide security and safety, economic and material well-being, psychological, physical and emotional well-being, and meet spiritual needs.
- Family function is affected by factors including the family's developmental stage, the influence of culture/ethnicity, and processes and behaviours within the family.
- Important processes in a family involve power and intimacy, role-structuring, communication, problem-solving, and change processes. Families lie on a continuum with healthily functioning families having high levels of capability at one end and poorly functioning families having low levels of capability with regard to these processes at the other end.

QUESTIONS FOR GROUP DISCUSSION OR STUDENT ASSIGNMENTS

1. How might the function of providing for the needs of individual family members be expressed in an isolated, single-parent family compared with an extended family? What are the implications for the adult/s and children in each case?
2. How might the function of reproduction and the raising of children be expressed in a same-sex family compared with a nuclear family? In connection with this, what issues might arise for each of these families?
3. How might the function of contributing to community well-being be expressed by a large extended family compared with a couple with no children? Identify any ethical issues involved.

● ● ●

6

Family Interactions

As discussed previously, a family constitutes a system. Even so, it is important to remember that the system comprises a group of individual family members, and that the interactions between these individuals will provoke responses and behaviour patterns among them and that these will have an influence on the family as a whole.

Figure 6.1 describes diagrammatically the way that an individual functions in the family. The individual family member will have their own perceptions of the family which will be influenced by their beliefs, norms, myths, values, and attitudes. Clearly, all of these will be conditioned by the individual's own personality traits. Additionally, an individual family member will have their own thoughts and behaviours, which enable them to do the best they can to meet their own needs in the context of the family. Individuals in the family will strive to get their emotional and physical needs met in a way that reduces their personal anxiety and helps them to feel comfortable within the

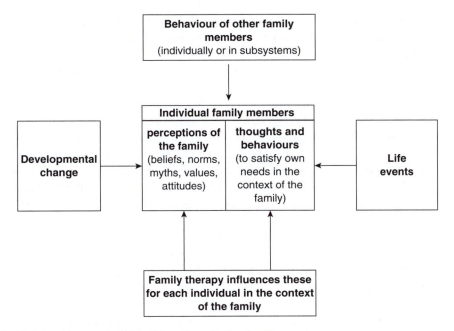

FIGURE 6.1   *How an individual functions in the family*

family system. Sometimes the way in which a family member endeavours to get their needs met may not be comfortable for other members of the family and may in fact be problematic for them. David can give a good example of this situation occurring from his own experience. He remembers being frustrated as a young child and behaving in a way that was problematic for the family. His siblings were much older than him. Because of this, he often felt excluded and unable to satisfy his need for interaction with other members of the family. To solve this problem, he discovered a way to get the attention of his elder siblings. He continually and deliberately did things to annoy them! Although he succeeded in getting his need for interaction satisfied, the outcomes for himself and the family were not generally positive. At the time, he was doing the best he knew to get his own needs met – but at a cost to himself and the family.

> **It is good to assume that most people are doing the best they can**

As counsellors, we will often be confronted by situations similar to the one described by David. In situations such as this, we think that it is almost always reasonable to assume that the family member/s in question are thinking and behaving in the best way they know how. Certainly, this is an assumption that we ourselves make when we are working as relationship counsellors. As counsellors, one way to assist the family is to help them to become aware of what they are doing and its consequences, and then to discover alternative ways of behaving which will meet their needs but with positive outcomes.

As illustrated in Figure 6.1, the individual family member's perceptions of the family, and their thoughts and behaviours, will be influenced by the behaviour of other family members, by developmental changes in the life of the family, and by life events or decisions that impact on the family as a whole. For example, a family relocating due to work opportunities or the sudden hospitalization of a family member will have an impact on the thoughts and behaviours of each family member. Where a family is involved in family therapy, the therapeutic process may also have an influence on each individual family member.

As a family interacts on a daily basis, each family member will be influenced by the behaviours of other family members. Similarly, subsystems within the family will be influenced by other subsystems. Consequently, when counselling families, it is important for the counsellor to consider the family as a dynamic, interactive system containing subsystems of one or more individuals, and to focus on patterns of relationship rather than primarily concentrating on individual behaviours and personalities. At times the counsellor may focus on individual behaviours and personalities, however generally it is helpful to consider the way problems affect the quality of the relationships and interactional processes occurring in the family.

Focusing on interactional patterns of relationship during counselling with a family necessitates paying attention to processes of communication and how family members talk and relate to each other. These processes, and their associated interactional patterns, are usually of more interest to the relationship counsellor than the detail and content of what family members are saying. Thus, while listening to the content of the discussion, the counsellor also needs to pay attention to the observation of the interactional patterns within the family. It is not surprising that families who come for counselling are usually focused on the detail and content of what is troubling them, as they are likely to feel strongly about these. Consequently, in the first instance, they are unlikely to recognize the processes and interactional patterns that are occurring. While listening to a family's discussion of their problem, the counsellor can raise the family's awareness of the interactive processes occurring between family members. If the family is to change, recognizing and understanding how these interactions within the family contribute to and/or maintain both helpful and unhelpful behaviours with regard to the problem is essential.

In can be helpful in identifying and understanding family processes to take into account some commonly observed family interactions, but before discussing these, it is useful to consider the relevance of cybernetics and attachment theory.

Cybernetics

Jackson (1959) drew attention to the relevance of cybernetic theory with regard to the way families function. The cybernetic concepts of linear and circular causality and of homoeostasis are very useful in enabling a counsellor to understand the processes occurring in families.

Homeostasis

Homeostasis has been described in the theory of cybernetics as the self-regulation that allows systems to maintain themselves in a state of dynamic balance. The notion of family homeostasis helps in understanding a family's tendency to resist change. As explained previously a family will naturally seek to maintain its stability and equilibrium. Unfortunately, although the natural tendency to seek homeostasis is essential in helping a family to stay on course and lead a stable existence, if change is to occur, homeostasis needs to be temporarily disrupted so that new patterns of relating can be developed and form the basis for a new homeostasis.

It is interesting to note that frequently a problematic symptom occurring within a family often performs a function in maintaining homeostasis. Strangely, existence of the symptom has a stabilizing influence on the family. Consider the example of a family where there is significant tension between the parents. It may be that in this family an emotionally disturbed child (the problem) is continually drawing attention to himself by engaging in unhelpful behaviours. By focusing their attention on the child and ignoring their marital conflict, the parents are able to maintain a stable relationship (homeostasis) though the cost to the child may be great. Unfortunately, we have found that this is not an uncommon scenario.

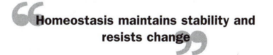

Homeostasis maintains stability and resists change

Although homeostasis remains an important concept in family therapy, it fails to take account of the natural human potential for creativity. This potential for creativity can be of considerable value in enabling families to discover for themselves adaptive ways in which to change.

Linear and circular causality

Linear causality describes a process where one event causes another. For example, event A (overspending) may be the cause of event B (bankruptcy). However, becoming bankrupt does not cause overspending. This is a good example of linear causality because whereas event A causes event B, it is clear that the event B does not cause event A.

Circular causality describes the situation that exists when event A affects event B, and additionally event B affects event A. Generally, circular causality begins with a precipitating event. Often in families the precipitating event occurs as a result of a family member making an effort to have their needs met. Here is a simple example of circular causality: if someone pays a second person a compliment (event A), this in turn may affect the behaviour of the second person, who might then be more likely to behave in a positive way to the first person (event B). As a result, good feelings may then flow around the positive feedback loop created (see Figure 6.2). Cybernetic theory suggests that it is preferable to use the concept of circular causality as opposed to linear causality as a basis for understanding the processes occurring in families.

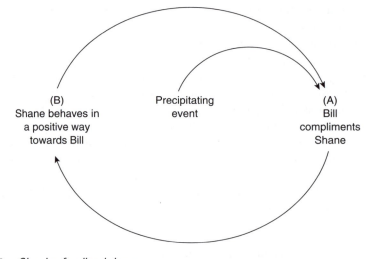

FIGURE 6.2   *Circular feedback loop*

The feedback process that occurs may gradually change, coming round to a new position. Sometimes the change can be so minutely different from the previous one that it is difficult for family members to recognize it. However, the new position may represent an important shift in the functioning of the family. For example, in the illustration above, the behaviour of the second person may change from being positive to behaviour which reflects a desire for a deeper and more meaningful relationship. Family therapy, in part, involves the promotion of positive feedback loops so that useful outcomes occur.

The concept of circular causality provides a helpful insight into family interactions

It is interesting to note that most families who seek counselling express their concerns in linear and not circular terms. Consider this example:

A mother comes to counselling complaining that her 4-year-old son is unmanageable even though the mother has instituted recommended behaviour management strategies. When these strategies haven't worked the mother has applied the strategies even more rigorously. This has had no positive effect whatsoever. Can you see how this mother is understandably locked into linear thinking (see Figure 6.3). She believes that by repeating the process and by doing more of the same the child's behaviour should improve, and because it doesn't, she sees her son as unmanageable. In her view, he has a problem and she would like the counsellor to fix this problem.

FIGURE 6.3   *The mother's linear understanding of the problem*

If we examine her situation in terms of circular causality we might recognize a feedback loop. The precipitating event can be seen as the child seeking attention by misbehaving. When he misbehaves the mother either withdraws or punishes him. The child feels rejected and seeks more attention by continuing to misbehave and possibly escalating his negative behaviour. If the counsellor is able to raise the mother's awareness with regard to her role in this feedback loop (see Figure 6.4), she has the opportunity to make decisions to change the process by introducing a new feedback loop (Figure 6.5). As the child receives attention, it is possible that he will become less demanding and the mother may be more likely to willingly provide the required attention.

Attachment Theory

Attachment theory provides an understanding of the unconscious and innate need for human beings to form close relationships. Initially, attachment theory was developed to describe the dependent relationship between a child and an adult (Bowlby, 1964). However, the theory is particularly relevant to both couple and family counselling as it helps explain the way in which adults need to depend on each other in seeking their own well-being. Additionally, many counsellors believe that the way couples deal with each other and their children reflects their attachment history.

Attachment theory assumes that infants become attached to their mothers or other objects that provide contact and comfort. It has been found that young children who are separated from their mothers experience a series of reactions that can be described as protest, despair, and finally detachment. Infants use their attachment figures as a

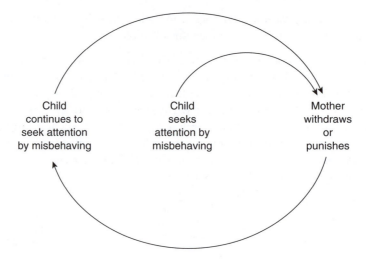

FIGURE 6.4   *A circular feedback explanation of the problem*

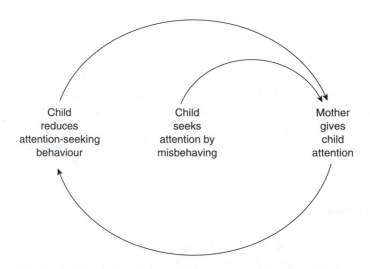

FIGURE 6.5   *Circular feedback describing a different way of dealing with the problem*

secure base for exploration. When an infant feels threatened, they will turn to the attachment figure for protection and comfort. Infants with secure attachment are confident in the availability of their caregivers and subsequently confident in their interactions in the world (Mercer, 2006).

Infants who are insecure display either an avoidance strategy or a resistant strategy. When using an avoidant strategy the infant inhibits attachment behaviour, and when using a resistant strategy the infant clings to the mother and avoids exploration. Infants experiencing insecure attachments may have had their attempts to attach rebuffed or met with indifference. As a result, such infants remain insecure about the availability of caregivers. Because attachment relationships are internalized, these early experiences shape expectations for later relationships of friendship, parenting, and romantic love.

> **Attachment theory is often helpful in explaining relationship dynamics**

Family counsellors can use attachment theory to inform their understanding of current relationships within a family. A child's misbehaviour might reflect an insecure attachment or a husband's avoidance might be due to ambivalent attachment, or a wife's animosity may be an expression of anxious attachment.

Commonly Observed Family Interactions

There are a number of commonly observed family interactions and it can be very helpful for a counsellor to recognize these. They include:

- interactions between subsystems
- boundaries and family rules
- alliances
- coalitions
- triangulation
- the double-bind.

Interactions between subsystems

There are many different subsystems within the family, such as the parental, marital, older children, and younger children subsystems, to name a few. Additionally, there may be subsystems resulting from alliances, coalitions, and triangulation.

In a nuclear family, the parents occupy two different subsystems. One is the spousal subsystem and the other the parental subsystem (Nichols and Schwartz, 2007). The spousal subsystem joins the couple together emotionally, psychologically, and sexually. In a family system it is usually expected that the boundary around the spousal subsystem will be strong so that the couple are able to have an intimate personal relationship with each other without intrusion from other family members.

In addition to belonging to the spousal subsystem the couple will also belong to the parental subsystem. In a nuclear family the parental subsystem will take responsibility for all aspects of parenting. The boundary around this system will be more permeable than that around the spousal subsystem. For example, if there is a considerable age difference between the children in the family, an older child or children may at times, under specific circumstances and with specific limits, be permitted to cooperate with the parental subsystem in helping to supervise and manage the behaviour of a younger sibling. In addition, the permeable boundary allows appropriate physical contact of an affectionate nature to occur between the parents and their children as well as the sharing of appropriate information.

The children of the family belong to a subsystem of siblings. Depending on the nature of the family, the boundary around this subsystem may be quite porous as friends of the children relate to one or more of those within the subsystem.

In some families, differences in gender are particularly important, and in such families there may be a clearly defined male subsystem and a female subsystem. The male subsystem may include the father together with boys in the family, and the female subsystem, the mother and girls. Clearly, these subsystems can be useful to family members as the male subsystem allows the males in the family to be supportive of each other while engaging in activities and discussions which are relevant for their gender. Similarly for the female subsystem.

Boundaries and family rules

Every system has a boundary, the properties of which are important in understanding how the system works. Most boundaries have some level of permeability; that is to say, some things can pass through them while others cannot. In families, boundaries are invisible barriers which regulate the amount and type of contact with others. Boundaries safeguard the separateness and autonomy of the family and its subsystems.

Problems can result when boundaries are either too rigid or too diffuse. Rigid boundaries are overly restrictive and permit little contact with outside systems, resulting in disengagement. Disengagement leaves individuals and subsystems independent but isolated. Enmeshed subsystems have diffuse boundaries. They offer heightened feelings of support at the expense of independence and autonomy.

Alliances

Alliances can be described as cooperative arrangements between two or more parties. For example, a father and son may both be keen on sailing small boats, so they may join together in this activity. Consequently, the alliance they have formed enables them to join together and to meet their shared needs.

Although alliances may have a positive impact within the family, it is not always necessarily so. Some alliances that are formed with a positive intention can have a negative impact on family functioning. Consider the example illustrated in Figure 6.6(a) where a mother and son have formed a close alliance. They may have joined closely together to satisfy their mutual needs. Unfortunately, in doing this, it is possible that a boundary emerges around them that excludes the mother's partner, the son's father. This might cause problems between the parents even though this may not have been the mother's intention.

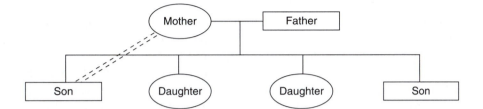

FIGURE 6.6(a)   *Mother-son alliance in a nuclear family*

Coalitions

A coalition is an alliance where two or more individuals in the family join together in opposing another member, or members, of the family. In the previous example of an alliance (Figure 6.6(a)), there would be a significant risk that the alliance between the mother and son could degenerate into a coalition against the father. For example, if the father tried to discipline the son, he might be resisted by the mother, who might want to support of the son. This would inevitably cause conflict between the mother and father. Interestingly, most but not all coalitions are cross-generational, as in the example just described.

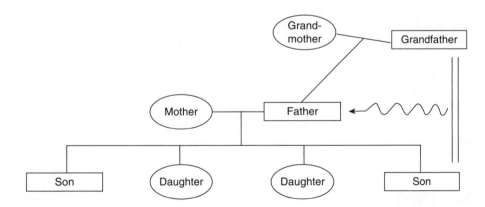

FIGURE 6.6(b)   *Grandfather–grandson coalition in a family*

An example of a cross-generational coalition is a coalition between a grandfather and grandson, as shown in Figure 6.6(b), where both join together to attack and/or undermine the father. It may be that every time the father tries to punish the son, the son seeks support from his grandfather, who supports and defends him while criticizing the father.

Triangulation

Triangulation occurs when difficulties occurring between two family members are not resolved directly between them but instead a third person becomes involved in the process. As an example, consider the situation where a mother and father have unresolved conflict between them. Whenever the tension begins to rise between them, instead of addressing the issues, they both focus on their daughter's behaviour, blame her for the tension in the family, and verbally attack her in order to deflect away from their own conflict.

Double-bind

The concept of the double-bind was introduced by Bateson, Jackson, Haley and Weakland (1956). This occurs when a member of the family receives contradictory messages on different levels of communication but finds it difficult to detect or comment on the inconsistency. This places the person in a double-bind, and in the view of Bateson et al. is 'crazy making'. Nichols and Schwartz (2007) emphasize that the double-bind is not simply the receipt of contradictory messages, but is a repeated pattern of communication experienced between two or more persons in an important relationship. For example, a negative message may be given, such as 'Don't do that or you will be punished' together with a second message, given at a more abstract level, conflicting with the first but also enforced by the threat of punishment. Thus the person is placed in a double-bind because whatever they do is likely to result in negative consequences. Bateson et al. (1956) give the following example of a double-bind:

A young man in hospital recovering from a schizophrenic episode received a visit from his mother. When he put his arm around her she stiffened, but when he withdrew, she asked, 'Don't you love me any more?' Clearly, the young man was in a double-bind because if he showed affection he would be rejected and if he didn't show affection he would be accused of not loving his mother.

KEY POINTS

- An individual's perception of their family is influenced by the behaviour of other family members, life events, and developmental changes.
- A counsellor needs to focus on the interactional processes occurring in the family while at the same time attending to the content of the family discussion.

- Homeostasis involves the natural tendency to maintain equilibrium and stability while resisting change.
- In order to maximize the possibility for change it is preferable to use the concept of circular rather than linear causality in describing family processes.
- Relationship problems can frequently be described in terms of attachment theory.
- Rigid boundaries tend to enhance independence and autonomy whereas flexible boundaries enable heightened feelings of support.
- It is important for relationship counsellors to understand family interactions such as the formation of alliances, coalitions, triangulation, and the double-bind.
- Encouraging clients to think in terms of circular rather than linear causality is advantageous in promoting change.
- Attachment theory enables understanding of how a client's attachment history might be affecting their current behaviour and relationships.

QUESTIONS FOR GROUP DISCUSSION OR STUDENT ASSIGNMENTS

1. Describe a family situation that you have witnessed where an underlying problem has provided stability for the family.
2. Discuss the way that developmental processes and life events can affect a family's functioning. Illustrate your answer with practical examples.

7

The Initial Contact with a Family Before Counselling Begins

In our experience as relationship counselling practitioners, although not essential, it is usually advantageous if contact is made with the family prior to the first family counselling session. We agree with Lowe (2004) that the first therapeutic conversations begin when the first contact is made. It is at this point that the initial joining can occur, practicalities regarding the counselling process can be negotiated, and useful information about the family can be obtained.

We recognize that some relationship counsellors prefer to have minimal, if any, contact with clients or referrers before the first meeting and to start from scratch at that meeting (Lowe, 2004). We are quite happy to do this, if that is what the client wants. Certainly, some clients will phone to make an appointment and are reluctant to enter into discussion at that time. However, many clients are uncertain about the counselling process and need reassurance, in particular in connection with their ability to influence the process so that it is comfortable for them. Consequently, we believe that it is often useful for a relationship counsellor to talk with a family member, or partner in a couple, prior to the first counselling session.

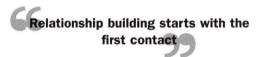

Relationship building starts with the first contact

Sometimes, referrals will come from outside sources, such as community agencies or government departments. In these cases, the counsellor needs to make a decision about the extent of the information they would like to have from the referral source. As counsellors ourselves, we have found it useful to have as much information as is offered from both the client family and/or referral sources. In gathering such information it is important to remember that the information provided by a family member or a referrer is that person's subjective perspective of the family. During the counselling process it is very likely that other perspectives will emerge as individual family members share their points of view.

Joining with the Caller

Often one member of a family will telephone to tentatively make an appointment for counselling. This is an opportunity for the counsellor to join with the caller and to help them to prepare themselves and their family for the first counselling session.

Can you imagine what it must be like for a family member, usually a parent, to take the initial step of contacting a counsellor to make an appointment for counselling? Before taking this step, it is quite likely that the family, and in particular the caller, have been troubled by a problem within the family for some time, have tried to solve the problem and have failed to do so. They may be uncertain about whether counselling is appropriate, and whether it is likely to help.

Many prospective clients see the counsellor as an expert and expect that the counsellor will tell the family what to do in order to solve their problem. We believe that it is more important for the family, in collaboration with the counsellor, to discover their own solutions.

In order to successfully join with the caller it can be useful for the counsellor to help the caller to feel at ease by inviting them to talk about their anxieties related to seeking counselling, and by listening to the information they provide about their family situation. Additionally, it is important for the counsellor to answer any questions the caller may have with regard to the counselling process. While doing this it is usually sensible to use reflective listening skills and minimal responses. In this way a comfortable relationship can begin to be established between counsellor and caller.

Being prepared for requests for counselling from new clients

It can be very helpful in gathering information about a family to use an intake form similar to that shown in Figure 7.1. Included on the form is a space for a genogram. This shows pictorially the membership and structure of the family, as shown in Figure 7.2. Where the information is available, the names and ages of children can be included on the genogram. Also boundaries around systems and subsystems can be drawn. Notes might be added regarding the problem, as described by the caller, alliances and coalitions, and the duration and nature of couple relationships. Drawing a genogram such as this can be very useful to the counsellor as names can be memorized before the first counselling session and genealogical relationships between family members are clear.

Addressing the caller's personal anxieties

While a telephone call from a member of the family should not be treated as a counselling session for that member of the family, it is important to let them voice their anxieties with regard to the counselling process. The counsellor also has an opportunity to explain broadly how the family counselling process will enable all members of the family to talk

INTAKE FORM

Family name:

Caller's name:

Address:

Phone number:

Genogram:

Caller's description of the problem:

Duration of the problem:

Referral source:

Outcome of the call:

FIGURE 7.1   *Example of an intake form*

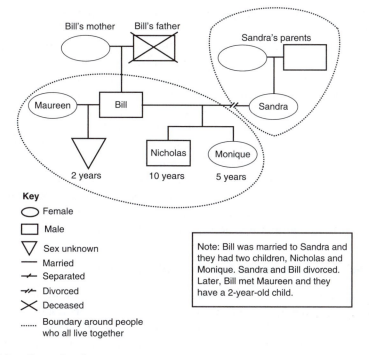

Key

○ Female

□ Male

▽ Sex unknown

— Married

⊢ Separated

⊬ Divorced

✕ Deceased

...... Boundary around people who all live together

Note: Bill was married to Sandra and they had two children, Nicholas and Monique. Sandra and Bill divorced. Later, Bill met Maureen and they have a 2-year-old child.

FIGURE 7.2   *Example of a genogram*

about the problem facing the family. Issues related to confidentiality may be discussed along with the rights of parents.

Making the first approach to a counsellor can be anxiety-provoking

Parents are often concerned about how to tell other members of their family that an appointment has been made for counselling. We believe that, as counsellors, it is important for us to be transparent in all our transactions and to encourage the family to do the same. Consequently, we believe that it is sensible and appropriate for all family members to be made aware in advance of the reason why they are coming to consult with a counsellor. It is not appropriate for family members to be persuaded to attend a counselling session under a false pretext as this is likely to be counter-productive, to alienate one or more family members from the counselling process, and to interfere with the building of a trusting relationship between the counsellor and the family. In order to avoid this occurring, we suggest that it is better for family members to be informed that by attending counselling problems which have risen in the family can be addressed with a view to achieving positive outcomes for both individuals as well as the family as a whole.

Sometimes parents have difficulty knowing how to encourage younger members of the family to come to counselling sessions, particularly if problems in the family relate to the behaviour of one of them. The parents often fear that unless they become firm in their requests that the young person will not attend or will attend with hostility and resentment. In such a situation it can be useful to suggest to parents that it may be helpful if they explain to the family that they themselves would like to attend counselling in order to help them deal in the best way with problems in the family. They can then say that they would like the other family members to come along with them so that everyone in the family can express their point of view and by doing so help in the counselling process. Giving such an explanation helps to make the counselling process more acceptable to younger members of the family as they are less likely to see the counselling process as confronting and stigmatizing for them.

Deciding who should attend the first counselling session

Sometimes a parent making an appointment will suggest that they would prefer to attend alone, or together with their partner, at the first session rather than with the whole family. While we prefer to have the whole family attend the first session, we believe that it is more important to arrange the process in a way which will best suit the clients. However, we are careful to explain why we believe that it would be helpful for the whole family to attend the first session; this would enable us to simultaneously collect points of view from different members of the family and help us to build a more comprehensive picture of what is occurring within the family. Also, if the parents come to the first session on their own, it may be more difficult for other members of the family to join with and trust us, as they may wonder what information we have already been given by their parents. After explaining why we would prefer to have the whole family present, we are equally interested in what the family believes is the best approach for their particular situation. By respecting and accepting the family's decision we find that the joining process is enhanced.

Terminating the call appropriately

As stated previously, it is not appropriate for an initial telephone conversation with a member of the family to be used as a counselling session. While listening to the anxieties of the caller and addressing issues related to the counselling process, it is sensible to limit the call by suggesting that further information might be disclosed during the first counselling session. The caller might also be made aware that as part of the integrative counselling model used, it is possible for counselling sessions for individual members of the family to be included in the process if that is deemed to be desirable.

Gaining information from referrers

Sometimes a third party who is not a family member will phone to make an appointment on behalf of a family. This person may be speaking as a friend of the family, or on behalf of an agency or government department. They may be a medical practitioner, school teacher, school counsellor, or of another profession. Information gained from such referral sources can be valuable because it provides another perspective on the family. It is essential to remember that this information comes from one perspective and is not necessarily of more value than any other individual perspective.

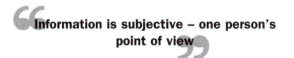

> **Information is subjective – one person's point of view**

Sometimes a person who is not a member of the family but is referring the family for counselling will phone to make an appointment for the family. When this happens, we tell the referrer that we would prefer a member of the family to contact us themselves to arrange an appointment time. However, we are flexible and in some cases will offer an appointment time to the referrer. The advantage in having a member of the family call to make an appointment is that this enables us to make a direct connection with the family, and to check whether the family are motivated to come for counselling rather than being directed to come for counselling against their will. In this regard we do recognize that under particular circumstances, such as where child abuse has occurred or is suspected, or where the possibility of such abuse occurring is considered likely, that families will be appropriately referred for counselling and may be reluctant to attend. In situations like this, we place great importance on building a relationship of trust with the family, while at the same time being open and honest about any limits to confidentiality which may be imposed upon the counselling process from external referral sources.

The usefulness of obtaining information before starting the counselling process

It can be advantageous for the counsellor to have information from other sources about the family prior to the commencement of counselling. This includes information about the family's history, typical behaviours of individuals in the family, and the family's cultural background. Such information may enable the counsellor, in collaboration with the clients, to guide the counselling session in a useful direction.

It must be remembered that information given by a referral source may be inaccurate and distorted because of the referrer's own agenda. However, such information is still useful because it is someone else's perception of what is happening. For example, we may have been told by a school headteacher that a child in the family is deliberately disobedient. Later, we may discover that the child has a high-order language problem and consequently has difficulty in understanding instructions, but is not generally being deliberately disobedient. Although the first piece of information was factually incorrect, it would have informed the counsellor with regard to what might have been happening in the child's life at school.

KEY POINTS

- Relationship-building takes place from the first contact.
- Reflective listening skills are useful when a family member phones for an appointment.
- Genograms are helpful when recording intake information.
- It is important for parents to be honest with families about why they are coming for counselling.
- It is helpful, but not essential, if the whole family attend the first counselling session.
- Information from referrers can be helpful but it must be recognized as being just one person's point of view.

QUESTIONS FOR GROUP DISCUSSION OR STUDENT ASSIGNMENTS

1. Imagine that a parent calls to make an appointment and tells you, the counsellor, that they are not intending to tell the family the correct reason for coming to counselling. Discuss how you would deal with this situation, taking into account any ethical considerations.
2. Imagine that your own family, or your family of origin, have agreed to attend counselling. Fill out an intake form complete with genogram. After completing the intake form, discuss any emotions that you experienced while doing this task, and any ideas that emerged as a consequence of completing the form.

8

Helping the Family to Communicate in the First Session

In this chapter we describe the first session of counselling using the CACHO model. Many of the strategies used when working with the family can also be used when working with couples, as will be discussed in Part Five. Whenever working with families, we strongly recommend the use of a co-therapist or a reflecting team. Consequently, the process to be described in this chapter will assume that the counsellor is working with such assistance. In our experience, working with the help of a co-therapist or reflecting team is more effective than working as a counsellor without assistance in enabling the family to discover ways of changing that suit them. The counselling process is brief and time-effective when working with a co-therapist or reflecting team. As a result, the family are more likely to become positively engaged in the counselling process and be optimistic about the possibilities for change than they would be if a slower process was used.

Preparation before Meeting the Family

As discussed in the previous chapter, counsellors often have information about a client family before the family arrives for counselling. This information may have come from a referral source or from a member of the family who phoned to make the appointment. The information may have been recorded on an intake sheet, as described in Chapter 7. Figure 8.1 shows an example of a completed intake sheet. The information on the sheet relates to a fictitious family. We will use this fictitious family to illustrate the CACHO model for counselling families. Prior to meeting the family it can be helpful for the counsellor and co-therapist or reflecting team to meet together to debrief with regard to any personal issues which may concern any of them personally, and to familiarize themselves with information about the family and the family's reasons for attending counselling.

When a member of a counselling team prepares to work with a family they may bring with them troubling personal issues of their own, and these may intrude on their ability to fully attend to the family. It is therefore good practice for team members to debrief by sharing the existence of any such issues with the team. Usually, by sharing these issues, they can be put to one side so that the team member can concentrate on the client family without distraction.

Sometimes, when familiarizing themselves with information about a client family, a member of the counselling team will find that personal issues of their own are triggered as a consequence of considering the family's presenting issue. There is then a risk that the team member's response to the family during counselling will be a response to their own issues rather than the family's. Once again, it can be useful for any team member troubled by such personal issues to indicate the existence of these to other members of the team. By doing so, they may be able to put intruding thoughts about these issues to one side.

It is important to make a distinction between debriefing with other team members in the way described and counselling to address personal issues. It would not be appropriate for debriefing prior to a counselling session to become a counselling session for the team member. While mentioning the existence of issues can be helpful in enabling a member of a counselling team to put these issues to one side, personal troubling problems need to be addressed in supervision or in a separate therapeutic setting.

Imagine that you are a member of the counselling team preparing to see the family described on the intake sheet in Figure 8.1. You might like to stop for a moment to consider what thoughts come to mind when you think about this family.

It is tempting to try to guess what is happening in the family, and you might have begun to think about any of the following possibilities:

- Sean doesn't want to be in this family and would rather live with his natural father.
- Sean resents the time Mark spends with Zachary because before Zachary was born Mark and Sean spent time together.
- There is a problem in Alice and Mark's relationship and they are triangulating Sean to avoid facing their own problem.
- Grandma resents Mark being in the family and is in coalition with Sean against Mark.

Obviously, there are many possibilities so it can be a mistake to jump to conclusions before meeting the family. What is important is to help the family to discover for themselves what is really happening in their family and to empower them to make decisions about how to deal with the problem. Even so, it is useful for the counselling team to take note of information recorded on the intake form. Because Alice initiated contact with the counsellor, it is important to remember that this information comes from Alice; it is her picture, and may be different from the pictures of other family members.

Greeting the Clients

Being friendly and relaxed when meeting a family in the waiting room helps to put the family at ease. This meeting is the appropriate time to greet each member of the

INTAKE FORM

Family name: JOHNSON

Caller's name: ALICE JOHNSON

Address: 62 SPANO ST, TAIGUM

Phone number: Silent number

Genogram:

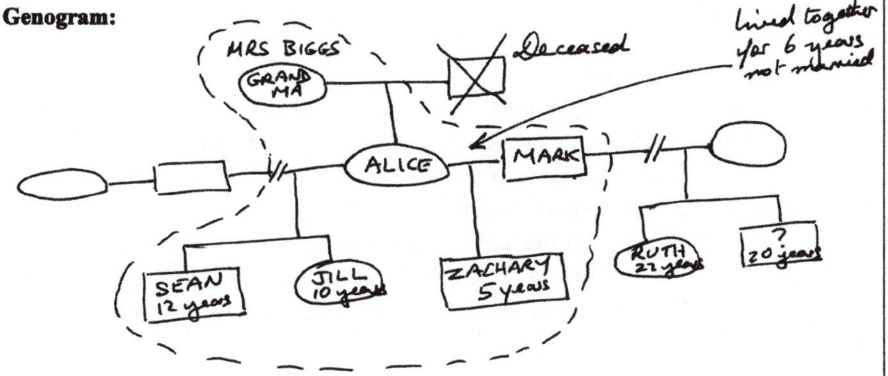

Caller's description of the problem: Alice phoned saying that she wanted counselling for Sean. Alice says that Sean's behaviour is destroying the family, with the result that Mark + she are contemplating separating "as this seems to be the only solution". Sean gets on with no-one except Grandma. He is disobedient + rudely insults Mark. Alice fears that Mark + Sean will become physically violent to each other because Mark thinks that Sean has been spoilt + needs to be "stamped on". Alice's mother (Grandma) strongly disagrees with Mark.

Duration of the problem: about 2 years duration.
When Mark first moved in 6 years ago Sean + Mark did things together (both liked sailing).

Referral source:
The family doctor: Dr D Richards

Outcome of the call:
Alice decided to ask the whole family to come to the first counselling session + then they will review the situation.

FIGURE 8.1   *Example of a completed intake form*

family individually and to get to know them by name. Also, it is an opportunity for the family to be introduced to the co-therapist or reflecting team members and for any questions regarding the counselling process to be answered. The family's consent for the use of a co-therapist or counselling team is essential, along with written consent for any proposed recording of the counselling session. It is important to be clear and transparent about the reasons for using a co-therapist or counselling team and/or recording, and about the way in which the co-therapist or reflecting team will be involved.

Joining with the Clients

Coming to counselling as a family presents the family with a new experience which is different from other experiences, and is consequently likely to be stressful. As pointed out by Lowe (2004), in this stressful family situation, the first meeting is likely to see most, if not all participants, operating initially from reactive postures, predisposed towards fight or flight and primed to react rather than respond. It is therefore critical that during this time of initial contact the counsellor places a strong emphasis on joining with each member of the family. This focus on joining is likely to reduce the family members' level of stress so that they can participate freely and willingly.

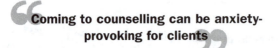

Coming to counselling can be anxiety-provoking for clients

The counsellor's initial goal is to encourage each member of the family to share with the rest of the family their pictures of the family and of what they believe to be happening within the family. To do this the counsellor needs to use a process which engages each individual in the family. Consequently, rather than listening for any length of time to one particular family member, the counsellor continually switches attention from one member to another. As the counsellor listens to each person it is important to *validate* each individual's picture of the family. By doing this, family members are likely to view the counsellor as an independent person who is able to see things from each individual member's perspective.

Throughout the family therapy process the counsellor will encourage family members to talk directly to each other whenever appropriate. This is important because as family members communicate with each other they have the opportunity to try to understand each other's points of view. In addition, the counsellor can observe the processes that are occurring between family members while they communicate.

Validating each family member's picture is essential in the joining process

Joining with younger members of the family

We have noticed that when parents take their children to see a doctor, teacher, or other adult for advice or help, generally, the parents do the talking and the children say very little. In some families, children are taught that it is not very polite to talk while adults are talking. When counselling families it is highly desirable to create and maintain good relationships with every member of the family, including the younger members, so that everyone has an opportunity, and feels free, to talk about their point of view.

Kathryn will describe hows she might empower Zachary, the youngest member of our presenting family (see Figure 8.1), to talk about his point of view:

As soon as the family were seated in the counselling room I would ask the parents, *'Is it okay with you if I talk with Zachary first?'* Almost always the parents will agree. I will then ask Zachary a circular question. I might say, *'Zachary, this is a difficult question and you may not be able to answer it, but can you tell me why you think your Mum and Dad have brought you all here?'* If Zachary tells me that he doesn't know the answer to my question, I will then follow up by asking, *'If you had a guess about why Mum and Dad have brought you all here, what would your guess be?'*

It might be that Zachary would be unable to give me an answer, in which case I would move to the next eldest member of the family, point out that Zachary doesn't know why Mum and Dad have brought the family here, and ask, *'Why do you think Mum and Dad have brought the family here?'*

Using this process empowers younger members of the family to take part in the conversation, and this will develop as I use more circular questions to engage other members of the family, including the parents.

Replacing Monocular Lenses by Multiple Lenses

When a family comes to counselling, each individual member will have their own picture of the family and of what is happening within the family. It is as though they are looking at their family through a single lens with monocular vision.

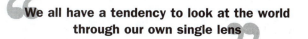

We all have a tendency to look at the world through our own single lens

As the counsellor engages each family member and invites them to describe their individual perceptions of what is happening in the family, other members of the family listen. As a consequence, family members begin to see each other's perceptions of their family. In this way, instead of individual family members having monocular vision and looking through one lens, they will hopefully begin to look through multiple lenses, seeing several different points of view.

An excellent way in which to help a family share their individual perceptions of the family with each other so that they start to see through multiple lenses is to use circular questions. Circular questions originated from the Milan systemic family therapy model (Selvini Palazzoli et al., 1980) which was described in Chapter 1.

The Role of the Family Counsellor

In some ways a relationship counsellor working with a family is rather like the conductor of an orchestra. The conductor doesn't play any of the instruments himself, but instead skilfully invites different members of the orchestra to play their instruments at appropriate times so that there is blending together of acoustic information from many different types of instrument. The conductor does take responsibility for guiding the musical process that evolves but has little control of the way that individual members of the orchestra play their instruments. Now we admit that this metaphor is not exact, but in some ways it parallels the role of the family counsellor.

Just as the conductor of an orchestra orchestrates the work of the musicians, so the counsellor needs to 'orchestrate' the process that occurs in a relationship counselling session. The counsellor needs to make decisions about what skills to use, when to use them and how to use them. Additionally, the counsellor needs to decide when to move the focus from one member of the family to another.

A relationship counsellor has a dynamic role

A relationship counsellor has a number of other important duties to perform while conducting a counselling session. These include:

- creating and maintaining a safe climate
- using skills which will enable the family to look through multiple lenses
- using skills which will raise awareness
- maintaining a respectful acceptance of each individual's point of view
- generating energy and interest in the counselling process.

Creating and maintaining a safe climate

Families frequently come for counselling when there are high levels of tension in the family. As a consequence, in counselling sessions, it would be easy for emotions to rise, increasing tension to unacceptable levels where members of the family may not feel safe in disclosing important information. Relationship counsellors therefore have a responsibility to manage counselling sessions in order to do everything possible to ensure that unacceptable levels of harmful emotion are not generated.

While we believe that it is important for counsellors to create a climate where families can be empowered to take responsibility for their own decisions, we also believe that it is essential in any relationship counselling situation for the counsellor to contain the counselling process. By adopting this position we believe that, as counsellors, we are behaving ethically and ensuring the physical, emotional, and psychological safety and well-being of our clients. Containing the counselling process involves using skills to manage situations so that positive outcomes are achieved.

Bubenzer and West (1993) are specific in stating that any system requires some behavioural management skills in order to operate efficiently and this also holds for couple and family counselling sessions. They make it clear that when counselling couples, for example, the counsellor's ability to implement behavioural management skills during a counselling session is usually summoned when one or both partners stop listening, fail to work at understanding one another and, instead, go forward into accustomed and problematic patterns of interaction. Similarly, in family counselling sessions the counsellor will need at times to use specific counselling skills to manage the counselling process.

We believe that it is not acceptable for a counsellor to tolerate abusive behaviour in a counselling session. Inevitably, there will be times, with particular families, when an individual or individuals in the family express anger aggressively or may use statements which are demeaning to another person, or others, in the family. However, when this occurs it is essential for the counsellor to calmly and with determination exert control. In extreme cases, the counselling session should be brought to a close. Where this is not considered necessary, the interactional process should be discussed so that positive outcomes are achieved.

> **Behaviour management is part of a relationship counsellor's responsibility**

Behaviour management by a counsellor can include controlling an individual's talk time and supporting a submissive or disempowered member of the family. Sometimes this can be done through the use of the alter ego process (see Chapter 9).

Using skills which will enable the family to look through multiple lenses

As discussed, an important goal for the counsellor in the first session is to elicit information which will enable family members to see each other's perspectives – in effect, to look through multiple lenses instead of a single lens. We believe that usually the best way to do this is through the use of circular questions, as described in Chapter 4. As explained in Chapter 4, using circular questions draws more than one person into the conversation at any one time. These questions also make it easy for the counsellor to move from talking to one person to talking to another. For example, the counsellor might ask, *'Jill, how do you see the relationship between Grandma and Sean?'* After receiving the answer from Jill, the counsellor can turn to Mark and ask, *'Do you agree with Jill's answer, or do you have a different point of view?'* It is also quite possible that either Sean or Grandma will want to offer their points of view rather than just letting other people talk about them and their relationship.

> **Circular questions are helpful in enabling a family to see through multiple lenses**

Using skills which will raise awareness

According to the Gestalt theory of change, change occurs through raised awareness. It is therefore important for the counsellor to make use of those skills that were described in Chapter 4. Such skills are particularly useful in helping to raise awareness while encouraging the family to communicate. These skills include:

- listening and observation
- reflection and validation
- making information newsworthy
- feeding back observed family processes
- reframing
- externalizing the problem.

Maintaining a respectful acceptance of each individual's point of view

If the counsellor is to engage each member of the family, they will need to pay attention to, and accept, each individual's point of view. Assuming that this task is successfully performed, it is likely that all the members of the family will see the counsellor as someone who is capable of being impartial, of accepting difference, and of being respectful. Moreover, the counsellor will not be seen as someone who wishes to impose their own point of view, beliefs, attitudes, or biases on the family, but will be seen as someone who wants to help the family discover what is best for them.

Generating energy and interest in the counselling process

It is inevitable that every counsellor will bring into their counselling sessions aspects of their own personality. We recognize that different counsellors have different ways of relating. Even so, we are convinced that for successful relationship counselling the counsellor's level of energy and interest throughout the counselling session is likely to impact on the family. The counselling process will inevitably be very serious at times, but we believe that it is appropriate and advantageous for humour to be introduced at appropriate times and, if the opportunity arises, for light-hearted conversation to be included when this occurs spontaneously. As a consequence, a warm, friendly relationship between the family and counsellor can be maintained. This requires a counsellor to be energetic in orchestrating the counselling process. When energy levels fall it can be useful to either introduce a new strategy, or check with the family about the direction of the session, or invite the reflecting team/co-therapist into the session, or to end the session.

Use of a Co-therapist

As explained in Chapter 3, while counselling is in progress the co-therapist (if one is used) observes from the observation room through a one-way mirror. During the counselling process the co-therapist may intervene by phoning through into the counselling room using an intercom phone. Additionally, at the end of the first session the co-therapist may be invited into the counselling room to give the family feedback, often in the form of a feedback picture.

Telephone interventions

Telephone interventions by a co-therapist can be used for any of the following purposes:

- to feedback processes
- to feedback interactional patterns
- to feedback observations of behaviour
- to draw attention to information that has been minimized
- to suggest a hypothesis to explain particular behaviours.

Detailed information regarding the use of a co-therapist and telephone interventions is given in Chapter 3. As explained in that chapter, after a telephone intervention has been made, the counsellor may decide to pass the intervention on to the family. In this case, a counsellor might say, 'Harry (the co-therapist) said that ...'. It is important for the counsellor to accurately repeat what the co-therapist has said. Having passed this message on, the counsellor can then make it clear that the message comes from the co-therapist, thus enabling the family to disagree more easily with the message if that is what they wish. Telephone interventions can be very useful in bringing the family's attention to information that they may have missed and in helping them to openly discuss the situation with each other.

Sometimes a counsellor will decide that it is not appropriate to pass the message from the co-therapist on to the family at the time it is given. It may be that what is occurring in the session is useful for the family and introducing a message may distract them from conversation that is helpful. It is appropriate for the counsellor at such a time to say to the family, *'Harry has just made a comment but at this stage I wonder if it would be more useful to continue talking about . . .'*.

Presentation of a feedback picture

During the first counselling session with a family, the counsellor will make a decision with regard to moving towards closing the session. At this point the counsellor can, with the family's permission, invite the co-therapist to come into the counselling room to give the family feedback about what the co-therapist has observed about the family, its interactions and behaviours. The counsellor will ask the family not to comment or ask questions while feedback is being given, but just to listen carefully, and then to talk about the feedback after the co-therapist has returned to the observation room.

Sometimes the co-therapist can give feedback verbally. At other times, the co-therapist can give feedback by drawing a representational or metaphorical picture on a white-board while talking about the picture. It is helpful for the family if the co-therapist is careful to explain that the feedback offered will only describe their picture of what is happening in the family, and that this picture may be quite different from the family's picture.

> **The co-therapist's picture is seen through their own individual lens**

The co-therapist's feedback provides an additional picture which family members can accept, reject or use in developing their own new pictures. It is not important whether they accept or reject the feedback picture. What the co-therapist's feedback picture does is to provide an additional lens which comes from outside the family system and which may be useful in contributing to their own pictures.

An advantage in using the co-therapist's picture is that the co-therapist is less engaged with the family than the counsellor and is able to provide another perspective which is likely to be a more detached view. The family's response to, and discussion of, the feedback picture helps in raising the family's awareness of what is happening in the family. Gestalt therapy theory suggests that such raised awareness will provide the family with an opportunity to change.

In presenting a feedback picture it is important for the co-therapist to:

- stress that every family member is doing the best they can – their behaviour is a response to the system and environment
- comment on the family's resources and competencies
- comment on individual family members' strengths

In giving feedback it may be useful to:

- comment on what has been noticed about how the family has responded as a result of any developmental or physical changes
- comment on what has been noticed within the family session with regard to processes and interactive patterns (here-and-now processes).

Examples of feedback pictures

Figures 8.2(a)–(d) are examples of feedback pictures (they are all representations of fictitious families).

FIGURE 8.2(a)   *Feedback picture*

Figure 8.2(a) shows a family where the mother suggested the family come to counselling because she was worried about the emotional state of the oldest son, who had withdrawn from all activities and was staying at home doing very little and looking very depressed. As a result of observing the first counselling session, the co-therapist drew the picture shown in the figure. While drawing the figure, the co-therapist said:

I am going to draw a picture to represent your family. It is my picture and I am not an expert on your family so I may be wrong. In my picture this is Dad. I have heard that he goes around the family singing. I have heard that he has a serious illness and believes he is at risk of dying. I am wondering whether he sings because he's worried about what might happen to the family if he were to die and this is his way of keeping worry at bay. I notice that Mum said that she does a lot of yelling. I'm curious to know whether it is her way of keeping worry out of her life by being angry because Dad's illness is threatening him. Next I notice that Simon stays at home and does very little. Is it possible that worrying makes him stay at home to keep a check on Dad to make sure that he's okay? I notice that Shane is also worried and wants to be given more information about what is medically wrong with Dad so that he can be less worried. Little Crystal seems to me to deal with her worry by being very affectionate to everyone in the family. From what I've seen, I get the impression that this family are all worrying about Dad but not talking to each other about their worries. I have drawn circles round each person in the family to indicate that everyone is worrying separately instead of talking to each other. I notice that although the family don't talk about their worries, they do talk about riding bikes, which they all enjoy and it seems as though this common interest ties them together. I have drawn two other boxes here with question marks in them because I am wondering if there are any other ways in which the family could support each other.

FIGURE 8.2(b)   *Feedback picture*

Figure 8.2(b) shows a family which came to counselling as a consequence of fighting between an older daughter and a younger daughter in the family. The co-therapist presented the picture in this way:

… I see your family is a very powerful family, like a family of lions. It seems to me the most powerful member of the family is Dad, who stands alone and is proud of his family. My impression is that Jennifer is very fond of her mother and really likes getting her mother's attention (so I've drawn hearts here). However, Susan would also like to have her mother's attention and this causes conflict between Jennifer and Susan. The way I have drawn the picture Mum is looking at Dad while Susan hides behind Mum's back seeking protection from Jennifer. Mum would like the girls to get along together, and is unhappy with Jennifer, who she believes should try harder as she is the eldest. I have drawn a circle around Jennifer because I don't think she wants to spend time with Susan, but wants to walk alone and develop a close relationship with her mother. I've heard that Dad is very heavily involved in his work to provide for his family so has little free time to spend with them. I'm curious about what might happen if that were to change.

FIGURE 8.2(c)   *Feedback picture*

Figure 8.2(c) shows a family consisting of a mother and her 16-year-old son. They came to counselling because the mother, Maude, was concerned about her very conflictual relationship with her son, Peter. It emerged in the counselling session that Peter wanted to have a good relationship with his mother but felt pressured to become the sort of person he didn't want to be. His goal was to lead a free lifestyle as an actor rather than going to university to study business management as his mother wanted. The co-therapist gave the following feedback:

I've noticed that you, Peter, are striving towards your goal of becoming an actor and don't want to be a conventional person who goes to university to study business management. I have drawn you in this balloon here to represent you doing the things you like in the way you like. I think that you are despairing, Peter, because you want your mother to accept who you are, and want a good relationship with her, but she wants you to be different. I think that you, Maude, are rather like an artist and Peter is your artistic creation. You have a particular dream for your son and would like to help him develop into the sort of person that you could be proud of; rather like a beautiful work of art that could be displayed in a conventional art gallery. You are despairing because having put so much effort into trying to help Peter become the person you want, he is turning out to be different. Because you really care about each other and want to have a good relationship you are both putting a lot of effort into trying to change each other. Unfortunately, it seems to me, that the more you try to change each other, the more you get into conflict.

Figure 8.2(d) shows a family which includes a mother, Andrea, a 17-year-old daughter, Kylie, a 15-year-old son, Leonard, and two younger children aged 6 and 7. Andrea brought the family for counselling because the younger children were out of control and their behaviour was troubling her. After watching the first counselling session the co-therapist gave the following feedback:

FIGURE 8.2(d)   *Feedback picture*

Kylie, my impression was that you didn't really want to be at this family counselling session. I think this is quite understandable because you have reached an age where you want to start being more independent and, as you explained, spending more time with your friends than at home. Andrea, I have heard that your husband left the family about six months ago and that before he left he was the most powerful member of the family. Once again, I think it is quite understandable that being on your own now you are not sure what to do. Because you're not sure what to do, I notice that Leonard has sensibly taken over, jumped up on this podium, and is doing his best to control the younger children. My impression is that you are not very comfortable with Leonard being on the podium, and although Leonard seems to enjoy being there at times, I sense that he is not too comfortable either.

Use of the Reflecting Team

The use of a reflecting team has been described in Chapter 3. During a counselling session members of the reflecting team observe and listen from an observation room through a one-way mirror and using a sound system. When the session reaches an appropriate point the counsellor and family and the reflecting team change places, with the reflecting team moving into the counselling room and the counsellor and family moving into the observation room. The reflecting team then hold a discussion regarding their observations from the counselling session. This discussion is held in accordance with the principles outlined below.

Examples to demonstrate ways of giving feedback in a reflecting team
Lowe and Guy (1999) suggest that while giving feedback reflecting team members should use language similar to that suggested in the following examples. These

statements demonstrate respectfulness, interest, tentativeness, creativity, and sensitivity. It is important to avoid statements that are patronizing, trivializing, judgemental, evaluative, or suggest that an expert opinion is being given.

- One thing I'm curious about…
- I wondered if…
- I was interested to see…
- A question I had was…
- I thought it was significant that…
- The thing that surprised me was…
- I noticed a change in… when…
- I wondered how… was able to do that.
- Bill said… but it did not seem to fit with his belief that…
- I noticed some themes emerging…
- I wondered what was happening for…
- I hoped (the counsellor) might ask about…
- I had a picture of… when the discussion was taking place
- I wondered what effect… might have had on the family, such as…

After the reflecting team have completed their discussion, usually limited to 10 or 15 minutes, the reflecting team once again change places with the counsellor and family. The family are now given an opportunity to discuss any issues that arise from the reflecting team discussion. A major benefit from using a reflecting team discussion is that the family get the opportunity to see their family from several different perspectives offered by the members of the reflecting team. In this way, members of the family have the opportunity to view their family through a number of additional lenses.

Example of a reflecting team discussion

Team member 1
I was interested to see that when Jerome mentioned how difficult it was for him to stay alone at home several other members in the family tried to help him overcome the problem.

Team member 2
Yes… I wondered if there have been times when Jerome has stayed at home alone in the past and not been worried.

Team member 1
…Yes and if he has, how was he able to manage that?

Team member 3
Yes… I had a picture of an army of defenders rallying to help and wondered if this was something that happens often in this family when someone is in trouble?

Team member 4

I noticed some themes emerging… when you mentioned an army of defenders it reminded me that during the session Anita talked in a proud way about how she helped protect her sister at school and also how Mum, although she finds herself working full-time, was proud of her beliefs about the importance of mothers staying at home instead of working so that they are there for the children.

Team member 2

I noticed a change in Jerome when the family tried to discover ways for him to feel more comfortable about staying home alone.

Team member 4

A question I had was if this family were to look at itself in 6 months time how would they know that the problem had been overcome?

As a result of such reflecting team feedback, the family's awareness of their individual and whole family strengths, resilience, and competencies might be raised. Also they might recognize possibilities and opportunities for change.

Ending the Session

As the session draws to a close the counsellor might indicate this by saying, *'I think this is a good time to end the session, but before we finish I'm wondering whether there is anything that you would like to ask or say'.* This gives the family an opportunity to comment on the session and to ask for information they would like to have.

Before the session finishes the counsellor might check whether the family would like to attend further counselling sessions or not. When asking about this, it is important to present both the possibility of coming back for another counselling session or sessions and the option of not returning for more counselling. For example, the counsellor may ask, *'Would you like to come back so that we can continue the counselling process or would you prefer to go away and see how things work out for your family?'*

If the family decide that they would like to come back for ongoing counselling, the counsellor needs to explain the process that is likely to be used. For example, the counsellor might say: *'If you do decide to come back again, I will use some additional strategies which I think may be helpful for your family. Also, depending on what emerges in the following counselling sessions, I might suggest that sometimes it might be useful for you if I, or another member of the counselling team, were to see one of you separately, or two or three of you together, rather than the whole family. However, if I, or another member of the counselling team, do see some of you on your own or in a small group, I suggest that we follow up with a whole family session after that. Of course, it will be your decision as to whether you would like us to work this way or whether you would prefer just have counselling sessions where the whole family attend each time.'* Notice that this information is presented in a way which offers the family a choice about the way the counsellor works. Chapter 10 describes how, when using the CACHO model, we integrate whole family work with individual and subgroup counselling.

Debriefing

After the family have left, it is recommended that the counsellor and reflecting team members should debrief. Similarly, if a co-therapist has been working with a counsellor instead of a reflecting team, it is advantageous for the co-therapist and counsellor to debrief together.

Debriefing can be useful for the following purposes:

* maintaining positive relationships between members of the counselling team
* exploring parallel processes
* identifying personal issues in team members triggered by the counselling process
* reviewing the counselling process
* exploring future strategies for raising the family's awareness.

Maintaining positive relationships between members of the counselling team

It is inevitable that sometimes issues will arise between members of a counselling team as a result of the counselling process. A member of the team may believe that it would have been better for the counsellor to have worked in a different way, or may believe that a member of the reflecting team used the reflecting team discussion inappropriately, in a way that would have been unhelpful for the family. Unless issues such as these are brought out into the open, discussed and resolved, it is likely that there will be disharmony within the counselling team.

Exploring parallel processes

A counselling team working with a family is at risk of developing similar unhelpful processes to those of the family in their own dynamics. Consider the situation where a family is attending counselling and where the parents believe that the children are not respecting their needs, while the children believe the same of their parents. It may be that one member of the counselling team, as a result of their own personal issues, joins with the parents and sees the children as behaving unreasonably, while another member of the counselling team joins with the children and sees the parents as behaving in an unhelpful way. The two members of the counselling team involved are at risk of becoming engaged in an unhelpful parallel process to that in the family, where their relationship and their roles will become compromised. Where such issues arise it is helpful for them to be brought into the open, in the context of the whole team, so that they can be discussed and resolved.

Identifying personal issues in team members triggered by the counselling process

It is certain that at times a member of a counselling team will have issues of their own triggered as a result of counselling or observing a family counselling session. For example, if a member of the counselling team has unresolved issues relating to abandonment by their mother when they were a child, these issues are likely to be triggered if a family presents where a child has been abandoned by their mother. In such a case, we believe that it is important for the counselling team member involved to take responsibility for the way in which these issues are managed. While debriefing within the counselling team may raise the team member's awareness of the issues, the team environment is not usually an appropriate place in which to resolve personal issues. Personal counselling or professional supervision provide appropriate and more comfortable opportunities for the resolution of such issues.

Reviewing the counselling process

Debriefing gives the counselling team an opportunity to review the counselling process, to recognize what was helpful in that process, and to look at alternative ways of working that might have been useful. It is by doing this that counsellors, co-therapists and members of a reflecting team are able to improve their practice so that they can provide the best possible service to their clients.

Exploring future strategies for raising the family's awareness

Debriefing can also be used to explore future possibilities regarding strategies that might be used in a future session to further raise the family's awareness with the goal of bringing about change.

KEY POINTS

- Preparation requires counselling team members to identify their own personal issues and put them to one side.
- Information received prior to meeting the family is generally only one person's point of view.

- After greeting clients, the clients need to be informed of the processes to be used and their consent obtained where necessary.
- A major goal is to encourage the family to share with each other their various pictures of the family and how it functions.
- The counsellor is responsible for creating and maintaining a safe environment.
- Skills to raise awareness need to be used.
- The counsellor needs to respectfully accept each individual's point of view.
- A co-therapist can provide feedback through telephone interventions and the use of a feedback picture.
- Reflecting team discussions are useful in helping the family to look at their family unit through a number of different lenses.
- Debriefing is essential in order to ensure the highest quality of counselling is maintained.

QUESTIONS FOR GROUP DISCUSSION OR STUDENT ASSIGNMENTS

1. Discuss with practical examples the issue of safety for members of a family. Explain why it is important for the counsellor to take responsibility for ensuring safety. Give examples of how a counsellor might behave in situations where safety might be compromised.
2. Discuss the difficulties that would be confronted by a counsellor who was working with a family without the assistance of either a co-therapist or a reflecting team.

9

Raising the Family's Awareness of Family Dynamics

As explained in Chapter 8, in the first session with a family we generally focus on helping individual members of the family to share their perceptions of what is happening in the family. What we try to do is to help members of the family begin to see the family in a different way. When they first attend a counselling session it is inevitable that each member of the family will see the family from their own particular perspective. It is as though they are each looking through their own individual lens, which is narrowly focused. Our goal is to help them to look through each other's lenses so that by looking through multiple lenses they will see a broader picture. In order to achieve this, we make extensive use of circular questions. These are particularly useful in helping to promote conversation between family members, and in enabling them to share their individual perceptions of the family and what is happening within it. Additional perspectives on the family are also offered by a co-therapist presenting a feedback picture or by a reflecting team's discussion.

Using the CACHO model of relationship counseling, the co-therapist presents a feedback picture at the end of the first session but not at the end of subsequent sessions. This enables the counsellor to refer to the feedback picture given at the end of the first session in later sessions to identify change. However, it is useful for the co-therapist to give verbal feedback to the family at the end of each session. This feedback can be particularly helpful in drawing the family's attention to positives which have been achieved between sessions.

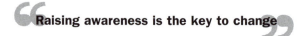

Raising awareness is the key to change

After the first session, strategies which will raise the family's awareness of what is in the 'here and now' are used, as we continue to rely on the Gestalt therapy theory of change.

Counselling Interventions

In the second and subsequent counselling sessions we use the range of counselling skills described in Chapter 4. In addition, we place emphasis on the following:

- the use of circular questions
- feedback of interactional patterns
- feedback of here-and-now processes
- feedback of observations of behaviour
- drawing attention to information that has been minimized
- telephone interventions when a co-therapist is used.

The use of circular questions

The counsellor asks questions of the family so that their responses will reveal the way the family is interconnected and the means by which it operates as a system, including beliefs about itself. As this information is generated, the family is then provided with an opportunity of becoming aware of its manner of interaction and relating (Street, 2006).

Feedback of interactional patterns

As a consequence of asking questions of the family, the family is likely to start to recognize some of their interactional patterns. However, families are likely to use explanations that are based on linear causality rather than circular causality (Nichols and Schwartz, 2007). Generally, explanations based on linear causality lead to a tendency to do more of the same, even if that is failing to achieve a positive outcome. By contrast, explanations in terms of circular causality are more helpful in enabling a family to recognize options for change that might lead to different and more positive outcomes, as explained in Chapter 6 (see Figures 6.3 and 6.4 on pages 67 and 68).

When a counsellor recognizes a circular process, it can be useful to draw a diagram to illustrate the process on a whiteboard for the family and to check with them whether they believe that this circular process is occurring or whether they have a different explanation. It is not important whether the family agree or disagree with regard to the process suggested by the counsellor. If they disagree, they have the opportunity to draw an alternative diagram to illustrate how they see things. By doing this, the awareness of the family is raised about what is happening in the here and now, with the consequence that they are empowered to make changes to the process that is occurring if they choose.

Feedback of here-and-now processes

As individuals, when we are involved in interacting with others it is often hard for us to recognize the processes that are occurring internally within ourselves, and in our relationships. For example, the counsellor might notice that whenever her father says something a daughter looks angry but sits quietly saying nothing. By feeding back to the daughter, '*You look angry when your father talks*', the daughter may recognize that she is angry and be able to talk about her anger. This feedback could also be given through the use of a circular statement, with the counsellor saying to a brother, '*I notice that your sister looks angry when her father talks*'. Such feedback is likely to raise the family's awareness of a here-and-now process which is occurring in the family.

Feedback is helpful in raising awareness

Feedback of observations of behaviour

The counsellor might have noticed that instead of paying attention to the counselling process and being involved in it, that an adolescent son continually sketches and seems absorbed by what he is doing. In this instance, an option would be for the counsellor to feedback their observation of the behaviour together with a circular question by saying, for example, '*Susan, I notice that Kevin seems very interested in his sketching. If you had to guess, what do you think he might be thinking?*'

Drawing attention to information that has been minimized

There will be times when information in a family will be minimized, often, but not always, when it is offered by someone in the family who is fairly disempowered relative to others. This minimization may be part of a circular process which is causing a problem for the family. Consider an example where parents have brought their family for counselling because of continual conflict between a teenage son, Maurice, and his younger brother, Michael. During the counselling session the teenage son might complain that while trying to do his homework he is continually being 'hassled' by a younger brother who presents as extrovert, happy and cheerful, and, as a consequence, is liked by his parents. The parents might minimize the teenage son's complaint by saying that the younger brother '*just wants to be friendly*', and that the teenager is nasty to his younger brother and always has had difficulty concentrating anyway. The counsellor might recognize that the teenager is not being heard in the family and that two circular processes are occurring, as shown in Figure 9.1. It could be useful for the family if the counsellor were to encourage them to work out the circular sequence by beginning to draw the sequence on a whiteboard at the point where Michael wants Maurice's attention and asking the family what they think might happen as a consequence for Maurice. If in collaboration with the counsellor they are able draw a figure which demonstrates the circular processes involved, they may recognize how they could replace these with more helpful processes.

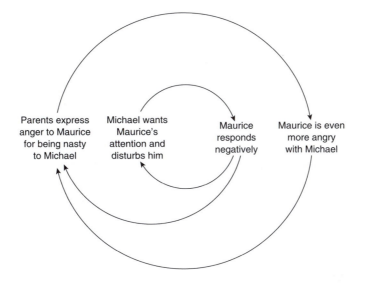

FIGURE 9.1   *Circular processes*

Telephone interventions when a co-therapist is used

As explained in Chapter 8, telephone interventions by a co-therapist who is observing through a one-way mirror can be very useful in a variety of ways in helping raise a family's awareness of what is happening in the here and now.

Meeting the Family Again

Frequently, change will occur in families between counselling sessions. As a result, when a family come to a second or subsequent counselling session it can be helpful to assume that change has occurred. As with the first counselling session, it is important to focus initially on joining with the family. If the counsellor is relaxed and the atmosphere is friendly, the family are likely to find it easy to join with the counsellor and to relax themselves.

After initially joining with the family it can be helpful to ask a circular question to investigate what changes have occurred in the family and what the effect of these changes has been. This can be done by asking either an openly directed circular question or a general circular question, such as: '*What's been better since you came here last time?*'

> **Change occurs between counselling sessions as well as during sessions**

Notice that the question assumes that something has been better since the family came last time. Often a member, or some members of the family, will confirm that some positive change has happened. However, as explained in Chapter 1 and reiterated in later chapters, because families seek homoeostasis there is often resistance to change. As a result, it is common for a family member or members to minimize the change and/or to suggest that the change only occurred as a result of a temporary family situation. For example, if we refer to the family described in the previous chapter (see Figure 8.1, on page 83), it might be that Grandma will say, '*I was surprised to notice that since we came here last time Sean and Jill have been spending time doing things together which they have never done before, and both of them seemed a lot happier.*' In response to this, Alice might say, '*Oh that's only because Jill has a new video game that Sean wants to play*' and, as a consequence, the change in Sean and Jill's behaviours and relationship may no longer be seen as important. In a situation such as this, the counsellor needs to make the change newsworthy.

Making change newsworthy

The idea of making change newsworthy comes from narrative therapy and solution-focused counselling (de Shazer, 1991). In terms used in these two counselling approaches, identifying change and making change newsworthy enables the family to thicken the preferred stories that the family have begun to create about themselves.

In order to make change newsworthy, rather than challenging the way the change has been minimized, the counsellor can express surprise that the change has occurred. The counsellor might say, '*I'm amazed to hear that Jill and Sean have been happily spending time together*', and then follow up by asking Jill, '*What did Sean do differently that enabled you to play happily together?*' and to Sean, '*Do you agree with what Jill says?*', and then ask, '*Sean, what did Jill do differently this week?*' Finally, having heard their answers and the discussion relating to their change, the counsellor can say, '*I really am amazed that you have both been able to change so quickly. How did you do it?*'

Having made the change newsworthy the counsellor is then in a position to support an optimistic point of view about the family's potential for change.

Strategies for Use in Second and Subsequent Sessions

The emphasis in the second and subsequent sessions of counselling is to intensify the awareness in the family in order to promote change. There are many strategies that can be used within the framework of the CACHO model to intensify awareness of the family. In this chapter we will discuss the use of the following:

- the genogram
- creative strategies.

Use of the Genogram

An example of a genogram is given in Figure 7.2 (page 77). Drawing a genogram on a whiteboard in collaboration with the family can be very useful in helping them to talk about their family, and in raising their awareness with regard to relationships and behaviours in the family.

Genograms can be used for a variety of purpose:

- to identify intergenerational behaviour
- to draw attention to alliances and coalitions
- to explore boundaries and structure
- to identify triangulation.

Identifying intergenerational behaviour

As described in Chapter 1, Bowen (1978) drew attention to the way that relationships, behaviours, and other factors affecting family dynamics are passed down from generation to generation. This transmission occurs spontaneously and is certain to have an influence on family functioning. If the family are helped to see how unhelpful behaviours and ways of relating have been passed down from previous generations, they have an opportunity to decide to replace such unhelpful inherited family dynamics with new behaviours and thus create a different way of functioning.

> **Family styles of functioning are passed down from generation to generation**

Consider an example. A family may have come to counselling because the parents are disturbed by the behaviours of their children. By drawing a genogram and encouraging the parents to talk about how it was constructed it might emerge that the father has come from a family which was very easy going with few rules, whereas the mother has come from a family where her father was a rigid disciplinarian who enforced very strict rules. The parents might become aware that they both had expectations that their family would be similar to their own families of origin. As a result of constructing the genogram, they would have become aware that they were not united in parenting their children. Having recognized this, the parents might decide that it would be useful for them to have a counselling session on their own to make decisions about how they would like their current family to function with regard to parenting.

Drawing attention to alliances and coalitions

During the process of constructing a genogram the family's awareness can be raised with regard to perceived alliances and coalitions within the family. These can be added

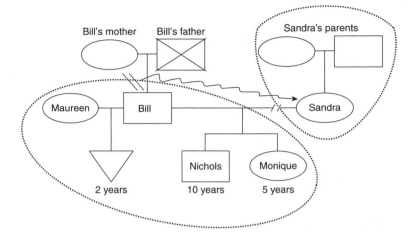

FIGURE 9.2(a)   *Coalition between Bill and his mother against Sandra*

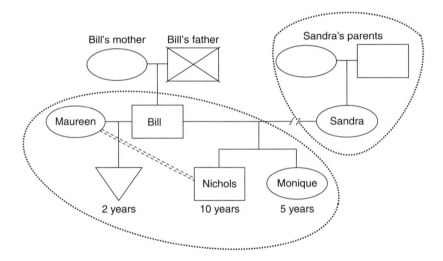

FIGURE 9.2(b)   *Alliance between Maureen and Nicholas*

to the genogram diagrammatically, as shown in Figures 9.2(a) and (b). In Figure 9.2(a), the double line between the Bill's mother and Bill, together with the wavy arrow pointing towards Sandra, represents a perception that the family has regarding a coalition between Bill and his mother, who join together in attacking Sandra. In Figure 9.2(b), the double dotted line between Maureen and Nicholas represents a perception of an alliance between them as they both have a strong interest in fine art and support each other's efforts to paint pictures.

It can be very useful in relationship counselling to draw attention to perceived alliances and coalitions. By asking circular questions, the counsellor can help the family discover the influence that any existing alliances and coalitions have on the functioning of the family.

Exploring boundaries and structure

The functioning of the family will also be affected by the boundaries existing in the family and the structure of the family. In Figures 9.2(a) and (b), boundaries around Maureen and Bill's family and Sandra's family of origin have been shown as dotted lines. There may be additional boundaries within the families. For example, there may be a boundary around Maureen and Bill, demonstrating that they are a couple and also parents. However, it could be possible that this boundary is fairly loose and permeable, and that a stronger boundary exists around Maureen and Nicholas as a result of them joining together in an alliance (described before). If this is the case, it alters the structure of the family from the preferred structure recommended by Minuchin (1974), where there is a strong boundary around the parental dyad. However, we need to recognize that each family is different and does not necessarily have to have a particular structure in order to function effectively. Raising a family's awareness of the boundaries within the family and the family structure empowers the family to make decisions, if they wish, with regard to changing these boundaries and the associated family relationships.

Identifying triangulation

Figure 9.2(c) represents triangulation where Maureen and Bill avoid confronting issues in their own relationship by drawing Bill's mother into their relationship. They might both complain continually about the only problem in the family being the intrusion of Bill's mother, her attitude, and behaviour. By concentrating on Bill's mother, they shift the focus away from their own relationship and achieve homeostasis, as described in Chapter 6, enabling the family to maintain stability but at an emotional cost to themselves and probably other members of the family. Using the genogram to identify the triangulation provides Bill and Maureen with an opportunity to explore and make changes to enhance their own relationship, and as a likely consequence promote harmony within the family.

Creative Strategies

There are an unlimited number of creative strategies which can be used when counselling families (Ruckert, 2000; Zinker, 1978). Counsellors who work experientially, and those who work in other creative ways, use strategies to enable a family to have an awareness-raising experience which will give them the opportunity to recognize more

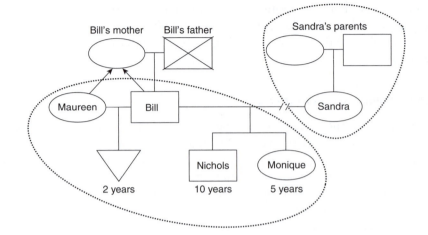

FIGURE 9.2(c)   *Triangulation of Bill's mother by Maureen and Bill*

fully what is happening in the family. As a consequence, the family may be empowered to make decisions for change. In this chapter we will deal with a limited number of creative strategies which we commonly use in second or subsequent counselling sessions with families. These are:

• family sculpture
• the use of cushions as symbols
• the use of other symbols
• role reversal
• the alter ego strategy
• counsellor/co-therapist open discussion.

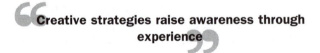

Creative strategies raise awareness through experience

Family Sculpture

The idea of using a family sculpture comes from Virginia Satir's Human Validation Process Model of family therapy (Satir and Bitter, 2000). Family sculpting increases each family member's awareness of how they function and relate to others and how others view them in the family. Through using family sculpture, relationships, processes, boundaries, alliances, coalitions, and interactions become evident.

Family sculpting gives family members an opportunity to express the way they view one another, to express how they feel about current relationships in the family, and to say how they would like relationships to be different.

Family sculpture is particularly useful in the following situations:

- where issues of power and/or intimacy are not being usefully addressed
- where family members are having difficulty expressing their opinions verbally
- where family members are intellectualizing and overlook the emotional component of their communication
- where family members' feelings are being denied expression by others, censored, or rationalized
- where the family have difficulty understanding verbal descriptions of their family
- where therapy seems to have lost its momentum.

There are three different ways of creating a family sculpture:

1. Using the family members directly.
2. Using coloured cushions.
3. Using symbols.

Family sculpture using the whole family

Before initiating a family sculpture, the family need to be invited to take part in the sculpture and decide if they believe that it would be a useful and helpful experience for them. The family also need to be informed about the process, what the activity will involve, and be given a clear message that it will be okay if they decline to accept the invitation. Initially the counsellor might say to the family:

'I wonder if it might be useful for this family to create a family sculpture? A family sculpture will give us all an opportunity to see what your family looks like in addition to talking about the family. It will involve someone in the family being prepared to act as a sculptor, who will arrange the remaining members of the family so that they stand in positions relative to each other to illustrate the way this family fits together. Would you like to try this approach or would you prefer not to do that?'

If the family accept the invitation, the family can be invited to stand up and move all the chairs and other furniture out of the way so that there is a clear space in which to create the sculpture.

The next step is for the counsellor to encourage a person in the family to be the sculptor. Often, it can be advantageous for a younger person in the family to be the sculptor as this engages the younger members of the family in the activity. The counsellor then invites the sculptor to begin arranging the family into a 'picture' that depicts how the family is in their view. The counsellor might say to the sculptor, *'I wonder if you would like to try, in the first instance, to be the sculptor? If I tell you what to do, would you like to be the sculptor, or would you prefer me to ask someone else?'*

The sculptor is then given the following instructions:

1. For the time being you are in charge here. When you move a member of your family to the new position I want them to do exactly as you tell them.
2. I want you to place each member of your family in a position next to other members of your family to demonstrate closeness. For example, if Jennifer is very friendly with Jason, you would put them close together. But if they didn't like each other you might put them a long way apart, or facing each other looking angrily at each other.
3. I also want you to put people in the family in positions which show who is powerful and who is not. For example, if Marcus is a very powerful member of the family, he might be standing on a chair above everyone else, and if he was a not so powerful member of the family he might be sitting on the floor with someone pressing down on him.
4. I would also like you to tell each member of the family what attitude, stance, and facial expression you would like them to demonstrate.
5. Finally, I want you to place yourself in the sculpture.
6. I would like you to do all of these things silently with no one in the family talking until the whole sculpture is complete.

The purpose of the sculpture is to represent closeness and distance, alliances and coalitions, and illustrate power dynamics in the family.

While the family sculpture is being created, the counsellor might facilitate the sculpting by asking particular questions such as:

'How close is your mother to your father?'
'Should they be touching or not?'
'Who is closest to your mother out of all the children?'
'Is she looking at them?'

Additionally, while the sculptor is preparing the sculpture, the therapist might give feedback about what is occurring. For example, the counsellor might say:

'I notice that your brother seems reluctant to be moved closer to his father.'
'Mum is smiling now that she is standing on the wooden box.'

When the sculpture is complete, the counsellor may ask questions and give feedback. For example, the counsellor might ask family members about their emotional responses to being in their positions in the sculpture, and may ask them where they would rather be in the sculpture. In giving feedback the counsellor tells the family what has been noticed about the arrangement, stances, and expressions.

Finally, the counsellor might ask the sculptor to rearrange the family in such a way that family relations are improved. For example, the therapist might ask:

'How could you change the sculpture so that it would feel better to be a part of this family?'

After discussing the original sculpture it can be useful to ask other members of the family whether they would like to change the sculpture, and if they want to, to allow them to do so.

Processing the sculpture

While the creation of the sculpture is in progress the counsellor can continually check how members of the family feel in positions they have been asked to take up. They may also be asked how they believe the sculpture should be. After the sculpture has been completed, the family should be asked to return to their seats and then invited to discuss the sculpture and anything that emerged for them as individuals while participating in the sculpture.

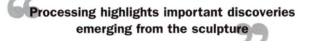

Processing highlights important discoveries emerging from the sculpture

Creating a family sculpture using the family members themselves as the sculpture can be a very powerful experience for the family and individuals within the family. As a consequence, the family's awareness of what is happening in the family is likely to be raised and it may be that individual family members will get in touch with and experience strong emotions which have previously been unexpressed. Although this is useful for those families where individual members are able to cope with an emotional experience of this type, for some families the experience is too demanding. If not skilfully managed by the counsellor, it might be of a negative value to the family. Where a counsellor judges that some family members are particularly vulnerable, it is better to use a less threatening approach, such as using cushions or symbols to create a family sculpture. These approaches are less direct as they externalize the family and allow family members to remain somewhat distant from the sculpture itself.

Family sculpture using cushions

In order to carry out a family sculpture using cushions, a pile of assorted cushions of various colours and styles is required. The process begins by asking each member of the family to choose a cushion to represent themselves. As each member of the family chooses a cushion they can be invited to describe the cushion. Through describing the cushion they will inevitably reveal the way they perceive aspects of themselves. For example, person might say, '*This cushion is soft and fluffy. It looks as though it has been knocked around a bit. It's embroidered in a fairly messy sort of way, so it's a bit like me.*' The counsellor might then ask, '*Can you tell me more, or would it be too difficult to do that right now?*' By asking this, the counsellor invites the person to talk more about themselves and also gives them an opportunity not to reveal information.

When each member of the family has chosen their cushion, one member of the family is selected to be the sculptor and to place the cushions in a pattern on the floor to symbolize the relationships in the family. Thus, if the sculptor believes that two members of the family are close to each other, their cushions will be placed close to each other, or may even overlap. If one member of the family is believed by the sculptor to be squashed by another member of the family, one cushion may be placed on top of the other to demonstrate the relationship.

After the sculptor has completed their work, other members of the family can be invited to comment on the sculpture. Also, they can be invited to move the cushions into different arrangements if they wish. Using this process, experiments can easily be carried out with regard to different perceptions of relationships by rearranging the cushions.

Family sculpture using symbols

Another way of creating a family sculpture is to use small objects, such as those used in a sandtray, in place of cushions. For full details regarding miniature animals and sand tray symbols please refer to our book *Counselling Children: A Practical Introduction* (3rd edn, Geldard and Geldard, 2008a). Also refer to Part Three where the use of miniature animals and symbols is discussed when helping children to talk about their relationships. The process is the same as that used when working with the cushions described above. The miniature animals or symbols can be used on the floor or on a table.

An example of a family sculpture

In order to describe an example of a family sculpture we will refer to Figure 8.2(d) on page 94.

As discussed in Chapter 8, this is a feedback picture given to a family by the co-therapist at the end of the first counselling session. With a family like this, it could be useful to create a family sculpture when the family return for the next counselling session. One member of the family could be invited to place the family members in a sculpture. In such a situation, the counsellor should not necessarily expect that the family sculpture will resemble the feedback picture given at the end of the first session because in the time between the first and second sessions change may have occurred. However, whatever the new arrangement, the family would be able to discuss how it felt for each of them to be in their position within the family. Through this raised awareness, the family would recognize that they can either continue to relate as they have been or that they could make some changes.

Use of Cushions as Symbols

It can be very advantageous for a counsellor to have a pile of cushions of various sizes, shapes, colours, designs, and patterns readily available in a counselling room for a number of purposes. For example, many practitioners in psychodrama rely heavily on the use of such cushions for a variety of experiential purposes (Vondracek and Corneal, 1995). Additionally, cushions are very useful when helping an individual family member explore relationships with others, either within the family or external to the family. Relevant strategies are described in Chapters 17 and 18.

Cushions can also be used in a family counselling session as symbols to represent emotions, situations, processes, memories, etc. For example, a cushion could be placed on the floor between a mother and daughter to represent a barrier between them. They could both be invited to talk about the barrier. Also, the cushion could be removed to symbolize the removal of the barrier and the mother and daughter could be invited to talk about how that felt. Thus they would be involved in an experiential exercise to explore the usefulness and problems created by the barrier and to look at how it could be removed, and what it would be like if it were removed.

At times in counselling sessions the whole family will not be present. This might be because some members of the family are not able or willing to engage in the counselling process, or because a deliberate decision has been made to hold a session with just a part of the family. In this case, it can sometimes be useful to use cushions to represent those members of the family who are not present. This gives an opportunity for dialogue to take place between a member of the family who is present and the absent member who is represented by the cushion. The strategy of dialoguing using cushions is explained in detail in Chapter 18 as it can be useful when helping young people to explore their relationships with their peers or with adults.

Use of Other Symbols

Symbols such as those used in a sand tray can be employed for a wide range of purposes when counselling families. Symbols can be used to represent:

- emotional feelings
- thoughts
- beliefs
- barriers
- secrets
- issues that are too difficult to talk about
- people
- obstacles to change
- solutions to problems.

Symbols are a valuable tool for the creative counsellor

A creative counsellor will find many other ways in which to use symbols. As an example, consider the use of symbols to represent issues that are too difficult to talk about. It may be that a son in the family is very depressed and his parents believe that this is affecting the family generally. In the initial session of counselling it emerges that there are a number of secrets in the family. In the subsequent session the counsellor can remind the family that it became apparent in the first session that there were secrets, or issues that were too difficult to talk about.

Each member of the family might then be invited to choose a symbol, or more than one symbol, from the set of symbols, to represent things that are too difficult for them to talk about. Once the symbols are selected and placed in front of the individuals concerned, family members can be asked if they are able to say something about their symbol or not. In addition, family members can be asked whether they would mind if other members of the family try to guess what their symbols represent. By following this process sensitively, and reassuring family members that they will not be pressured to disclose what their symbols represent, it is possible that some disclosures of important information may occur. Paradoxically, sometimes having permission not to talk about a secret is more likely to result in the secret being disclosed.

Sometimes the family will be unable to disclose anything about their symbol or what it represents. In some cases individual family members may wish to engage in individual counselling where they feel safer and more able to talk about the difficult topic represented by the symbol.

Even when the family members are unable to talk about the hidden meanings of their symbols the exercise can still be useful. Family members can decide what impact the things these symbols represent have on the family, whether these put blocks between relationships in the family, and what they fear would happen if the hidden information was disclosed.

Role Reversal

Role reversal involves inviting members of the family to exchange seats with each other and to imagine that they are the other person. They are then invited to role-play each other in dialogue regarding the issues that are impacting on their relationship. During this process the counsellor needs to coach the role-players, and to pause the process at appropriate points to check how each participant is feeling and whether the process is useful. It can also be useful to use circular questions addressed to those members of the family who are observing the role-play to see what they believe may be happening in the relationships, and to enquire about their own experiences, feelings, and thoughts, resulting from their observations of the role-play.

Role-play techniques can also be combined with the alter ego strategy (see below), although the latter strategy is not confined to role-play situations.

Alter Ego Strategy

The alter ego strategy, or psychodramatic technique of doubling, can be used when advocating for an individual family member in a family or subgroup session, and when encouraging the expression of feelings (Vondracek and Corneal, 1995).

Informing the family in advance

As a counsellor, it is important to explain the alter ego process to the family in advance by informing them that you will make "I" statements on behalf of a member of the family. It is also essential that the family member in question understands that they can either agree with the statement or challenge it.

Advocacy

At appropriate times during a family session the counsellor may notice that a family member is unable to share their point of view, or that a family member is censoring their point of view as a result of the family interactional patterns and processes. Using the alter ego strategy, the counsellor may stand near them and say the words that it appears they are unable to say. They are then invited to either reject or accept the counsellor's words. When using this process the counsellor needs to be careful to be even-handed rather than joining with any one member of the family in particular. For example, if the counsellor acts as alter ego for a son talking to his mother, the counsellor should follow up, if it is appropriate to do so, by acting as alter ego for the mother when she replies.

Expressing feelings

When using the alter ego strategy to encourage the expression of feelings, the counsellor stands near the family member who is addressing the others, and uses stronger language and emotional expression to more accurately convey and amplify the emotional feelings of the person concerned. For example, a member of the family might say, *'I'm disappointed by what's happened'* while at the same time appearing to be very angry. The counsellor might stand beside the person saying loudly and with emphasis, *'I am very angry about what's happened'*.

Counsellor/Co-therapist Open Discussion

The use of a counsellor/co-therapist open discussion is explained in Chapter 3. In many ways, such a discussion is similar to the discussion between reflecting team members when the family is observing. In the counsellor/co-therapist open discussion, the co-therapist is invited into the counselling room to have a discussion with the counsellor. They share their views with each other openly with regard to the family and its functioning. In doing this they use the guidelines that apply to a reflecting team discussion, as described in Chapter 3. The goal is to raise the family's awareness of what is in the here and now, while helping the family to recognize that each family member is doing the best they can. In the process they raise possibilities for the future.

Closing the Session

As mentioned previously, it is our practice to use a feedback picture towards the end of the first counselling session with the family. However, we prefer this picture to act as a reference point for the family so we do not provide a feedback picture in subsequent counselling sessions.

Where a co-therapist is involved, the counsellor can invite the co-therapist into the counselling room near the end of the session to give verbal feedback. This verbal feedback will focus on positive changes that the co-therapist has noticed, and on helpful possibilities for the future that have been raised during the session. Emphasis is placed on helping family members to feel good about themselves by positively connoting the family and its members, and their ability to succeed in discovering and putting into place helpful alternatives for the future.

When using a reflecting team, the process in subsequent sessions will be similar to that described in Chapters 3 and 8.

Discussion regarding ongoing appointments

The session needs to end with a discussion regarding future appointments, if the family believes that these are necessary. At this point it might be decided that it would be useful to have some individual sessions with particular members of the family or perhaps some small group sessions involving only some members of the family. For example, if two brothers have relationship problems, it might be useful to see them in a counselling session where they can discuss their relationship with each other in the safety of the counselling environment. When choosing these options it can be useful to inform the family that where individual or subgroup counselling sessions occur, that outcomes from these sessions may be brought back into the whole family in a later joint session. However, detailed information about what is discussed in individual and subgroup sessions will remain generally private, unless there is good reason to share this with parents because parental or safety issues are involved.

KEY POINTS

- The ongoing goal in family relationship counselling is to raise awareness of what is in the here and now.
- Counselling interventions include the use of circular questions, giving feedback, and making information newsworthy.
- The counsellor assumes that change has occurred since the previous counselling session.
- Family members will often attempt to minimize change that has occurred.
- Important strategies include use of the genogram, family sculpture, role reversal, the alter ego strategy, and counsellor/co-therapist open discussion.
- Family sculpturing can be done by the family members themselves, or by using cushions or other symbols.
- Symbols can be used creatively to help raise the family's awareness through experiential exercises.
- Ongoing appointments can be made for the whole family, individuals in the family, or subgroups of the family, if necessary.
- Individual or subgroup counselling is later integrated into whole family counselling.

QUESTIONS FOR GROUP DISCUSSION OR STUDENT ASSIGNMENTS

1. Choose an object as a symbol to represent some information that no one else knows about. Without disclosing the information itself describe the symbol as you initially think about it and when you think about it more deeply. Add more information. Describe the experience of going through this process.
2. Create a family sculpture of your own family, or your family of origin, using symbols or miniature animals. Discuss this sculpture and any emotional feelings that you are prepared to disclose which emerged during your creation of the sculpture.

10

Integrating Individual Counselling with Whole Family Work

In this chapter we will discuss our practice framework. This involves working not only with the whole family using the CACHO model, but also with individuals and subgroups within the family. For example, we might decide to work with two of the children together, or with the parents on their own, or with a mother and son. After working with an individual family member, or with a subgroup of the family, we integrate this counselling work with the counselling work we are doing with the whole family. This practice framework differs from traditional frameworks which draw strong distinctions between individual counselling and family therapy.

Nichols and Schwartz (2007) note that individual counselling and family therapy each offer an approach to treatment and both have their virtues. They state that in individual counselling treatment should be directed at the person and their personal makeup. They maintain that family therapists, on the other hand, believe that the dominant forces in our lives are located externally, in the family. While we broadly agree with their definition of individual and family counselling and the purposes of each, we believe that the personal issues of individuals interact with the family, and that the family influences the personal issues of family members. As stated by Andreozzi (1996), while we might focus primarily on relationship phenomena, we must also consider the individual in the family. Consequently, it seems logical to us for counselling to address both the personal issues of the individual and family issues. This can be done through using an integrated combination of family counselling and individual counselling.

> **Personal issues interact with the family – the family influences personal issues**

We will now discuss in more detail our reasons for believing that integrating individual and subgroup counselling with family counselling is preferable to working exclusively either with the family or with individuals in the family on their own.

Limitations when Counselling the Whole Family

While counselling a family as a group can be very powerful in helping to improve a family's functioning, this style of counselling does have its limitations.

In our experience, problems in families often arise as a result of the personal needs of individual members of the family not being satisfactorily addressed. As a consequence, the individuals concerned experience emotional distress and may behave in ways which are a response to their unmet needs but are unhelpful for the family as a whole. We are frequently confronted by situations in family counselling where a family member who is experiencing troubling thoughts or emotions is unable to talk about their issues in the company of other family members, even though their issues are affecting the family's functioning.

Even if an individual family member is able to talk about relevant personal issues which affect the family during a family counselling sessions, it may not be appropriate to deal with these issues in the context of the whole family. When counselling a family, we need to keep the whole family engaged in the counselling process and this may be difficult or impossible if a significant amount of time is spent addressing the issues of only one member of the family.

Consider some examples where individual and subgroup issues might need to be addressed privately rather than in the context of the whole family:

Example 1

A member of the family may not feel safe disclosing information. This is particularly likely to happen in families experiencing domestic violence, where a child or parent is too frightened to talk about what is actually happening in the family. In this situation, the counsellor might recognize that information is not being disclosed and notice a significant power imbalance in the family. Individual or subgroup counselling might then enable family members to start talking about their fears and issues.

Example 2

As a consequence of raised awareness during a family counselling session, a mother might start to recognize that her own unresolved issues regarding sexual abuse are impacting on the way that she relates to some members of her family. She might realize that it would be advantageous for her to be able to address her issues privately in individual counselling.

Example 3

While participating in a family sculpture (as described in Chapter 9) a mother and father might be concerned to discover that in the sculpture they were placed a long way apart from each other. They might recognize that other family members are troubled by the separateness and realize that they need to address their relationship issues through couple counselling. It would not be appropriate for this to occur in the presence of their children, so separate couple counselling sessions could be arranged instead.

The examples illustrate the need to provide for counselling for subgroups or individual members of the family when carrying out family therapy.

Individual counselling

Individual counselling can be useful for addressing:

- personal issues
- personal behaviours
- sensitive relationship issues.

All human beings have personal issues which may have their origin in childhood experiences or as a consequence of life events. Personal issues are not only troubling for the individual, but also inevitably have consequences regarding the individual's relationships with others. For example, a young person who has been traumatized by loss earlier in life might have been unable to resolve the trauma and be troubled by their memories. A consequence of the loss might be that they have become hyper-vigilant in looking after their possessions and they try to be in control of their surroundings at all times. This vigilance and need for control is likely to be problematic for other members of the family. Individual counselling in such a situation might enable the young person to resolve their issues and to recognize the way their behaviour is impacting on other family members. This enhances the possibility of change occurring within the family.

Sometimes relationships in families are affected by sensitive issues which are difficult, if not impossible, to discuss in the presence of the whole family. For example, inappropriate sexual contact may have occurred between two siblings in a family. Both parties may be too anxious and embarrassed to be able to talk about this except in an individual counselling session. However, unless the issue is resolved, there is likely to be ongoing tension within the family which may also affect other family members who are not aware of what has occurred.

Subgroup counselling

Subgroup counselling can be useful for addressing:

- relationship issues between two or more family members
- subgroup needs and issues
- parenting issues.

It is quite common in families for troubled relationships between two members of the family to have a negative impact on the functioning of the family as a whole. Although in some cases it is possible to resolve such issues within the context of the whole family, in other cases the two members concerned may feel exposed and vulnerable if they try to resolve their relationship issues with each other with other members of the family present.

> **Relationships within a subgroup can impact on the family as a whole**

In some families, a subgroup in the family will have common needs or issues which are not being addressed. This is particularly likely to occur when a subgroup is in some way disempowered and unable to be open in talking about their needs or issues. For example, consider a family where there are two late aged teenagers and two younger children. The younger children may feel bullied by the teenagers and believe they are not supported by their parents when they have tried to complain. During family counselling the counsellor might recognize that these children do not seem to have a voice in the family. A counselling session or sessions with the younger children might enable them to disclose their issue and talk about their needs. The counsellor can then work to enable them to be heard and to get their needs met within the context of the whole family in later sessions.

In some families it may emerge that part of the problem relates to parental issues. These may be relationship issues between the parents, or differences with regard to parenting styles. It is clear that such issues cannot sensibly be addressed within a whole family counselling session. Consequently, it can be useful in situations such as this for the parents to have counselling sessions for themselves.

Integrating Family, Subgroup, and Individual Counselling

Figure 10.1 illustrates the process that we use when integrating work with individuals or subgroups with whole family counselling.

The first family counselling session

As illustrated in Figure 10.1, we prefer to have the whole family present at the first session if this is acceptable for the family. This enables the counsellor to join with the family and begin to identify processes and interactive patterns within the family. As discussed in Chapter 8, the first session enables the family to share their individual perceptions with each other so that, in effect, they move from looking through monocular lenses to looking through multiple lenses. During this first session the family's awareness is likely to be raised with regard to issues that can be addressed.

The second and subsequent family counselling sessions

In the second family counselling session creative strategies and other techniques are used to help intensify the raising of awareness in the family. This is likely to influence the perceptions, thoughts, behaviours, and relationships within the family.

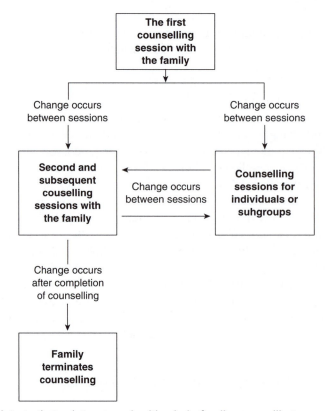

FIGURE 10.1   *Integrating subgroup work with whole family counselling*

The process will hopefully enable the family to experiment with and experience new interactive patterns.

Prior to the second or subsequent family counselling sessions, and with the agreement of the family, some individual and/or subgroup counselling sessions may be held. When offering the option of individual or subgroup counselling, the counsellor may wish to explain to the whole family that after individual or subgroup counselling those involved will be invited to share whatever they wish to share from their sessions with the family, but that it is possible that there may be information which they wish to keep private. Consequently, issues with regard to keeping information private and not sharing with the whole family may need to be addressed.

Individual and subgroup counselling

As explained earlier, counselling sessions for individual family members may be used for addressing sensitive personal issues and behaviours, and relationship issues. Subgroup counselling can be used for addressing relationships between two or more family members, subgroup needs and issues, and parenting issues.

While working with an individual or small group, the counsellor needs to prepare the individual or small group for the work of integration.

The process of integration

When considering how to integrate individual or subgroup work into the wider system, it can be helpful to collaborate with the family members involved in the individual or subgroup sessions with regard to how integration is best achieved so that it will result in positive outcomes. One option is to integrate work from an individual or subgroup counselling session into the whole family system in a family counselling session. Another option is to integrate information from an individual counselling session or subgroup session into a larger subgroup by bringing the smaller systems together to share the information, beliefs, and ideas that evolved in the individual or small group work.

During the work of integrating information from an individual or subgroup counselling session into the wider system, the counsellor's role is to act as a facilitator in enabling family members to share information with each other. Discussion needs to be encouraged regarding the information that is to be shared with the wider family system and that which is to remain private. This discussion is important because before sharing information with the wider system the likely consequences of doing this need to be explored.

Sometimes it will not be necessary to carry out the work of integration within a counselling session because, as a consequence of individual or subgroup work, family members may spontaneously resolve issues between counselling sessions.

Ethical decision-making

When conducting individual and subgroup counselling there are limits to the right to confidentiality due to ethical considerations. For example, if a member of the family is threatening to harm themselves, or another person, or damage property, the counsellor has an ethical responsibility to disclose this information to the appropriate person or authority. Similarly, parents have a right to know if there are important issues relating to their child's safety, general well-being, or mental health. In such instances, we believe that the child should be given a choice about the way in which sensitive information is disclosed. For example, they may wish to disclose the information themselves, or they may wish the counsellor to help them in making the disclosure, or they may want the counsellor to make the disclosure in their absence.

There are ethical limits to confidentiality

Ethical decisions with regard to confidentiality are not simple. We believe that it is essential for counsellors to practise according to a professional code of ethics, which provides guidelines on decisions relating to duty of care. Counsellors may find that it will sometimes be inevitable that they will need to pass on confidential information to others in the best interests of individuals and the family. We believe it is best to be transparent with families regarding our duty of care responsibilities by explaining limitations concerning confidentiality before individual or subgroup work begins.

Advocacy

At times, a counsellor may need to be an advocate for one family member or a subgroup during the integration process. This is particularly the case with children, who may need the help of an advocate to be able to share relevant information with others in the family, especially with their parents. At the end of an individual counselling session with a child, the counsellor can discuss with them whether or not they want to share the information they have disclosed in their individual counselling session with the family, or with some members of the family, or whether they wish to keep this information private. We believe it is helpful if they are given the option of keeping the information private rather than just being asked whether they want to share the information as some children will automatically agree when asked a question instead of considering alternatives. If they decide that they do want to share the information, the next step is to encourage them to look at the possible consequences of their disclosure. Naturally, it is possible that, having thought about the consequences, they will change their minds and will be unwilling to share.

Sometimes when the child decides to share information with their parents or other members of the family they are apprehensive about doing this even though they want to go ahead. In this case the counsellor can give the child the options below, as we believe that the child should have some level of control over the process of disclosing personal or sensitive information, particularly where there are issues with regard to safety. When sharing information the child can:

- invite the relevant family members into their counselling session to share the information
- share the information in a family counselling session
- share information with the assistance of the counsellor as an advocate
- consent for the counsellor to share information with the family with the child present.

If the child decides to make the disclosure of information themselves, it may be helpful to ask them what they will say and how they will say it. The counsellor might then decide to help the child by coaching them in the most appropriate way of passing the information on.

When acting as an advocate for the child, it is important to first discuss with the child the implications of doing so, and then to agree with the child about what is to be said and how it is to be said.

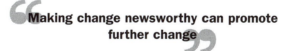

"The alter ego strategy can be helpful when advocating on behalf of a family member"

Sometimes it can be useful, when helping a child who is having difficulty being heard by other members of the family when disclosing information, to use the alter ego strategy, as described in Chapter 9. Consider, for example, a situation where a child is trying to tell their parents that they do not feel safe when in the company of an elder stepbrother, but the parents are discounting the importance of the child's information. The counsellor might stand beside the child and say on their behalf, '*I'm very frightened when I am with him and I would like your help in protecting me.*' Because this information is coming from the counsellor it is more likely to be heard and less likely to be discounted.

When using the alter ego strategy with a child it is sensible to talk with the child in advance about the strategy and to let the child know that it is fine to disagree with what the counsellor says when acting as alter ego.

Change occurs between counselling sessions

Much of the change that occurs in families engaged in family therapy occurs between counselling sessions, as is illustrated in Figure 10.1. This is inevitable because during counselling sessions individual perceptions of family members change due to raised awareness. The possibility of using new behaviours is discussed and these can often be spontaneously implemented. It is important to capitalize on this between-session change so that it is recognized, with the result that further change is promoted. Often families will minimize changes that have occurred. For example, someone in the family might have pointed out that Jason's behaviour has been much better. However, another member of the family might respond, '*Oh yes, but Jason was on holiday last week and we took him to Movieworld so he got everything he wanted.*' This statement detracts from the information that Jason has changed by minimizing the change that has occurred.

"Making change newsworthy can promote further change"

In order to ensure that change is recognized, valued, and will continue, we need to make change newsworthy, as explained in Chapter 9.

KEY POINTS

- Individual counselling is helpful in addressing personal issues.
- Family counselling is helpful in addressing family relationships and functioning.
- Integrating individual, subgroup, and family counselling provides a more complete service for clients.
- Individual and subgroup counselling sessions can occur between family counselling sessions when required.
- Information from individual and subgroup counselling can be integrated into family counselling where appropriate.
- Advocacy may be required on behalf of children disempowered by adults.
- Change may occur within counselling sessions and also between counselling sessions.
- Making change newsworthy enhances the possibility that change will continue.

QUESTIONS FOR GROUP DISCUSSION OR STUDENT ASSIGNMENTS

1. Discuss the advantages and problems relating to integrating individual, subgroup, and family counseling. Illustrate your discussion with practical examples.
2. With reference to family therapy theory, explain why it is advantageous for family counsellors to make change newsworthy and explain why families may be resistant to change. Use practical examples to illustrate your explanations.

Part 3

Relationship Counselling for the Child

In this part of the book we will discuss individual counselling for a child in order to help the child to talk about family relationships. This will include discussion of ways to help the child to talk about their relationships with their parents, brothers, and sisters. Additionally, the discussion will address the child's relationships with peers, teachers, and other adults. Practical strategies involving the use of media and/or activity, together with counselling skills, will be described.

11

Helping the Child to Talk about Their Relationships

Unfortunately, it is often the case that children are disempowered within their families. Additionally, where they develop unhelpful behaviours as a response to stress in the family they may become scapegoated, stigmatized, or pathologized by other family members. Children often do not have the skills to enable them to talk about and satisfactorily address their emotional issues through conversation with their parents or other family members. It is also often difficult for them to talk about such issues in counselling sessions as they may believe that there will be negative consequences for them if they disclose sensitive family issues.

As relationship counsellors, it is essential for us to do what we can to enable all family members, and particularly children, to resolve their relationship issues within and outside the family. In order to help children resolve their relationship issues a counsellor needs to build a relationship of trust with the child. If this is to be successfully achieved, the first step is to contract with the child's parents or carers in the presence of the child about the process of working individually with the child. As a consequence, the child is aware that the parents approve of them engaging in individual counselling, and give permission for them to talk freely about their worries.

Before counsellors work with children it is essential for them to have a sound theoretical background and to receive practical training under the supervision of a counsellor who is qualified and experienced in working with children. We recommend that new counsellors who wish to work with children might like to read our book *Counselling Children: A Practical Introduction* (2008a).

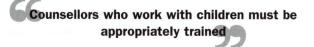

Counsellors who work with children must be appropriately trained

It is advantageous if the child–counsellor relationship is an exclusive one. Therefore, when working with a co-therapist, we prefer the co-therapist to become the child's counsellor so that the child has an individual personal counselling relationship with a person who is not directly involved in working with the rest of the family. This helps in enabling the child to trust the relationship, and to feel more confident in speaking freely about troubling issues. Similarly, when working with a reflecting team, it can be useful for one of the team members to act as counsellor for the child.

Contracting with Parents

Contracting with parents begins when the counsellor who is working with the family discusses with them the possibility of providing individual counselling sessions for a child with another member of the team acting as their counsellor. At this stage issues of confidentiality can be discussed. This discussion can include an explanation that if the child is to be able to talk freely about things that trouble them, they will need to have some confidence that what they talk about will be private and details of their conversation will generally only be disclosed to parents or other people with the child's permission. However, there are ethical limits to this confidentiality and parental rights need to be respected, so parents and child need to be informed that there may be times when it is important for information to be passed on. Our preferred approach is to explain that in such instances we will discuss with the child how and when the information is to be shared with others. We do this so that the child does not become disempowered but has control over the way in which information is shared with other people.

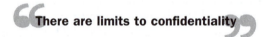

There are limits to confidentiality

When we need to pass information on to parents or other people, we remind the child of our discussions regarding sharing information with others. We identify the information we believe is important and then ask the child what it will be like for them when the information is passed on. We then explore both positive and negative consequences of sharing so that the child is fully aware of what outcomes there might be. We address the child's anxieties about sharing the information and invite the child to make decisions with regard to the timing and conditions surrounding the disclosure. This enables the child to experience some level of control pertaining to the sharing of information. The following questions can be useful in this process:

- Would you like to tell your parents yourself, or would like me to tell your parents?
- Would you like me to be present while you tell your parents, or would you like to tell your parents on your own?
- Would you prefer me to tell your parents with you present, or would you prefer me to tell your parents without you being present?
- Would you like this to happen today, or at another time?

The Purpose of Individual Counselling

When counselling a child it is essential for the child to understand that there are specific goals to be achieved through counselling. Unless the child is aware of the reason for spending time with the counsellor, the child may just see counselling sessions as a time to play or to enjoy using media. Helping the child to understand why they are to spend time in counselling is best done in the presence of the parents, or alternatively the whole family. The counsellor might say to the parents, *'I think that it might be useful if the counsellor Bronwyn, who is observing from behind the one-way mirror, were to spend some time with your daughter, Alexandria, because it seems to me that Alexandria has some worries of her own and it might be helpful for her to be able to talk about these privately with Bronwyn. I wonder if you think this might be helpful for Alexandria or not?'* If the parents respond positively, the counsellor might also invite Alexandria to consider the possibility of working separately with another counsellor. It is important for the counsellor to explain that if Alexandria spends some time separately, she will be able to use activities and toys to help her to talk about herself, her school, friends, and family. This process makes the purpose of counselling transparent so that both the child and parents are clear about why individual counselling for the child has been proposed.

Attributes of the Child's Counsellor

A counsellor for children should be congruent, in touch with their own inner child, accepting, and emotionally detached. Children are very good at recognizing people who are not congruent and who are trying to play a role which is not consistent with the rest of their personalities. However, if the counsellor is congruent, they are likely to be seen by the child as trustworthy.

If a counsellor is to join with a child, they must be able to get in touch with their own inner child so that they can connect appropriately. Additionally, counsellors must be able to give their child clients permission to be who they are, and to be accepted as they are without the counsellor showing either approval or disapproval. As explained more fully in Geldard and Geldard (2008a), counsellors need to have a level of emotional detachment when working with children. If a counsellor becomes emotionally involved with the child, then they are likely to become emotionally affected by the child's issues in a way which is apparent to the child, and this will not be helpful.

Combining Media and Activity with Counselling Skills

When counselling adults it is sufficient for the counsellor to engage in conversation with the client using appropriate counselling skills. By doing this the client is likely to disclose their troubling issues to the counsellor. Generally, this approach will not enable children to talk about their worries. In order to help them to get in touch with emotional issues and talk about them we need to engage them in the use of particular media or activity so that their interest is captured and they are able to use the media or activity to help them focus on what is of importance to them. In order for the counsellor to engage with the child and help the child to talk about their worries, while the child is using media or is engaged in an activity, the counsellor needs to use suitable counselling skills.

> **"Counselling children requires the use of media or activity and counselling skills"**

Joining with the Child

For a counsellor to join with a child they must be capable of:

- creating a trusting relationship
- selecting and using media or activity
- providing the facilities and opportunities for free and/or meaningful play
- using appropriate child counselling skills.

Creating a trusting relationship

While providing a level of openness, warmth, and friendliness, and showing an interest in the child and what the child is saying and doing, as explained previously, the counsellor needs to remain both congruent and grounded, with a level of emotional detachment which makes it safe for the child to talk about their troubling issues.

In the process of joining it can be useful for the child to be provided with choices and options about how the first counselling session with them should begin and proceed. It is highly desirable during the joining process to help the child to understand the nature of the child–counsellor relationship so that they know what the expectations are; otherwise they will not feel secure and comfortable in the relationship. For example, it can be helpful for the counsellor to enquire about the child's experience in the whole family session/s and to explore the difficulties of participating in the family group discussions. Joining is primarily about creating a relationship which meets the child's needs in the counselling environment so that the child will feel comfortable enough to engage usefully in the therapeutic process.

Selecting and using media or activity

The joining process can be enhanced by the selection of suitable media or activity. In this regard it may be useful to give the child some options about what sort of media they would like to use, or what sort of activity they would prefer to engage in. Typical, media for use when carrying out relationship counselling with children includes:

- miniature animals
- symbols in the sand tray
- clay
- drawing and painting.

The use of the media and activity for relationship counselling with children is discussed further in Chapters 12 and 13.

Providing the facilities and opportunities for free and/or meaningful play

For younger children, typical media and activity include:

- puppets and soft toys
- imaginative pretend play.

These will be explored in more detail in Chapters 12 and 13. To work effectively with puppets and soft toys, and involve the child in imaginative pretend play, it can be very helpful to have a suitably equipped play therapy room. This might include child-size furniture and associated items, puppets, dolls, and dressing-up materials. By providing these items, the child is able to create stories about families using the puppets and dolls, and to role-play family members using the dressing-up materials, as will be described in the later chapters.

Using appropriate child counselling skills

In order to engage a child so that the child can talk about the troubling issues which are affecting their behaviours and relationships with others, the counsellor needs to invite the child to make use of particular media, or to take part in a particular activity.

Giving instructions

Once the child has decided on one of the alternatives, the child needs to be given clear instructions about how to use the media. Otherwise they will not know what they are supposed to do, and the therapeutic process is unlikely to proceed usefully.

Structuring the session

When a child first has a relationship with a counsellor they will be unsure about what is expected of them unless they are clearly told. Consequently, the counsellor needs to talk to the child about any alternatives that are available. The counsellor might say to the child, *'If you like, we can spend some time using these miniature animals, or alternatively we can use these things and put them into the sand tray'*. By giving the child choice the child will feel as though they have some control in the situation. Giving the child direction also enables the child to feel safe and secure because the child knows that the counsellor, who is respected by their parents, is in charge and will take responsibility for what happens in the session.

Once engaged in this way, the counsellor can make use of a variety of counselling skills, including:

- giving instructions
- observation
- making statements
- active listening
- the use of questions.

> **Children need direction in order to feel secure in the counselling situation**

Observation

A counsellor can observe the child's behaviour, mood, intellectual functioning and thought processes, speech and language, motor skills, and also their relationship with the counsellor. These observations will provide the counsellor with useful information in understanding the child's thinking, emotional state, and behaviour.

Making statements

While the child is actively involved in using media, it is often sensible for the counsellor to observe rather than intrude on the child's process. However, it can be useful for the counsellor to match the child's body language and to sit beside or opposite them so that they are aware that the counsellor is engaged with them. Occasionally, the counsellor might feedback what they have observed. For example, by making statements such as those below the counsellor provides the child with an opportunity to articulate how they feel or explain what they are thinking.

'I notice that you seem to be having difficulty deciding which object to choose.'
'You look sad when you do that'.

Active listening

As when counselling adults, active listening involves matching body language, the use of minimal responses, reflection, and summarizing. Generally, these micro-skills should be used sparingly but sufficiently to demonstrate to the child that the counsellor is paying attention and is interested in what they are doing and saying.

Use of questions

Questions should be used only when necessary because if the counsellor asks too many questions the child will be likely to rely on the counsellor to ask more questions rather than staying with their own process and talking about what really matters for them.

A problem with questions is that they tend to lead a child in a particular direction and this may take them away from thinking about and disclosing their most troubling issues.

Generally, 'why' questions aren't very useful when working with children because they invite interpretative answers which tend to deflect the child away from their internal processes. 'What' and 'how' questions are preferred because they invite the child to share information which is not contaminated by contrived explanations. Explanations distract the child from the true essence of the story and allow them to deflect away from painful experiences.

KEY POINTS

- Children can be dis-empowered, scapegoated, stigmatized, or pathologized by other family members.
- Counsellors working with children need a sound theoretical background and practical training under the supervision of a counsellor who is qualified and experienced in working with children.
- The child needs a level of privacy in order to be able to talk freely but there are ethical and parental limits to confidentiality.
- It is important for the child to understand the purpose of counselling.
- Counselling children involves the use of media and/or activity together with counselling skills.
- Giving the child directions enables the child to know what is expected of them and helps them to feel secure.

QUESTIONS FOR GROUP DISCUSSION OR STUDENT ASSIGNMENTS

1. Discuss the ethical issues related to confidentiality for children who are being counselled. Explain under what circumstances you believe that information should be passed on to the parents or others. Identify problems which might arise as a result of disclosing information to parents or others.
2. Discuss two or three alternative ways of dealing with a situation where the parents want a child to have individual relationship counselling but the child is reluctant to separate from their mother. Explain the advantages and disadvantages associated with each alternative.

12

Exploring the Child's Relationships with Parents and Siblings

As described in the previous chapter, counsellors working with children need to join with the child and engage them in ways that will enable them to feel comfortable with and interested in the counselling process as it evolves. Although joining is obviously required at the start of the session, we believe that the process of joining is an ongoing one where the child continually needs to be re-engaged so that their interest and involvement is encouraged. Reynolds (2005) points out that most children will not sustain intense therapeutic work throughout the length of a counselling session, so she suggests varying the activities used so that the child remains engaged.

Children inhabit a different world from that of the adult and are at a different developmental level. They don't share the adult preference for language and verbal communication and the rules of adult conversation just don't apply to how children relate. Children like to communicate through play and creative activities as well as through conversation (Sharry, 2004). If we are to engage children in suitable activities or in the use of particular media, we need to be aware of the developmental stage of the child. Activities and media that may suit a younger child may not suit an older child. Consequently, when exploring the child's relationships with parents and siblings, we will describe different ways of working with children who are developmentally average in their general abilities and fall into the following age groups:

- age 7 upwards
- age 5–7
- below age 5

Working with Children of Age 7 Upwards Using Miniature Animals

Usually when working with children in this age group we will use miniature animals to help the child to talk about their perceptions of their family and relationships within the family.

To use this approach we need a selection of small plastic toy animals and other creatures. It is advantageous to have a wide variety in this selection, including animals and creatures of different sizes, colours, and appearance. Some of these will look aggressive, others will look friendly, and some will look neither friendly nor aggressive and more self-contained, like a tortoise. In our selection, we have:

- domestic, farm, and wild animals
- dinosaurs of various types and sizes
- reptiles, including snakes, crocodiles, and lizards
- insects, including spiders, ants, and grasshoppers
- Sea creatures, including turtles, dolphins, and whales.

Where possible, we include male, female, and baby animals. We only include animals that are able to stand freely without support because children become frustrated and distracted when animals fall over.

Using miniature animals to explore relationships in the family

Usually we invite the child to sit with us on the carpeted floor of our play therapy room and to have a look at the animals and other creatures. After the child has had time to examine the animals and become familiar with the range, the counsellor might say, '*I'd like to find out something about you and your family, and I thought that I could do this if we were to use these toy animals.*' Having received the child's response, the counsellor might say, '*First, I would like you to choose the animal which is most like you*'.

Be unhurried

It is better to allow the child plenty of time to choose the animal rather than hurrying them. If they have difficulty, the counsellor might select two or three animals and ask, '*Are you like this animal, or more like this animal, or not like either of them?*'

Once the child has chosen their animal, the counsellor can say, '*Tell me about that lion (or whatever animal is chosen)*' or '*What is that lion like?*' Hopefully, the child will respond by talking about the personal characteristics of the lion. For example, the child might say, '*This lion is very fierce and can get very angry*'. Sometimes a child who is developmentally immature will not be able to describe the lion in terms of personal characteristics but will instead will make a concrete statement about the size and physical attributes of the lion, such as, '*The lion has a nice tail*' or '*The lion has big teeth*'. In this case, we would recognize that this particular strategy is not suitable for this child and would use the strategy described in the next section for a younger child.

If the child has been able to describe the personal characteristics of the animal, the counsellor might follow up by asking, '*Can you tell me more?*' The child might then reply,

'*This lion has lots of friends*'. The counsellor might follow up in this case by asking, '*Is there anything else you can tell me about the lion?*' and get the response, '*The lion and gets angry when other people annoy it*'.

In using this approach, the counsellor refers to the animal selected as 'the animal' or, for example, 'the lion'. The counsellor does not call the animal by the child's name, and does not imply that the animal is the child even though the animal has been chosen as being *most like* the child and will be used to represent the child. Referring to it as 'the animal' or by its name allows the child to distance themselves from the chosen animal, so that although it represents them in some ways, it is not the same as them. They can then project qualities, characteristics, and behaviours on to the animal with safety. The animal – not the child – becomes the owner of negative, positive and unacceptable attributes. This enables the child to feel freer in attributing negative and undesirable behaviours which they may recognize in themselves but may not be ready to own.

As counsellors, we need to be careful not to project our own ideas on to the animals chosen by the child. For example, the child might choose a panther, which the counsellor sees as aggressive. However, the child might see the panther as powerful but friendly, and not aggressive.

Once the child has selected the animal which is most like them, the counsellor encourages the child to select other animals to represent each member of their family. The same procedure is used as before, with the counsellor making requests such as '*Now choose the animal which is most like your mum*'. As each animal is chosen, the counsellor asks the child '*What is that animal like?*'

As each animal is selected, the child is encouraged to place it in front of them. Eventually the child will have a group of animals to represent their family. When the group is complete, the counsellor should note the placement of the selected animals and make a statement about how they have been arranged. For example, the counsellor might say: '*Your animals are all in a straight line*' or '*Your animals are all in a circle with the zebra in the centre*'. Often, when a counsellor makes such an observation, the child will spontaneously talk about the meaning which is associated with the arrangement of the animals. For example, the child might say, '*All the other animals are watching the zebra because she likes to play tricks on them*'.

Sometimes a child will not respond to the counsellor's feedback statement about the arrangement of the group of animals. In this case, the counsellor might say to the child, '*Arrange the animals in a picture so that I can see what your family is like*'. The intention is to encourage the child to arrange the animals so that the arrangement provides a metaphorical picture of the family.

Once a child has arranged the animals into a picture, the counsellor can begin to explore the relationships between the animals in the group. For example, the counsellor may begin to explore the relationship between the dog (representing the child) and the dinosaur (representing the child's father). The counsellor might ask questions like: '*I wonder what it is like for the dog to be next to the dinosaur?*'

Later the counsellor might ask: *'What is it like for the dinosaur to have the dog next to him?'* and *'How does the horse* [representing the child's mother] *feel about the dog and dinosaur being together?'* It could also be useful for the counsellor to ask the child how they think the other animals in the group feel about this arrangement. The process can be extended by asking the child to move the dog (if that is the animal the child chose to represent themselves) to a new position near another animal. Similarly, the child can be asked to move other animals into different positions in the group. In this way, the various relationships within the group can be explored.

While giving the child instructions and exploring the relationships in this way, the counsellor is careful not to move the animals, but instead to ask the child to move them. We believe that by doing this the child develops a greater sense of ownership about the story which they are telling, and is more likely to feel in control of the process and be more in touch with their perceptions.

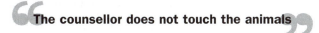

The counsellor does not touch the animals

Sometimes a counsellor may notice that a child is reluctant to move an animal into a particular position. The counsellor might then use reflection to feed this observation back to the child by saying, *'You seem to be unhappy about moving the duck next to the snake'*. By feeding back this information to the child, the counsellor is able to raise the child's awareness of important feelings. After each animal is moved, the child is again asked questions about the feelings of various other animals with regard to the altered position. Thus, the child, in an indirect way, shares their picture of their family, and of their family's relationships, with the counsellor.

As well as exploring current relationships, the counsellor can explore how the child might feel about absences of family members. For example, the counsellor might say to the child, *'I would like you to move the dinosaur and put him behind your back'*. The visual picture that appears for the child is now one where there is an absent dinosaur (father).

The miniature animals can be used to help the child to explore their ideas about what would make relationships within the family more comfortable. This can be done by inviting the child to put their animal in a place where the animal will feel most comfortable in relation to other members of their family.

It can be useful to invite the child to place their own animal close to an animal which has already been identified as worrying for them. Thus, the child can fully experience the resulting feelings and deal with them.

When the counselling session is drawing to an end, we find that it is useful to invite the child to arrange the animals in a way that will enable all the animals to feel most comfortable. The counsellor might say, *'I'd like you to rearrange your animals into a new picture so that all of the animals will feel happy and comfortable'*. This enables the child to leave the session feeling comfortable about their work and with a sense of closure around the issues of relationships within their family.

Generally, when using miniature animals, the counsellor shouldn't advise, interpret or congratulate the child while they are telling their story. Similarly, expressions of surprise, approval or disapproval would intrude on the storytelling and might influence it so that it would cease to be authentically the child's. The counsellor needs to take the child's story seriously and to communicate respect for it. This is true even when it is clear that factual information in the child's story is completely wrong. It is only by having the opportunity to tell their story, in their own way, that the child can later move forward to test their perception of reality.

The projective nature of working with miniature animals

When using the miniature animals the counsellor is relying on a projective technique to help the child to express what they are unable to say clearly. Projective techniques are an avenue to inner thoughts and emotions. They are also cognitive as they reflect modes of perception and thought processes aside from idiosyncratic content (Waiswol, 1995).

Projective techniques are typically divided into five groups (Linzey, 1959), one of which is the category of *expressive techniques*, in which the subject is required to organize and incorporate a particular stimulus into a self-expressive process, such as storytelling, role-playing, psychodrama, dance, etc. These techniques are relevant for counsellors of children when using miniature animals.

When using the miniature animals we invite the child to tell us a story about themselves, their family, and family relationships using the stimuli (miniature animals) to express themselves. When eliciting these stories using projective techniques, Linzey (1959) suggests attending to several dimensions which are important for understanding the internal world of children. These are:

- *Imagined real*: in a 'real' story, we have components of reality that are very likely to come from the child's world, for example reference to television, or a foster family. In an imaginary story, we have components that are probably imagined, for example living in a forest, or the whole family dying. A counsellor needs to be aware that the child's story may be an imagined, or hoped for, story and not reality.
- *The child in the story*: the counsellor needs to observe how the child views themselves in the family.
- *Emotions in the story*: the emotional content in the story needs to be checked with regard to the child's and other family members' emotions.
- *The object of interaction in the story*: the counsellor needs to explore the interpersonal relationships between the animals so that the child has an opportunity to talk about them.
- *Characterization of the interaction*: the counsellor needs to take note of themes regarding interactions, for example themes of power, intimacy, rescuing, and victimization.

- *Coping and problem-solving in the story*: the counsellor needs to observe how the responses of the animals reflect an ability to cope.
- *Direction of the story*: the counsellor needs to check whether the child believes there is a possible optimistic outcome.

The sequence of questions described previously when working with children using miniature animals reflect how these dimensions can be drawn out.

Throughout the process involved in working with miniature animals, the counsellor never refers to the group of animals selected as 'the child's family' and never uses the names of members of the child's family. This might inhibit the child in the allocation of attributes, behaviours, thoughts and feelings to the animals, and might block the child's ability to freely explore the relationships between the animals. The process is projective, with the child projecting ideas from their family on to the animals, but having the freedom to exaggerate or modify those projections. By using this projective technique, the child is likely to access ideas and beliefs which may have been suppressed into their unconscious because of fears about the consequences of recognizing those ideas and beliefs.

Because the process is projective, the child will make connections between relationships and behaviours in the animal group, and relationships and behaviours in their own family. In so doing, they are likely to make important discoveries about relationships within their family, and to want to talk about these.

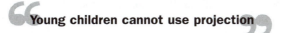

Young children cannot use projection

It needs to be recognized that because of its projective nature the strategies described for working with miniature animals are not suitable for use with younger children. The child needs to be functioning at least at a concrete operational level where storytelling is primarily in the area of association and connection among symbolic representations and feelings (Singer and Revenson, 1996). Using miniature animals involves some cognition because of the design of the activity, which involves matching animal characteristics with human behaviours and characteristics. Younger children tend to produce concrete responses and are unlikely to be able to project their ideas about various family members on to the animals. Instead, they are likely to talk directly about the selected animals and their characteristics. Further, children under the age of 7 have limited ability to abstract and predict. They have little understanding of motive or intent and therefore find it difficult to project other people's behaviours on to the animals. Younger children are functioning at a pre-operational level where, while the child is able to represent the world through symbols, these symbols are interpreted from the child's own perception and involves magical thinking to make sense of the world (Singer and Revenson, 1996).

Counselling skills needed

The counselling skills described in Chapter 11 are required when using miniature animals. Here are some examples to demonstrate the use of these skills when working with miniature animals.

Observation and reflection of feeling

The counsellor might say: '*I noticed that you looked happy when you put the monkey and the goat together.*'

Observation and a statement

The counsellor might use a statement to feed back to the child an observation of significance by saying '*I notice that the chicken is the furthest one away from the rhinoceros.*'

Use of open questions

The counsellor might ask: '*What is it like for this animal when the dinosaur is standing in front of him?*'

Use of repetition

At times, while working with miniature animals, the counsellor may repeat word-for-word phrases used by the child to encourage the child to tell more of their story. Consider an example where, after moving a cat next to a hen, a child says: '*The elephant doesn't like that.*' If the counsellor repeats, '*The elephant doesn't like that*', then the child is likely to think about what they have said and to explore their ideas and feelings more thoroughly.

Bringing about relationship change

Working with the miniature animals is likely to bring family relationship issues affecting the child into the open so that the child can talk about these. It may be that through raised awareness of the issues the child will begin to make changes to troubling relationships. However, it is more likely that the troubling relationship issues will need to be addressed in a joint counselling session involving the child either with a parent or parents, or with another sibling or siblings, or in the context of the whole family, as will be discussed later in this chapter.

Working with Children of Age 5–7 Using Symbols in the Sand Tray

When exploring relationship issues with children who are not developmentally mature enough to use a projective technique we cannot use the miniature animals in the way previously described. Our preference when working with children in the 5–7 age group is to use symbols representing family members in a sand tray.

Even though we cannot use the miniature animals projectively, we can use them as symbols to represent various family members. Alternatively, we can use small figurines, or other symbols, to represent family members. When we use either miniature animals or figurines or symbols to represent family members, we refer to them directly by the names of the family members represented, as we are not using a projective approach. Thus if Daddy is represented by a horse, we refer to the horse as 'Daddy'.

Equipment and materials needed

The equipment and materials required for sand tray work include a sand tray, symbols, and figurines. For practical information regarding the use of sand tray work for counselling children with emotional problems, we suggest that you might like to refer to our book *Counselling Children: A Practical Introduction* (Geldard and Geldard, 2008a). Useful information regarding Jungian sand play is also offered by Ryce-Menuhin (1992).

The symbols used in sand tray work consist of a variety of small objects which are chosen because they have properties that enable them to easily assume symbolic meaning. We have collected our symbols over a period of time, so that they include many different types of object. For example, among our symbols are:

- many general items such as pebbles, feathers, candles, a padlock, a small pyramid, ornaments, a horseshoe, a pencil, a crystal ball, a torch battery, etc.
- small toys such as plastic trees and fences, aeroplanes, cars, and trains, etc.
- male and female figurines, superheroes such as Catwoman, Power Rangers, etc.
- miniature animals, as described previously.

Sand tray work provides the child with an opportunity to use symbols, within a defined space, to tell their story about their family and relationships within the family. The child can re-create in the sand tray events and situations from their past and present which may have impacted or currently impact on their relationships in the family.

When helping a child explore relationships within their family, each family member is represented by a symbol. Additionally, symbols are used to represent any specific items or people that may be part of the child's story, such as roads, houses, TV sets, furniture, cars, and fences. As mentioned earlier, younger children are functioning at a preoperational level where, while the child is able to represent the world through symbols, these symbols are interpreted from the child's own perception and involves magical thinking to make sense of the world (Piaget, 1948/1966). As a consequence, the symbols may also be used to represent less tangible concepts, such as secrets, thoughts, beliefs, wishes and emotional barriers. In summary, the symbols can be used to represent people, and concrete or intangible and abstract concepts which have a place in the child's story about their family.

> **Family relationships can be explored in the sand tray**

Using sand tray work, the child can explore themes and issues relating to their relationships within the family, as illustrated by particular events and situations. They have the opportunity to act out those things which are not, or were not, acceptable to them. Sand tray work gives the child the possibility of gaining a cognitive understanding of relationships within their family, to develop insight about these relationships, and to gain mastery over past and current issues and events.

Using the sand tray to explore relationships in the family

Because of the tactile and kinaesthetic experience of working in the sand tray, most children seem to engage readily in the task. When exploring family relationships with a child we usually start by inviting the child to choose a symbol for each member of their family. We then ask them to tell us a story about their family and as they tell us a story to put symbols in the sand to illustrate their story. For example, the child might start by saying, '*This is my brother, Aaron (picking up a symbol that represents their brother). He spends most of his time in his bedroom.*' In response, the counsellor might say, '*Put Aaron in the sand and choose something to make a bedroom for him and put that in the sand.*' As a consequence, the child might pick up a necklace from the symbols box to represent Aaron's bedroom and place the necklace around the symbol representing Aaron in the sand. As the child continues to tell their story the counsellor will continually encourage the child to select symbols to represent all those things that make up part of the story.

As the story proceeds, the counsellor can use the counselling skills described in Chapter 11 to help the child continue telling their story. For example, the counsellor might give feedback such as, '*I notice that you have put the symbol representing Samuel right next to the symbol representing your mother.*' As a result of this feedback the child might say, '*Yes, Samuel takes up all of Mummy's time and she never has time for me.*' Similarly, the counsellor might reflect what they perceive as the child's emotional state by saying, '*You seem to be very sad when you tell me that.*' The child might respond by saying, '*It's just not fair that I get into trouble and Samuel doesn't.*'

As the picture in the sand tray develops, the counsellor can notice the qualities of the various relationships, taking particular notice of strengths, weaknesses, distances, closeness and boundaries. Additionally, the counsellor can note any absences of significant others from the picture. Again, the use of feedback statements by the counsellor will help to raise the child's awareness of their situation so that they can deal with related issues.

Sometimes, while a child is working on their picture, they will talk about it spontaneously. Generally, the counsellor observes quietly as the child creates their picture. However, if the child does not talk about what they are doing, after observing for a while, it is appropriate for the counsellor to indirectly invite the child to talk about their story by using a statement to feed back what the counsellor has observed. For example, the counsellor might say: *'You've been very careful when making your picture'* or *'Your picture looks very crowded'* or *'Your picture is very busy'*. These statements are non-intrusive and are likely to encourage the child to talk about the picture, without directing them to one particular part of the picture. Sometimes, however, statements like the above are not sufficient and a question will be needed.

Feedback statements not only allow the child to talk about the picture, but also raise the child's awareness of their internal processes as they construct the picture. Their awareness of issues, thoughts and feelings is intensified and, consequently, they are able to bring these into focus so that they may be addressed.

Before asking questions, the counsellor should remember that it is important to sit quietly and to observe, rather than to interrupt the natural flow of the child's process. However, at appropriate times, during pauses, questions can be used to help the child to explore more fully or in more depth certain parts of their picture or story. Here are some examples of useful questions:

'Can you tell me about your picture?'
'I wonder what's happening over here?' (pointing to an empty space in the sand tray)
'Can you tell me more?'

> ## Allow time for the child to carry out their work in the sand

It is important for the counsellor to allow the child to develop their picture without intruding on the process or attempting to interpret the child's picture. Equally, it is important for the counsellor not to make assumptions about the meanings of symbols or objects in the sand tray story. It is better to explore the meaning which the child gives the symbol. For example, the counsellor might ask, *'Can you tell me about this rock?'* In response, the child might say, *'That's the church, where we get lots to eat.'* In this way, the child's awareness of issues and developments in their story is raised.

Counselling skills needed

The counselling skills required when working with symbols in the sand tray are described in Chapter 11. Here are some more examples of the use of the skills.

Observation and reflection of feeling
The counsellor might say: *'I noticed that you looked worried when you put Andrew in your picture.'*

Observation and a statement

The counsellor might use a statement to feed back to the child an observation of significance by saying: '*I notice that Monica and Jacob are a long way away from your Daddy and Rachel.*'

Use of open questions

The counsellor might ask: '*What do you think it is like for Mark when Uncle Harry comes into his bedroom?*'

Finishing the work

The counsellor needs to judge when the time is appropriate for ending a piece of work in the sand tray. Good indications of this are if the child stops work spontaneously, or when the child is unable to develop the story any further. Alternatively, it may be that the child has identified specific issues with regard to relationships in the family which need addressing. The counsellor can then summarize what has emerged from the work and affirm the child for the way they have told their story. The child can then be given an opportunity to dismantle the picture themselves or to leave the picture for the counsellor to dismantle after they have left. It would be inappropriate for the counsellor to dismantle the picture in the child's presence because it is the child's story. To do so would be intrusive and might lead to undesirable symbolic interpretations by the child. However, it is important for the child to know that the picture will not be there when they return for another counselling session.

Bringing about relationship change

Working with symbols in the sand tray is likely to bring family relationship issues affecting the child into the open so that the child can talk about these. In this age group, it is doubtful whether raised awareness of the issues will be sufficient to enable the child to begin to make changes to troubling relationships, as developmentally the child is unlikely to have the social skills required to achieve this. Consequently, the relationship issues will need to be addressed either with parents, or with other sibling/s, or in the context of the whole family. Further discussion regarding the integration of the individual counselling work with the wider system is included later in this chapter.

Working with Children of Below Age 5 Using Imaginative Pretend Play

When exploring a young child's experience of family relationships we prefer to use imaginative pretend play which is the naturally occurring play of young children between the ages of 3 and 5. Young children enjoy pretending to be someone else, such as a doctor examining a patient or a mother feeding her children. In their play, they dress up and make use of props, for example, empty food packets when they are pretending to be shopping. Thus, they combine the use of objects, actions, words and interactions with imagined people to produce a drama.

> **Young children naturally use imaginative pretend play**

Although very young children between the ages of 2 and 3 can mimic the roles of familiar adults in their lives, they need to use real objects, or toy replicas of them, in their representational play. Older children, from age 4 and upwards, rely less on real objects in their imaginative pretend play. In this age range, they are generally able to use unrelated objects to symbolize, or take the place of, objects which are involved in their play (Heidemann and Hewitt, 1992). For example, a wooden block might be used as a telephone. These older children are also capable of substituting actions for objects in their imaginative pretend play. For example, a child may raise a clenched fist to their mouth as a substitute for a cup when pretending to drink. Because older children are able to engage in abstract thinking, they can easily play the roles of fantasy characters, such as superheroes, monsters and fairies.

In imaginative pretend play the whole child becomes totally involved in acting out a character within an imagined situation. The child becomes an actor in the fullest sense.

Imaginative pretend play sometimes, but not always, includes the use of social skills. When social skills are involved, we refer to the play as socio-dramatic play. The use of social skills occurs when using imaginative pretend play in the form of verbal and non-verbal interaction between the counsellor and the child while the child is role-playing.

By using imaginative pretend play, a child can act out significant observations with regard to their life, the people in their life, and the relationship dynamics of their family.

When focusing on relationship counselling, imaginative pretend play can be used to enable a child to express underlying thoughts or thought processes, to experience cathartic release, to develop insight about and gain mastery over past and present issues and events, and to practise and develop new behaviours.

Materials and equipment needed for imaginative pretend play

We need to have a wide variety of props so that we can prompt children to enter into specific imaginative pretend play scenarios which are individually relevant and which might achieve the goals listed above. Some props need to be directly representational and realistic so that younger children can use them easily; others can be less representational, for use by older children.

We have in our play room the following equipment and materials to encourage imaginative pretend play (some of these are also listed in Chapter 16):

- child-size furniture and associated items (e.g. toy stove, table and chairs, doll's pram, plastic crockery, etc.)
- dolls, soft toys and associated items (doll's clothes, feeding bottle, etc.)
- dressing-up materials (e.g. hats, wigs, jewellery, doctor's bag, masks, magic wand, etc.)

Using imaginative pretend play to explore relationships in the family

Whenever a child uses imaginative pretend play to experience a make-believe world, they can experiment by using an unlimited variety of roles and behaviours. They can spontaneously change from acting out one role to acting out a different role. The relationship counsellor's responsibility is to provide an environment in which the child can create and enter an imaginary world, and then use the experience therapeutically with regard to their own family experience. The counsellor can use the relationship between the child and themselves to help the child to participate in, and benefit from, imaginative pretend play.

The counsellor has a choice of roles and that choice may significantly influence the therapeutic effectiveness of the play. We need to remember that most young children don't need an adult to be present as a play partner. However, they do need someone to provide time, space, props and, with regard to relationship counselling, to introduce themes and experiences. They need someone to act as a facilitator to help them to start playing, sustain their play, modify and extend it so that it is goal-directed.

Children who have limited play skills may benefit by the counsellor joining in their play to help them to improve their play skills. For the child with limited play skills there are three alternative roles which the counsellor can assume. These roles are described in *Counselling Children: A Practical Introduction* (Geldard and Geldard, 2008a).

Starting the imaginative pretend play session

Before starting the session, we make sure that the play therapy room is set up with the equipment and materials which will be needed to stimulate imaginative pretend play. When involved in relationship counselling we will usually set out the child-sized furniture in a way that suggests a family home, and have soft toys available to represent the members of a family.

When the child enters the room, we usually begin by saying something like: *'Today, we are going to spend some time playing with the things in this room.'*

Because the equipment and props are appealing to most children, the child will generally begin to explore what is available. The child will usually select some of the props, and begin to dress up and to imitate particular characters. Younger children usually move straight to the 'home' corner, where we have the kitchen, and begin to play roles that are familiar to them. For example, they may pretend to cook a meal as a mother or start to look after a baby doll. When the child begins to engage in this kind of play, the counsellor can engage in play with the child, if appropriate, or simply observe the child, the themes and the sequences of the play. The counsellor can then choose opportunities as the play progresses to suggest that the child create a family using the soft toys and create a story around family life. While this is in progress the counsellor can make statements, ask questions and provide feedback about what the child is doing. Through asking the child to create a family in the imaginative play, the child is likely to re-create situations, themes, and relationship patterns that occur in the child's own family. When troubling situations arise in the imaginative play, the counsellor can ask how one particular family member feels, and/or what they would like to happen. Additionally, the counsellor might ask, '*Is it sometimes like this in your family?*'

> **Imaginative pretend play inevitably draws on the child's own experiences**

Imaginative pretend play allows the child to create an imaginative story which will inevitably draw on their own experiences in their family. This will occur spontaneously as the child creates a script and directs the 'players', both animate and inanimate. These players include themselves, the dolls and soft toys, and perhaps even the counsellor. In the drama some children will spontaneously express their wishes, fantasies and fears, and the counsellor can retain the role of observer. However, for other children the counsellor can enrich the fantasies, wishes and ideas of the child through co-play. The counsellor might do this by exaggerating the role assigned to them, or by behaving in a paradoxical way and thus encouraging the child to become more forceful in expressing the ideas, fears, wishes or fantasies being acted out. However, the counsellor needs to stay strictly within the role assigned to them by the child, otherwise they will intrude on and inhibit the child's personal expression.

The counsellor can help a child to express underlying thoughts or thought processes by observing the child's play without interference. The child is then allowed, through free association, to use the imaginative pretend play time to explore unconscious wishes or desires. During this process, it is useful for the counsellor to reflect thoughts, feelings and content back to the child. For example, the counsellor might say: '*When Dolly is naughty she gets locked in her room. I wonder what it would be like for her to be locked in her room?*' This enables the child to explore their own issues about being trapped.

Imaginative pretend play is a way of giving a child an opportunity to act out feelings and problems, and thus to achieve emotional release or catharsis. When this happens, the imaginative pretend play is in itself the therapeutic intervention because the process of play is healing in itself. When seeking to achieve this goal, the therapist needs to be totally non-directive and must provide a safe environment and an empathic relationship with the child.

The counsellor can invite the child to use imaginative pretend play to re-create an unpleasant or painful family experience where the child felt helpless and disempowered. As this is acted out in the form of a mini-drama, the child can be encouraged to be more actively involved in events that may previously have been experienced passively. This can be achieved by inviting the child to repeat the mini-drama several times. With each repetition, the child is encouraged to experiment with new behaviours which are more powerful and involve taking more control. Thus, the child moves from a victim position and gains a sense of mastery over events that had been threatening.

Imaginative pretend play can be useful in enabling the child to develop insight into current and past events, or to take risks in developing new behaviours, to practise using new behaviours, to build self-concept and self-esteem, and to improve communication skills. For a fuller description of the use of imaginative pretend play for working therapeutically with emotionally disturbed children please refer to Geldard and Geldard (2008a).

Integration of Individual Counselling Work for the Child with Family Counselling

During an individual counselling session with a child information often emerges that could usefully be shared with other members of the family in order to improve family functioning. When this occurs the child needs to be given options with regard to sharing information with other members of the family. We would like to reiterate that we believe that it is preferable for a child to have a choice about what information is shared and how it is shared. However, this must be subject to the right of the parents to have information and any ethical requirements, as discussed in Chapter 11.

> "Children may be disempowered if they are not given choice"

We believe that it is desirable for the child to be able to make their own decision, if possible, with regard to how to address relationship issues. Consequently, the counsellor will need to explore with the child various alternatives, as described in Chapter 10.

Helping the child to talk with parents

Often a child will have information which is best shared only with their parents, certainly in the first instance. In this case, near the end of a counselling session with the child, the counsellor might ask them whether they would like their parent or parents to be invited into the counselling room. Where a child has been using miniature animals or symbols and the sand tray, the child might like to show a parent the arrangement of the miniature animals or symbols and to use these to share information. Clearly, counsellor discretion is required when doing this, and the child needs to be asked what the likely consequence of sharing in this way could be. Similarly, a child who has been involved in imaginative pretend play might like to explain to a parent what has happened in the imaginary family in their play, and the counsellor can extend their explanations by asking whether anything like this happens at home.

Sometimes it can be more useful to arrange a separate counselling session involving only the parent/s and child, where information can be shared and discussed and therapeutic work can focus on the parent–child relationship, as discussed in Chapter 13.

In all situations where the parents and child together are sharing information, the counsellor needs to act as a facilitator, creating a safe climate for all involved. The counsellor ensures that sharing is done in ways which are productive and helpful. It is important that all parties recognize that each of them is doing the best they can, even if that does have some unsatisfactory consequences for the family.

KEY POINTS

- When counselling children we need to use media and activity in conjunction with counselling skills.
- Miniature animals are useful for helping children explore family relationships from the age of 7 upwards.
- Working with miniature animals involves projecting thinking which much younger children have not developed.
- Symbols in a sand tray can be used to help children aged 5–7 explore family relationships.
- Imaginative pretend play can be used to help children below age 5 explore relationships within their families.
- When integrating individual counselling for the child with subgroup or family work it is preferable to give the child a choice about what information is shared and how it is shared, taking into account parental rights and ethical issues.

13

Addressing the Child's Relationships with Parents and Siblings

During an initial or subsequent family counselling session (as discussed in Chapters 8 and 9), the awareness of the family might be raised with regard to the unsatisfactory relationship between one, two, or more of the children, in the family. Similarly, the awareness of the family might be raised with regard to an unsatisfactory relationship between one, two, or more of the children in the family and their parents. During this process members of the family would have an opportunity to share their pictures of what was happening in their problematic relationships and it might be that through this

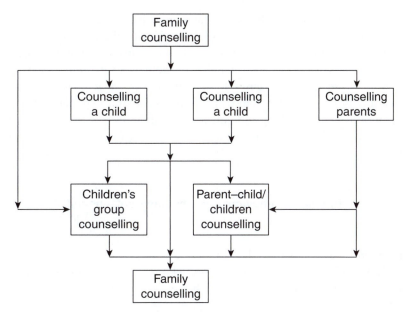

FIGURE 13.1   *Options for counselling a family*

discussion changes would occur spontaneously, either during the family counselling session or subsequent to that session.

It might be helpful at this stage to look at how to address children's relationship issues with other members of the family when spontaneous change does not occur.

Figure 13.1 shows diagrammatically some options that might be used where relationships between two or three children in the family are disruptive or unhelpful. The options would need to be negotiated with the family to suit their individual and family needs, and might include the following:

1. Whole family counselling.
2. Counselling for individual children.
3. Group counselling for the children concerned.
4. Counselling for the parents with regard to the problem.
5. Counselling for the parent/s and child/children.
6. Family counselling to integrate and complete the work.

Whole Family Counselling

As discussed earlier, during a whole family session unsatisfactory relationships between children in the family may be resolved either within the counselling session or between sessions. Unfortunately, where unhelpful behaviours, beliefs, and attitudes of two or more children have become established over time, it may be that the issues cannot be resolved initially at a whole family level. This is because the individual children involved may have intrapersonal emotional issues which may be too difficult to explore in a whole family setting. In such a case, it can be helpful for a counsellor to suggest some options regarding the ongoing process of counselling. The counsellor might negotiate with the family about the option of undertaking individual counselling and/or group work with the children involved, and perhaps offer separate counselling for the parents to help them address their issues and make decisions about how to manage the situation.

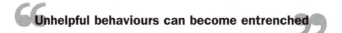

"Unhelpful behaviours can become entrenched"

In this chapter we will assume that a family has negotiated a process similar to that shown in Figure 13.1, where individual counselling for the children is the next step while the parent/s also have counselling with regard to parental issues.

Counselling for Individual Children

Counselling for each individual child provides an opportunity for the child to freely express their feelings and thoughts without fear of criticism or unsatisfactory consequences. The counselling processes described in Chapters 11 and 12 are useful when helping children to do this. As explained in Chapter 12, depending on the developmental ages of the children, it is recommended that either miniature animals, or symbols and the sand tray, or imaginative pretend play are used.

During individual counselling work with children it is possible that some emotional issues may be spontaneously addressed through raised awareness. However, where behaviours, beliefs, and attitudes have become entrenched, individual work with one child may not be sufficient to produce satisfactory change as the relationship issues may need to be directly addressed through joint counselling with other children concerned. Consequently, it may be useful to provide a group counselling session with the siblings who are involved in the relationship.

Group Counselling for the Children Concerned

There are some limitations with regard to group counselling for children. Most importantly, it is unlikely to be helpful to try to run a group counselling session for siblings who are at different developmental stages. In such a situation, it may be more useful for joint counselling sessions to be held between an older child and the parent/s, and then for the parents to consider their alternatives with regard to managing the behaviour of their children (as described in Chapter 20).

Group counselling for siblings is likely to be most effective when they fall into the age range of 7–12 years, so we will discuss ways of working with siblings in this age range.

For some older children it may be possible to use approaches that are suitable for young people, as described in Chapter 17. However, generally, when working with children, it is sensible to engage them in an activity. Being engaged in an activity allows the children to work quietly at times. This can be particularly useful when children in a group are experiencing high levels of stress, or are thinking about their troubling issues, or considering what they would like to say. Without an activity, silence can be embarrassing for them and may lead to an early termination of the session without the resolution of issues.

> ❝ **Activity engages the children and enables them to cope with silence** ❞

As described in our book *Counselling Children: A Practical Introduction* (Geldard and Geldard, 2008a), there is a wide variety of media and activity to choose from when working with children. Usually our preference, when involved in relationship counselling with two or three siblings, is to work with clay. We select this medium because it can be used interactively with each child working on their own to produce a sculpture, or working in conjunction with others to produce or modify sculptures. The nature of clay as a medium allows for change within the session. The shape, size and structure of sculptures can change, providing a metaphor for how change can occur in relationships. Additionally, individual sculptures can be combined into a group sculpture. Because clay can be used collaboratively, working with it may encourage the children to interact and communicate with each other with the consequence that relationship issues are likely to emerge and can be addressed.

Using Clay to Address Relationship Issues between Siblings

For full details regarding counselling children using clay refer to Geldard and Geldard (2008a). Soft, pliable clay is required and it is important for it to be conditioned so that it is moist but not too wet and not too dry. Suitable clay can be bought from craft shops in blocks. The clay can be cut using nylon thread attached to handles at each end, to slice through the clay. In can be helpful to have tools for sculpting the clay, such as wooden spatulas and plastic knives and forks, although this is not essential as clay is easy to mould by hand.

Usually we prefer to work with clay on a vinyl floor, rather than on a table, so that the children can move around easily and join with the clay, working right beside it, and moving among the sculptures they produce. It is possible to work on a tabletop, although in this case the work will inevitably be more constrained.

Starting work with clay

A good way to start work with a group of siblings is to invite them to make friends with the clay, as suggested by Violet Oaklander (1988). First, we get each child to cut off a piece of clay for themselves, and we also cut off a piece of clay for ourselves so that we can demonstrate what to do. We then suggest that the child follow our instructions as we say with appropriate pauses, 'Role the clay – flatten it – pinch it – pull it to pieces – gather it all up together and roll it again – poke a hole in it with one finger – tear a piece off and make a snake – wrap the snake around one finger.' This exercise gives the children permission to mould the clay into any shape and to become familiar with handling it.

Having made friends with the clay, there are several options which can be useful when carrying out relationship counselling. These include:

- making a family sculpture in the clay
- making a sculpture to illustrate whatever is most troubling in your relationship with your sibling/s
- making a sculpture to illustrate how you feel right now.

Making a family sculpture in the clay

The next step is to ask the children to each make a shape to represent themselves. It is important to give instructions that allow the child to be creative. For example, 'I want you to make a shape in the clay to be you. It doesn't have to look like you with arms, legs and a head, but could be any shape. It can be big or small, round or square, or any other shape. It might have holes in it or pieces sticking out of it. It really doesn't matter what it looks like, but make a shape to be you.'

Constructing the family

Once they have made their own shapes they can be invited to make shapes for other members of the family who are not present. They might need to negotiate about who makes what shape, or they might decide to make each shape as a joint effort.

The next stage is to ask them all to put their sculptures into a picture or arrangement with the other sculptures. In other words, to make a family sculpture with the clay which illustrates their view of the family.

Making use of the clay work

While the clay work is progressing the counsellor can carefully observe how the work is performed, the attitudes and behaviours of the children, and how they relate to each other. While being careful not to intrude on the creative process or to interrupt communication unnecessarily, the counsellor can use counselling skills to help the children gain awareness of each others' sculptures, and help them to talk to each other about their relationships. As they talk about things that trouble them in their relationships, the counsellor can make use of circular questions to check with each child how they think the other/s feel.

> **Counselling skills enable the children to talk about their relationship issues**

Additionally, during this process it can be advantageous if positive interactions are identified with regard to the way the children relate to each other and seek solutions to their problems. Encouraging the children to recognize positive interactions help them to focus on solutions rather than problems during this process.

Making a sculpture to illustrate whatever is most troubling in your relationship with your sibling(s)

An alternative to making individual sculptures and a family sculpture is to begin reminding the children that this counselling session has been arranged so that they can try to discover ways to have a better relationship with each other. Having done this, the counsellor can ask the children to sit quietly and to think about what it is that troubles them in their relationship with each other. When they have had time to think about this, they can be invited to make a shape, or a number of shapes, in the clay to represent what it is that troubles them about their relationship with a brother/s or sister/s.

Once they have made their shapes, the counsellor can use circular questions to ask the children to comment on each other's shapes and to see if they can guess what the shapes represent. As a result, discussion can ensue with regard to those issues that are contributing to uncomfortable relationships, and the counsellor can then encourage the children to see whether they can discover solutions which would lead them to feel happier. The children can be invited to swap their individual sculptures, to change the sculpture, and to illustrate their solutions using the clay.

Making a sculpture to illustrate how you feel right now

When using this strategy with children first invite them to sit quietly and to try to get in touch with how they feel emotionally inside. Having done this, the children can be invited to make shapes in the clay to represent their emotional feelings. Once again, the counsellor can use circular questions to ask the children to comment on each other's shapes and to see if they can guess what the shapes represent. Discussion can then follow with regard to the situations and behaviours that cause the feelings and the children can be encouraged to see whether they can discover solutions which would lead them to feel more comfortable. The children can be invited to make solutions from the clay for each other which can be attached to or incorporated with the original sculpture.

Counselling for the Parents with Regard to the Problem

As discussed in this book, parents usually make appointments for family counselling because they are troubled by what they perceive as problem behaviours by one or more of their children. Consequently, when helping children to address their problems it is usually sensible for the parent/s to be given on opportunity to explore their own issues with regard to their children.

The single parent

Single parents often feel responsible, helpless, and vulnerable to criticism when they believe that one or more of their children is behaving in unhelpful ways. Many single parents have little support, although some have extended family support or a supporting network of friends.

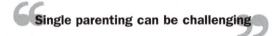

Single parenting can be challenging

In working with a single parent, the counsellor has an opportunity to help them to address their intrapersonal issues, particularly with regard to their role as a parent. Single parents do not often have the support of a partner in parenting their child or children, and as a consequence they often can be unsure about whether their parenting strategies are appropriate or not. A counsellor can help them to review the effectiveness of their parenting, particularly in terms of circular processes, as discussed in Chapter 6. They can be encouraged to explore alternative solutions and be given positive messages about their success in coping on their own.

Parents in a couple relationship

Because parents each come from their own family of origin, they often have different expectations with regard to their roles, their attitudes to behaviour management of their children, and their expectations of their children. These issues are discussed in Chapter 20. It can be useful for parents to have counselling for themselves as a couple with regard to their parenting when there are relationship difficulties between siblings in the family. If the parents have different approaches to managing these problems, it can make it more difficult for a satisfactory resolution of troubling issues to be achieved. Consequently, a couple can gain by discussing their parenting issues in a counselling session separate from the whole family.

Counselling for the Parent/s and Child/Children

Sometimes, after working separately with a child or children, and also with the parents on their own, it may be that sufficient progress has been made for the work to be completed in a whole family counselling session. At other times it may be advantageous to have a counselling session with the parent/s and child or children before integrating the work into the whole family system.

When a child and parent are alone together in a counselling session without other members of the family present, the counsellor has an opportunity to focus directly on the child–parent relationship and to observe it as it is acted out in the session. This live observation is necessary to understand the impact that the parent–child interaction has on both the parent's and the child's functioning. Sometimes the parent–child relationship becomes dominated by the problem, and as a result focuses exclusively on the child's negative behaviour, while disregarding the child's good behaviour and inherent strengths (Bailey and Sori, 2005). When this occurs it can be useful to externalize 'the problem', to shift the focus from the child's behaviour to how 'the problem' affects the relationship between the child and their parent. An example of externalizing can be found in *Counselling Children: A Practical Introduction* (Geldard and Geldard, 2008a). This example explains how to work with a parent and child with regard to helping a child whose angry outbursts are impacting on their relationship with the parent. In the example, 'anger' is externalized as an angry monster (the monster-in-me) and together the parent and child are encouraged to discover ways to collaboratively join forces to prevent the monster from continuing to damage their relationship.

When conducting such a counselling session, a therapist's job includes acting as a facilitator to enable discussion to occur between the parties involved. In this situation it may be necessary for the counsellor to act as an advocate for the child, as explained in Chapter 10. However, it is also important for the counsellor to respect and support a parent's right to make decisions on behalf of the child.

Family Counselling to Integrate and Complete the Work

As illustrated in Figure 13.1, after working separately with the parent/s and children it is usually advantageous to integrate the work into the whole family. Without involving the whole family in the changes that have occurred as a result of individual and subgroup work there is a possibility that some family members will unconsciously or consciously seek to maintain the original homeostasis in the family. Because some family members have not been involved in decisions that have been made with regard to behaviours and relationships between others, they may sabotage positive outcomes unintentionally by responding to situations using old, unhelpful patterns of relating. In addition, there may be unrecognized and uncomfortable consequences for some members of the family if changes are introduced without their knowledge.

> " **Without integration into the whole family
> changes may be undermined** "

Before setting up a family counselling session to integrate and complete the work it is advantageous to discuss with family members who have participated in subgroup counselling what information is to remain private within the subgroup and what information is to be shared with the family as a whole. Clearly, it is better if as much information as possible is brought into the open so that the family processes are transparent. However, it needs to be recognized that sensitive personal information may be disclosed in subgroup work and it may not be appropriate for this to be shared with the whole family.

During the whole family counselling session the counsellor can facilitate the sharing of information by subgroup members. The counsellor can invite family members to share with the whole family the things they have learned or discovered from their personal counselling sessions. Circular questions can be used to invite other family members to enter into discussion about the implications of choices or decisions that have been made with regard to solving the difficulties in the family. At this point it is possible that new and different solutions will emerge as family members once again share each other's pictures of their family.

Future family sessions can be used to monitor changes that have occurred and to make positive changes newsworthy so that they are maintained.

KEY POINTS

- Some relationship issues are best resolved in a small group setting.
- Individual counselling for a child enables them to explore and address personal issues that may be affecting their relationships.
- Counselling two or more siblings needs to involve media, activity, and counselling skills.
- Clay can be used in a variety of ways to help explore sibling relationships.
- Parental issues are best explored separate from the family as a whole.
- Integration of some group work is essential to ensure that changes are not undermined and to include all family members in decisions regarding changes.

> **QUESTIONS FOR GROUP DISCUSSION OR STUDENT ASSIGNMENTS**
>
> 1. Using the CACHO model, a co-therapist or reflecting team is usually involved. Discuss the advantages and any associated difficulties which might arise when the family counsellor works separately with the parents while the co-therapist or reflecting team members work with a child or children.
> 2. Identify and describe possible sensitive issues which might arise when counselling a subgroup, and discuss the reasons why these issues might or might not be suitable for discussion in a whole family session.

14

Addressing the Child's Relationships with Peers, Teachers and Other Adults

It is common for parents to take a child to see a counsellor as a consequence of poor relationships with peers or as a result of concerns or complaints by teachers or other adults about the child's behaviour. Some children have very low self-esteem, with the result that their parents are worried about them. Others have poor social skills and are unable to make friends or may behave as bullies or may be bullied.

The Role of Parents

Frequently, teachers will complain about, or have concern for, a child's behaviour at school, either in connection with their relationships with other children or in connection with their behaviour in class. It is not uncommon for parents to feel responsible for their child's problems and to develop a sense of guilt, shame or embarrassment. As pointed out by Andreozzi (1996), helping a parent to deal with these feelings is sometimes the first hurdle to overcome in working with families with symptomatic children.

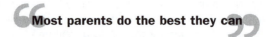

"Most parents do the best they can"

We believe that most parents do the best they can in raising their children. Although some parents may be limited in their parenting skills, knowledge and experience, it is unhelpful if they feel responsible for those things they cannot control, or do not know how to control, with respect to their children. As counsellors, our job is to help parents discover for themselves ways of parenting that are comfortable and have socially desirable outcomes, and to recognize when and how to respond.

Managing undesirable behaviour

We have noticed in our practice that when a child's behaviour is causing concern for their teacher it is common for the child's parents to believe that they are being blamed and are held responsible for that behaviour. We recognize and support the need for teachers to fully inform parents about their children's behaviours so that they can attend to their children's needs in appropriate ways. However, a parent cannot be responsible for managing a child's undesirable behaviour when the child is not in the parent's care but is at school under the care of teaching staff. While welcoming information from the school with regard to their child, the parent needs to be clear about what they can do to influence their child's behaviour in the school context and what they cannot. We have found that it is often helpful for a parent to recognize the limits of their responsibility for their child when the child is at school.

Sometimes a parent will believe that when their child misbehaves at school the child should be punished at home. This is of concern for two reasons. First, this means that the child is likely to be punished twice, once at school and once at home. If the behaviour occurred at school, the consequences experienced in the school environment are more likely to influence future behaviour at school. When the child comes home, it is more helpful for them to enter a supportive environment where they can talk about what happened to them without feeling criticized, while at the same time being reminded that their behaviour did lead to negative consequences at school. The home environment is potentially a place where the child can feel free to talk about those things that have been uncomfortable for them during the day without fear of further punishment. Counsellors can usefully help parents explore the limits of their responsibilities with regard to managing their child's behaviour when the child is not directly in their care. Additionally, it can be useful to help parents learn to recognize how to meet their children's needs so that their children can develop and change in adaptive ways. This can sometimes be achieved by reminding parents about how to encourage and reinforce socially desirable behaviours, as discussed in Chapter 20.

The Development of Social Skills

Sometimes children who have poor relationships with peers and adults have difficulties with social skills, and they may also have low self-esteem as a consequence. A child's self-image and self-esteem are dependent on the child's skills in relating to peers and adults. These skills contribute to self-esteem because a child with good social skills is likely to build satisfying relationships and to receive positive feedback from others. A child with poor social skills is likely to have unsatisfactory relationships and to receive negative feedback.

Many of the children who come to counselling with their families have poor social skills. Consequently, these children have had dysfunctional interpersonal relationships. Often, they have also engaged in socially unacceptable behaviours which have resulted in painful consequences for them.

It is clear that poor social skills lead to problems, not only in childhood, but also later in life, so it is very important for children with poor social skills to receive appropriate help to improve their skills so that they can enjoy their social interactions and feel good about themselves.

The following characteristics are typical of children experiencing relationship issues with peers or other adults. In whole family counselling some of these behaviours may have been observed by the counsellor or reflecting team. Often it can be observed that children:

- don't adapt their behaviour to accommodate the needs of others
- tend to choose less socially acceptable behaviours
- have difficulty in predicting the consequences of their behaviours
- misunderstand social cues
- are unable to perform the social skills required for particular situations
- often have an inability to control impulsive or aggressive behaviour.

There are three components to social skills training which are essential if the training is to be effective and useful:

1. We need to help the child to gain clear ideas about what constitutes socially adaptive behaviour.
2. We need to help the child to discover how to use appropriate social skills.
3. We need to help the child to generalize the skills learnt, so that they can be put into practice in the various social situations of the child's own environment.

In addition, there are three areas which need to be addressed when training children in social skills:

1. They need to be able to identify their own and other people's feelings if they are to relate adaptively.
2. They need to be able to communicate effectively in ways which validate their own needs and are respectful of others' needs.
3. They also needs to manage their own behaviour effectively so that it is socially acceptable.

These skills, which have been developed from the 'Emotional Intelligence' research and literature of Mayer and Salovey (1997), are often referred to as social-emotional competencies.

Identifying and expressing feelings

To function adaptively, so that they can relate easily with others, children need to be able to identify their own feelings, identify other people's feelings and express their own feelings. Quite often, we find that children are unable to label the feelings which they are experiencing. For some children, this may be because they have had confusing information about feelings. For example, a child might have been told by their mother that they were 'just tired' when they were actually behaving in an angry way. Other children may have difficulty recognizing the differences between feelings which are fairly similar. For example, feeling disappointed might be confused with feeling sad, and feeling embarrassed might be confused with feeling shy.

Communicating effectively

Once a child can identify their own feelings and recognize the feelings that other people are expressing, they need to learn how to express their own feelings clearly and appropriately. This means expressing feelings in ways which are comfortable for both the child and any other party involved.

When children can identify feelings in themselves and in others, and can begin to express their feelings appropriately, they are more likely to be successful in communicating with others and this has positive consequences for their relationships. Social communication involves an exchange between two (or more) people. Necessarily, one individual initiates the communication and the other responds. In early childhood, this peer interaction is based on shared play activities. However, as children grow older, the interaction becomes more focused on peer acceptance and intimacy. Friendships tend to move from being physical, with a focus on actions, towards relationships with an increased awareness of the feelings and emotions of others. In middle childhood, between the ages of about 7 and 11, children have more social contacts and are able to identify 'best friends'. With the establishment of best friends they begin to demonstrate commitment to each other. Aggressive interactions tend to decrease and friendships tend to involve more verbal interaction. At this stage, it is important for children to be able to communicate adaptively, or they will not be able to establish satisfying social relationships. Additionally, they need to learn to deal with the emotional consequences of situations that inevitably occur in childhood, such as being left out, being ignored, being in demand as a popular child, or being ridiculed.

Self-managing behaviour

To be socially competent a child must be able to identify and express feelings, develop skills to communicate successfully with others, and at the same time be aware of, and manage, their own behaviour. Being aware of their own behaviour helps them to be sensitive to feedback cues from others, and to be aware of the timing and pace of their own behaviour during interactions. In managing their own behaviour they need to be able to understand and recognize consequences, to recover after social errors, to present themselves in a way which is socially acceptable, and to reinforce their own social behaviours in a positive way.

Relationship Counselling for the Child

In order to address the relationship issues that a child may be experiencing with peers, or teachers, or other adults, it is recommended that one or more of the following might be used:

- symbolic sand tray work
- cognitive behavioural therapy
- worksheets
- group work.

Symbolic sand tray work

Often when working with a child on relationship issues in the school context, we prefer to use symbols in the sand tray rather than miniature animals, as discussed in Chapter 12. This enables us to gain a better understanding of the context in which the relationship problems occur whereas when using miniature animals the focus is more closely on the interpersonal qualities of the relationships.

Imagine that a child is having a relationship problem with a group of peers at school. We might start by asking the child to use symbols to create a picture of school in the sand tray, including the places where conflict with peers arises. As the child selects symbols, we would observe and use feedback statements and reflection to encourage the child to tell us about their picture.

Consider an example. A child has used symbols to represent their classroom, a playground, and a sports field. In giving feedback of observations, the counsellor may say something like:

'I notice that you were very careful in setting up the playground.'
'The sports field is a long way from your classroom.'

Once the picture is complete, a counsellor can ask the child to select a figurine to represent themselves and figurines to represent their peers, the teacher, and anyone else important in the story. After the child has put the figurines into the picture the counsellor might give the reflection and feedback like this:

'You looked worried when you put the teacher in the picture.'
'I notice that your friends are a long way away from you.'

In response, the child might say, *'My teacher never takes my side. Instead he sticks up for Stephen and Jasmine who are picking on me.'* Or, *'My friends run away when Stephen and Jasmine are around.'*

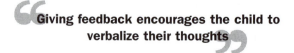

Giving feedback encourages the child to verbalize their thoughts

We would then encourage the child to tell us a story using the symbols in the sand tray about a typical day's events, starting from the beginning of the day and describing the way that conflict eventuates. Once this has been done, in order to help the child get in touch with the relationship issues, we would invite the child to engage in a dialogue between themselves and their peers as it would occur at school. While engaged in this dialogue we would ask the child to place a finger on the figurine which they imagine to be talking – either themselves or one of their peers. We would encourage the child to say what they would like to tell their peers and also explore the likely peer responses and consequences of doing this. By encouraging the child to express what they would like to say, we would hopefully enable the child to express their anger and to experience some cathartic release. When exploring the consequences of their own actions, we would help the child to think about alternative ways of behaving and talking, which might have better outcomes.

A similar approach can be used to help a child to deal with relationship problems with a teacher or other adult.

For additional details concerning sand tray work refer to Chapters 11 and 12 and our book, *Counselling Children: A Practical Introduction* (Geldard and Geldard, 2008a).

Cognitive behavioural therapy

During relationship counselling work, as described above, we might introduce ideas from cognitive behavioural therapy by challenging some of the child's self-destructive beliefs and helping the child to replace these by more constructive beliefs. Common self-destructive beliefs held by children are:

- I will always be treated fairly
- I should always win
- I should always get what I want.

Alternative, more helpful beliefs to these are:

- I deserve to be treated fairly but this won't always happen and I am big enough to cope with this
- If I win half the time I am doing quite well
- I won't always get what I want and when I don't I'll make the best of things.

> **Challenging self-destructive beliefs may be useful in improving relationships**

It is often likely that children who experience difficulties with peers or adults will have beliefs that are irrational. Such beliefs were described by Albert Ellis (2001), who was the founder of rational emotive behaviour therapy. These beliefs are, at the very least, unhelpful. If a child is to develop satisfactory relationships, they will first have to start to think more positively.

Consider an example. Imagine that we are working with a young girl called Amy whose emotional problems stemmed from feeling displaced in her peer group by Carolyn, who is a new girl at Amy's school. Amy has at least two unhelpful beliefs. One unhelpful belief is that she believes that her friends don't like her. But most importantly, another unhelpful belief is that she believes Carolyn has displaced her in the group. In Amy's case, both of these beliefs could well be incorrect and are certainly unhelpful. However, we need to be careful not to challenge beliefs that are based on accurate information. If it had been true that Amy's friends didn't like her, then instead of challenging the belief we would need to help Amy deal with the sad reality that her friends didn't like her, and to help her to make sensible decisions about how to behave so that life would be more comfortable for her.

However, if I believed that Amy's friends did like her, I might ask her what led her to believe that they didn't. Amy might indicate that they would sometimes ignore her. I would explore the logic behind Amy's thinking and invite her to consider alternative beliefs. I would raise her awareness of other possible beliefs, which in some way she may be overlooking or failing to identify. For example, I might ask her whether she thought that her friends might be focusing more on helping Carolyn adjust to being a new person in the class.

Reframing the way a child perceives their situation helps them to view their world more constructively. Notice that this is done by accepting the child's picture, but then expanding it to include additional information so that the child can perceive their situation differently.

I would ask her what her friends would need to do to convince her that they did like her. I would then suggest that she experiment so that she could explore her relationship more fully with her friends so that they could all feel more comfortable.

Amy's belief that Carolyn had displaced her in the group would be central to her emotional problems and would be certain to result in unhelpful behaviours by Amy in her school. I would encourage her to think about what she might need if she was the new girl in the school, and what she needed now. I would explore the strengths she had in herself with regard to being a friend and companion. I would try to help her to be proud of herself as a person who was capable of, at times, looking after and welcoming newcomers into her school.

My goal would be to help Amy to change her unhelpful beliefs about her peer group, so that instead of seeing herself as displaced, she would see herself as having an important role in the group and as being an important member of the group. By helping her to think differently about her role in the group, it is possible that she would no longer need to continually engage in attention-seeking behaviour, and would feel more comfortable in the long term. However, because she had used unhelpful behaviours for a while, she might continue to use them unless they were directly addressed. Consequently, once we have addressed a child's self-destructive beliefs, it is important to help them to look at their options and choices with regard to their behaviour. There are a number of ways of doing this, including using worksheets.

The use of worksheets

Most children are familiar with worksheets because they are commonly used in schools for teaching purposes. Activities involving worksheets have many different forms, including answering questionnaires, working on quizzes, finding words, joining dots, looking for differences between pictures, finding hidden items in pictures, and matching similar items. Some worksheets include measuring scales, such as pictures of thermometers, or continuum lines which stretch from one extreme to another, to measure attitude, performance or other criteria. Clearly, well-designed worksheets are inviting for children, who enjoy using them. Most importantly, from the counsellor's point of view, worksheets act as a springboard for discussion because they tend to draw out and focus the child's thoughts about particular issues or behaviours. When working specifically on social skills development, worksheets can be used to help a child to:

- begin to look at particular issues, so that these issues can be explored
- consider new ways of thinking and behaving
- explore, understand and develop problem-solving and decision-making skills
- make choices about how they might respond to a particular social situation or event, and to explore the possible consequences of these responses
- recognize differences between old and new behaviours
- affirm and/or reinforce concepts, ideas, beliefs and behaviours which have been explored or discussed during family counselling
- develop a plan so that learnt skills are generalized into the child's environment.

In individual counselling, we use worksheets to help the child to think about their current behaviours and the consequences of those behaviours. We help them to recognize alternative behaviours, and to make choices about how they intend to respond to particular social situations in the future. Worksheets for use by counsellors working with children to address social skills issues can be found in *Counselling Children: A Practical Introduction* (Geldard and Geldard, 2008a). Working individually gives the child an opportunity to examine their own responses and choices without pressure from others. Clearly, this is an individual task, as each child is different, and has their own unique social environment. Once the child has chosen appropriate skills for use in particular situations, we can help them to devise a plan of action. In this plan the child needs to decide on the best time to use the selected skills within the various situations of their environment. Thus they are able to think about ways in which to generalize learnt social skills into the various settings of their own unique and individual environment.

After the child has attempted to carry out their plan of action, they can be invited to evaluate the success of the plan, and to modify it if necessary for future use. We can also help the child to think about possible responses to any new problems that may arise as a consequence of their use of new social skills.

Group work to address social skills

As mentioned earlier, sometimes children who have poor relationships with peers and adults have difficulties in executing social skills and may also have low self-esteem as a consequence. In such cases, it can be useful for them to be engaged in group work. As pointed out by Sharry (2004), group work with children and adolescents is particularly useful in settings such as schools, colleges, after-school services, or community youth centres, where there is a big enough pool of referrals from which to create a therapeutic group.

As might be expected, it is difficult to improve social skills by working with children individually because social skills involve the use of interactional behaviours. However, group programmes can be useful in helping children improve their social skills.

There are a number of important reasons for promoting social skills. Where children are unable to build social relationships with others, they are likely to experience anxiety in social situations and they may withdraw. Children with poor social skills may be rejected by their peers and have an increased risk of emotional and behavioural difficulties. Research findings suggest a strong relationship between social competence in childhood and social, academic and psychological functioning (O'Rourke and Worzbyt, 1996). We also know that children with poor social skills are unable to initiate and maintain interaction with others in a positive manner. As a consequence, they are likely to be ignored, or suffer rejection. They may be actively disliked, blamed and maltreated by other children. Consequently, they are often depressed and unhappy children. On the other hand, children with adaptive social skills are likely to be popular, have friends and be happier. There is therefore a strong case for addressing social skills deficits in children. Additionally, an emphasis on teaching social skills to children has grown in recent years because of the importance of socially effective behaviour on subsequent development (Rose and Edleson, 1987).

Often children who have difficulty with social skills may exhibit some of the following problems, as described by Gajewski and Mayo (1989):

1. *A skill deficit*, which indicates that the child has not acquired the necessary social skill. For example, a child may be unable to appropriately accept a compliment because the child has never been taught to say 'thank you'.
2. *A performance deficit*, where the child has the skill, but doesn't perform it because of anxiety, low motivation, or feelings of incompetence.
3. *A self-control deficit*, where the child lacks adequate behaviours to control impulsive, disruptive or aggressive social behaviour. In this case, the child's lack of self-control interferes with the performance of learnt skills.

When running groups for children we recommend that there should be two leaders in each group, with one of them taking the primary leadership position and the other, whom we call the sweeper, looking after practical arrangements such as organizing any equipment and materials required, and attending to the special needs of individual children if these arise. Group programmes need to be varied so that they maintain the interest of the children while also being goal-directed. The group leader needs to use counselling and facilitation skills, including those described earlier in this book, and needs to be responsible for managing behaviour in the group so that the children feel safe.

A specific programme designed to address social skills is described in *Working with Children in Groups: A Handbook for Counsellors, Educators and Community Workers* (Geldard and Geldard, 2001).

KEY POINTS

- Parents cannot be responsible for their child's behaviour when the child is not directly in their care.
- Helping a child to tell their story in the sand tray is useful in relationship counselling.

- Dialoguing between figures in the sand tray can be cathartic and enable the child to discover new ways of relating.
- Young children can be helped to improve their relationships through imaginative pretend play.
- Group work is extremely useful in helping children to address self-esteem and social skills problems.

QUESTIONS FOR GROUP DISCUSSION OR STUDENT ASSIGNMENTS

1. Explain how you would work as a counsellor with a single parent who has low self-esteem as a result of receiving negative feedback about the behaviours of her children. Describe the theoretical approaches and counselling skills you would use.
2. Discuss how you would work in relationship counselling with a child who is both a bully and being bullied. Would you involve the parents or other family members in the counselling process? Explain the reasons for your decision.

Part 4

Relationship Counselling for Young People

Young people go through one of the most difficult developmental stages of their life as they enter into and pass through adolescence. When they were children their parents were generally in control of their lives and made major decisions for them. In adolescence, however, they strive to individuate and to be given more opportunities to make their own decisions and take responsibility for their lives. Yet they lack maturity and experience and face many challenges as they are confronted by new situations. One of the most difficult challenges confronting young people is that associated with establishing, maintaining, and adapting to changes in relationships with others.

Young people are challenged by the relationships within their own families as they strive to establish their own individuality. They also have to deal with the problem of peer pressure while trying to build and maintain positive relationships with their peers.

In this part of the book, we will describe the use of a proactive approach to counselling. We have developed this approach for counselling young people as it suits the young person's developmental stage and enables a counsellor to join effectively with them. We will also consider ways to help a young person with the changing relationships they have with their family, with their peer relationships, and with their relationships with teachers, employers and other adults.

15

Helping Young People to Talk About their Relationships

When involved in relationship counselling with adults we can, if we wish, rely primarily on verbal counselling skills, although we may also introduce experiential and creative methods. When helping children to talk about relationship issues, as discussed in Part Three, we find it useful to use media and activity in conjunction with counselling skills. When counselling young people we need to recognize that they are in a stage of life called adolescence. They are neither children nor adults, they are in transition between being a child and being an adult. If we are to engage them so that they will talk to us about their relationships we need to offer them a special type of client–counsellor relationship. Also, outcomes of counselling can be enhanced if we use a particular process of counselling which is compatible with typical adolescent communication processes, so that they become engaged with interest and will participate willingly and enthusiastically.

As counsellors, it is useful to remember that young people are in a process where they are trying to establish their own identity and beginning to individuate from the family. Consequently, many young people are reluctant to openly express their personal issues in front of the whole family. This problem can easily be overcome by offering the young person individual counselling as part of the complete family relationship counselling process.

> **In adolescence a young person individuates**

Young people have more complex cognitive processes and more advanced cognitive skills than children. Consequently, a counsellor can employ more advanced cognitive intervention strategies than those that can be used with children. Although it is sometimes helpful when counselling young people to make use of media and activity, care must be taken to respect the maturity and self-image of the young person. Also, it is important for the counsellor to respect the young person as an individual who wants to take responsibility for their own decisions rather than someone who wants to be told what to do.

In order to meet the special counselling needs of young people we have developed a particular proactive approach for counselling adolescents which matches their developmental stage and enables a counsellor to join effectively with a young person. This approach is described in detail in our book *Counselling Adolescents: The Proactive Approach* (Geldard and Geldard, 2004).

There are a number of important features of the proactive approach for counselling young people. In the proactive approach the counsellor:

- is authentic and open about themselves
- draws on existentialist philosophy and constructivist thinking
- is proactive in introducing creative, experiential, cognitive, and psycho-educational strategies
- is responsive to the young person's developmental needs
- works within the young person's framework and constructs
- matches the adolescent style of communication
- uses particular counselling skills.

Being Authentic and Open

For young people the quality of the counselling relationship is critical in influencing outcomes and client satisfaction (Eltz, Shirk and Sarlin, 1995; Kendall and Southam-Gerow, 1996; Shirk and Kaver, 2003). During adolescence a young person's relationships with adults will be different from when they were children and they may be unsure of the expectations. Consequently, if an adolescent client is to feel relaxed and have a sense of trust, the counsellor will need to be congruent, open and honest, sincere and respectful. By demonstrating these characteristics, an authentic person-to-person relationship can be created.

Authenticity requires the counsellor to remain in touch with who they are as a person so that the young person is able to genuinely connect in a one-to-one relationship. While the counsellor fulfils the counsellor role, the relationship with the young person may be compromised if the counsellor uses the role as a mask behind which they hide their real self.

> " A counsellor for young people needs to bring their own personality into the relationship "

As is natural in their developmental stage, young people are generally resistant to talking openly with adults, particularly professionals. In order to engage a young person in open discussion it is desirable for the counsellor to meet the young person in a way which enables them to be comfortable in expressing themselves openly because young people value equality and mutual respect in relationships. This does not diminish the importance of the counsellor fulfilling their role as counsellor in enabling the young person to explore their issues and find solutions, and in being able to share relevant information obtained through life experience and training.

Drawing on Existentialist Philosophy and Constructivist Thinking

The existentialist view is that the only way human beings can make sense of their existence is through their personal experiences. Human beings are free to choose and are therefore responsible for their choices and actions (Spinelli, 1996). These existentialist assumptions fit neatly with the adolescent stage in life, where the young person wants to be responsible for making their own choices and is making sense of their life through their personal experiences.

Constructivism is a theory which is useful in helping explain how we set about and try to make sense of the world in which we live (Fransella and Dalton, 1990). In constructivist terminology, human beings form *constructs* which encapsulate their concepts about their world. These constructs or personal interpretations of the world are not fixed but are revised and replaced as new information becomes available to the individual concerned. Each of us behaves like a scientist, formulating hypotheses, using our experiences to test them out and, if necessary, revising them (Winter, 1996). This is precisely what young people do.

Because the existentialist and constructivist views are closely aligned with the way in which most young people experience their world and think, it is advantageous if counsellors working with young people are able to adopt an existentialist and constructivist approach.

Being Proactive in Introducing Creative, Experiential, Cognitive, and Psycho-educational Strategies

Many young people are restless and uncertain during the counselling process and need to be actively engaged. It is usually not sufficient for the counsellor to be only a quiet listener. Some young people quickly become impatient and bored so the counselling process needs to be dynamic. This requires spontaneous behaviours combined with creativity. It is advantageous if the counsellor can be quick, flexible, and opportunistic. This means responding quickly and actively through the selection and use of appropriate skills and strategies so that opportunities are not lost. Thus the counselling process becomes energized.

> **Being proactive enables a counsellor to join with a young person**

To create the dynamic process described above the counsellor optimizes possibilities in the session by being proactive in making use of symbolic, creative, cognitive behavioural, and psycho-educational strategies, in conjunction with counselling skills. Detailed descriptions of the use of each of these strategies when counselling adolescents are included in our book *Counselling Adolescents: The Proactive Approach* (Geldard and Geldard, 2004).

Symbolic strategies

Symbolic strategies include the use of metaphor, ritual, symbols, sand tray, and miniature animals. These strategies are helpful in keeping a young person engaged, interested and enthusiastic with regard to the counselling process. Symbolic strategies particularly appeal to young people because using symbols challenges the young person's new-found cognitive skills of abstraction and the use of imagery. Also, symbolic work can help a young person to disclose material that may otherwise be inaccessible or difficult for them to talk about.

Creative strategies

Creative strategies include the use of art, role-play, journals, relaxation, imagination, and dream work. Many adolescents use artistic methods to express themselves and to convey meaning about their lives to others. For example, young people are often seen sketching and/or using graffiti to express themselves, release emotions and convey messages to other people. Creative activities require personal involvement on the part of the young person and must therefore be chosen to suit the interests, abilities and needs of the particular person.

When using either creative or symbolic strategies, the technique itself is of limited value unless the work is carefully processed by exploring thoughts, emotional feelings, and attitudes and beliefs which emerge during the process. Specific counselling skills that are useful during the processing of an activity are explained throughout this book, and in particular in Chapters 16–18.

Cognitive behavioural strategies

Cognitive behavioural strategies that are particularly useful for helping young people explore relationship problems include challenging self-destructive beliefs and assertiveness training. These strategies appeal to many young people as they can be helpful in enabling them to use cognitive processes to moderate their emotions and alter their behaviours. Frequently, relationship problems for young people stem from unrealistic expectations and/or an inability to appropriately ask to have their needs met. Consequently, these strategies are particularly useful with regard to improving relationships.

Psycho-educational strategies

Psycho-educational strategies include those activities that provide information to explain relationships, explain behaviour, and help to change behaviour. These strategies are helpful in enabling young people to learn about life and to help them to regulate their behaviours. Young people are on a journey of self-discovery and are mostly hungry to learn about themselves and their relationships with others. When using these strategies it is important to encourage the young person to participate actively in learning the new information using processes which are largely ones of self-discovery.

Responding to the Young Person's Developmental Needs

As discussed previously, young people are generally moving from a situation when their lives are mostly controlled by others to a situation where they have more autonomy and responsibility. Therefore the role of the counsellor includes inviting and allowing young people to express their autonomy and individuality within the counselling experience. The young person's choice about how to use the counselling session within mutually agreed limits regarding what is relevant and appropriate is essential. Many young people find that one session of counselling is useful in addressing the immediate issues confronting them. Consequently, they are in a position to decide whether to come to further appointments or not. Contracts can be collaboratively negotiated so that the young person is equally responsible for arranging ongoing appointments.

Working Within the Young Person's Constructs

When we work within the young person's constructs, we mean that we will listen to their story and will accept it at face value as the adolescent's truth, even if the story stretches our credulity. Although we will be totally accepting of the story and will not challenge its veracity, if there are inconsistencies in the story we will draw attention to these and explore them (out of genuine curiosity), provided that the client is happy to do this. Young people often tell counsellors stories which are difficult to believe. However, such stories are constructs which the young person is currently using to make meaning of their life and to help them understand their relationship with the world.

> **Believing the young person enables them to
> explore and amend their constructs**

If, as counsellors, we are to help young people to move ahead to the point of review-ing and exploring the meaning of existing constructs, it is essential that we accept what the young person is saying. Adolescents often feel that they are misunderstood and not believed by adults. As counsellors, if we behave in ways that match their stereotypical per-ceptions of adults not believing their stories, then the possibility of building a helpful counselling relationship will be diminished. It may be useful for you, the reader, to return to Chapter 1 for a review of constructivist theory and constructive family therapy.

Matching an Adolescent Style of Communication

There are two important ways in which a counsellor can match a young person's style of communication and consequently enhance the joining process:(1) through self-disclosure and (2) the use of digressions in the conversation.

Self-disclosure

Have you ever listened to a group of young people in conversation? If you have, you may have noticed that they are continually self-disclosing with regard to their own experiences, and that the use of self-disclosure helps them to join with each other. Some adults commonly experience the feeling that they are on a different wavelength from a young person, and consequently find communication with them uncomfortable at times. However, as pointed out by Bertolino (1999), in instances when communication seems to be difficult, self-disclosure can sometimes provide the necessary connective tis-sue. Self-disclosure can also be helpful in other ways. Not only can it bring to light the 'humanness' of the counsellor, but it can also help to normalize the experience of the client. According to some reports, a counsellor's openness through self-disclosure can contribute directly to change.

The value of self-disclosure to young people is described by Buhrmester and Prager (1995), who point out that through counsellor self-disclosure young people are able to evaluate for themselves the appropriateness and correctness of their opinions, attitudes, beliefs, values, and standards, as they share their thoughts with someone else.

> **Counsellor self-disclosure helps to establish a
> trusting, person-to-person relationship**

We recognize that in the past many counsellors believed that it was not acceptable for a counsellor to disclose information about themselves to a client. This attitude was originally promoted by Sigmund Freud because he believed that the therapist should be a blank screen, and that if this was not the case the therapeutic work would be compromised. However, when using a proactive counselling model with young people we believe that there can be considerable advantages in a counsellor being prepared to make appropriate self-disclosures. When a counsellor shares personal information with an adolescent, the young person is implicitly invited to relate to the counsellor as an equal. They are likely to see the counsellor as a real person who has feelings and experiences which may have some similarities to their own.

The most difficult questions about self-disclosure are 'when?' and 'how much?' (Leveton, 1984). There do need to be some clear limits to counsellor self-disclosure. It is not appropriate or ethical for the counselling process to lead to an undesirable closeness with the client or over-involvement by the counsellor. We think that the 'when' and 'how much' questions can be answered by recognizing that it is not appropriate for a counsellor to share sensitive personal information or to self-disclose about their own past or present problems unless these are minor and resolved. The focus must always be on the client's issues.

Digression

If you have listened to young people in conversation with each other you may have noticed that they tend to frequently digress from a topic of interest, talk about something else, and then return to the topic. By digressing they are able to deal with new thoughts without putting them on hold. Digressing serves a number of purposes:

1. Because adolescents are continually revising their constructs, they are often trying to grapple with many different ideas at the same time. When a new idea comes into their consciousness they feel impelled to deal with it straight away.
2. Digression enables a young person to temporarily move away from something that is troubling for them. By changing the topic they can stop talking about issues which are emotionally disturbing and instead talk about less troubling things. They may then return to talking about the emotionally troubling issues later. If they felt pressured to continue to talk about painful issues it is likely that they would shut down the conversation altogether.

We have noticed that when young people are talking with peers, digression is often a mutually employed process. It is usually accepted as normal behaviour rather than being inappropriate (Geldard, 2006).

> **Actively joining in a digression enhances the person-to-person relationship**

As counsellors, we can make use of digression to help us join with a young person. When they change the subject, rather than trying to immediately bring them back to the topic of conversation, we can actively join in the digression. For example, while discussing a painful relationship a young person might change the subject by saying, *'I've got a pot plant just like yours in my bedroom'*. The counsellor might then join in a discussion about the plants by saying, *'I bought that from the big nursery in Keppel Street. Where did you get yours?'* The discussion might then include how the plants are thriving and whether they need much looking after. After an appropriate length of discussion the counsellor might use a transitional question, as described later, to check out whether the young person is willing to return to the earlier topic of conversation. By using this approach, the conversation is compatible with the normal adolescent style of conversation, the young person does not feel pressured to talk about difficult issues before they are ready, and by sharing everyday information the joining process is enhanced.

Relevant Counselling Skills

The basic counselling skills listed in Chapter 4, and other skills described in that chapter, are useful when carrying out relationship counselling with young people. A number of additional skills are described in our book *Counselling Adolescents: The Proactive Approach* (Geldard and Geldard, 2004). Of particular value when relationship counselling with young people are the following:

- transitional, choice and Guru questions
- normalizing.

Transitional, Choice and Guru Questions

When working in a group setting with a young person and another member of the family, circular questions are very useful. However, when working with the young person individually the most useful questions are probably transitional, choice and Guru questions.

Transitional questions
As discussed earlier, adolescents generally like to digress in their conversations. Transitional questions are useful in inviting them to return to a previous topic of discussion. Examples of transitional questions are:

'You started to talk about the way your brother intrudes on your privacy, and I'm wondering whether you would like to tell me more about that?'
'You were telling me how angry you feel towards your stepfather, and I would be interested to know what that anger is about. Would it be helpful for you to tell me about that anger?'

Choice questions

Choice questions have their origin in reality therapy (Glasser and Wubbolding, 1995). These questions make it clear that the young person has a choice about the way they think and behave, and may also draw attention to the consequences of decisions.

These questions are particularly useful when counselling young people with regard to relationships. Commonly, a young person will be locked into a particular way of thinking and behaving with the belief that they have no choices themselves, and that it is up to the person with whom they are having a relationship problem to change. Rational emotive behavioural therapy can be used to challenge the expectation that the other person will change. It can be followed by the use of one or more choice questions. For example, the counsellor might ask:

'What other choices could you make in responding to your stepfather?'
'What do you think the consequences would be if you were to ignore your brother?'
'What would the consequences be if you were to talk to him about what troubles you?'
'What will be the consequence for you if you decide to continue to try to make your mother behave differently, and what will be the consequence for you if you decide to give up and accept what she wants in this instance?'

Guru questions

Young people are usually very keen to give each other advice, and to receive advice from their peers (Geldard, 2006). However, when advice is given or received in this way there is little expectation that the advice will be followed. Advice-giving is generally involved when peers help each other to think through alternatives. When young people come to counselling, they will often ask a counsellor what they should do. Sometimes it may be useful for the counsellor to make a suggestion of what they should do, but in making this suggestion to qualify it by saying something like:

'I don't know whether this would work for you. What do you think?'
'This is only an idea for you to think about because you might come up with a better solution?'

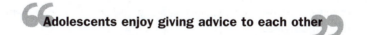

Adolescents enjoy giving advice to each other

Guru questions invite the client to be their own adviser. For example, if a young person called Andrew were to ask a counsellor, *'Do you think I should apologize to Fred?'*, the counsellor might then invite Andrew to take part in an experiment – to get up from his seat, stand in a new position facing his seat, and to imagine that he is a Guru, a very wise person. The counsellor might then say to Andrew, who is imagining he is a guru, *'Guru, you are a very wise person and I want you to give Andrew some advice. Imagine that he is sitting in that chair* [the chair Andrew was sitting in] *and tell him what to do.'* Many young people will enjoy this approach as it invites them into an advisory position. They often find that in that position they are able to offer themselves useful advice.

Normalizing

Normalizing is another counselling skill that can be very helpful to an adolescent with a relationship problem. Because young people have limited life experience they are often unaware of what is normal for most people. It is common for young people to believe that at times they are different from other young people, and this can affect their self-esteem. For example, a young person might say: *'I should be able to get on with my mother and I can't. My friends like her, but I argue with her all the time.'* In such a case it could be useful for the counsellor, before working on the relationship problems between the client and his mother, to normalize the situation. This could be done by explaining that at this stage in life it is normal for the young person to want to individuate, and it is also normal for parents to resist the young person's attempts to individuate, so some level of conflict is almost inevitable. Once this normalization statement has been absorbed by the client, the client may be more ready to enter into direct relationship counselling with his mother so that both of them are able to feel more comfortable in their relationship.

KEY POINTS

- The proactive counselling approach matches the adolescent development stage.
- A counsellor for young people must create an authentic person-to-person relationship.
- An existentialist philosophy and constructive thinking is appropriate when working with young people.
- Being proactive involves introducing creative, experiential, cognitive and psycho-educational strategies.
- In responding to a young person's developmental needs the counsellor needs to believe the client, and match the adolescent's style of communication.
- Self-disclosure by the counsellor enhances the person-to-person relationship.
- Actively joining in digression enables the counsellor to maintain an ongoing person-to-person relationship.
- Counselling skills of particular relevance to young people when considering relationships include transitional, choice and Guru questions, and normalizing.

QUESTIONS FOR GROUP DISCUSSION OR STUDENT ASSIGNMENTS

1. Use anecdotal examples to illustrate the importance of existentialist philosophy and constructivist thinking when working with young people.
2. Discuss the value of self-disclosure in counselling and illustrate this using an anecdotal example. Include in your discussion the ethical issues involved and the influence that these may have on a counsellor's decision to self-disclose.

16

Attending to the Young Person's Relationships within the Family

In order to be able to effectively attend to a young person's relationships with their parents and siblings, we need to have a clear understanding of the nature of adolescence. In adolescence, the young person moves from being part of the family group towards being part of a peer group and to standing alone as an adult (Mabey and Sorensen, 1995). Thus, the young person moves from dependency to independence, autonomy and maturity. There is a gradual transformation or metamorphosis of the person as a child into a new person as an adult. Inevitably, as a consequence the young person faces not only biological changes but also cognitive, psychological, social, moral, and spiritual challenges.

Cognitive changes

During adolescence the young person moves from the limitations of concrete thinking to being able to deal cognitively with ideas, concepts and abstract theories (Dacey and

Kenny, 1997). They continually explore, challenge, and change their constructs about the way they view their world. They develop egocentric thinking to the extent that they may have the idea that everyone is watching them as though they were on stage (Elkind, 1967). They may have the idea that they are both unique and invulnerable and at times feel omnipotent, all-powerful, and that they cannot be hurt. This is all part of a complex process of becoming a separate unique individual on a journey which leads to adulthood. Unfortunately, these beliefs, and in particular the sense of uniqueness, make it difficult for adolescents to believe that anyone else is capable of understanding them or how they are feeling. This has important implications for counsellors as in order to join with young people we first need to get their trust.

In adolescence, young people develop the ability to think logically and to make judgements based on logical thinking. Of particular importance to relationship counsellors is that several studies suggest that adolescents can be taught to improve their capacity for critical thinking (Eisenberg et al., 1999) and critical thinking can be useful when helping a young person to the evaluate relationship issues and the behaviour of others. Thus, part of the relationship counsellor's role may be to help a young person to find ways to improve their ability to use critical thought processes.

Young people develop the ability to use creative thinking which can be divergent and flexible, and enables them to consider remote possibilities and a variety of solutions to the same problem. Because they are developing their creative thinking abilities, many young people are particularly attracted to the use of creative strategies so these can be particularly useful in relationship counselling.

Psychological changes

Perhaps the most important psychological task for a young person is the formation of a personal identity. The psychological change involved in the formation of personal identity is certain to have implications on the young person's relationships with others, and in particular with family members. This is because the process of individuation necessitates the development of relative independence from family relationships, and an increased capacity to assume a functional role as a member of adult society (Archer, 1997).

> **To address a young person's relationship problems we need to understand the adolescent development stage**

Because they are on a journey of self-discovery young people are continually adjusting to new experiences, encounters, and situations, while at the same time adjusting to biological, cognitive and psychological changes. This is often both stressful and anxiety-provoking for them. It is not surprisingly, therefore, that adolescents demonstrate a decreased ability to tolerate, assimilate and accommodate change. The adolescent development stage is therefore characterized by emotional reactivity and a high intensity of emotional response (Shave and Shave, 1989). This makes it difficult for young people to control and modulate their behavioural responses, which at times may be inappropriately extreme. Such emotional fluctuations are certain to impact on relationships, and to address these, cognitive behavioural strategies can be useful when working with young people.

Social changes

A young person is challenged to make changes to their social behaviour as a consequence of the expectations of society, parents, family and peer groups. Unfortunately, most parents are not prepared for their child's shift from childhood to adolescence. As a consequence, unrealistic expectations may develop, with the result that there are likely to be tensions within the family and this inevitably places strain on family relationships.

Moral and spiritual changes

During adolescence young people develop a sense of human rights and develop clearer ideas about what they believe in and what they are prepared to stand up for. Such moral and spiritual changes inevitably affect a young person's attitude to others and to the behaviour of others. This will impact on relationships within the family where other family members may not share the young person's expectations or beliefs.

Ways to Attend to the Young Person's Relationships in the Family

If, as counsellors, we are to be helpful in attending to a young person's relationships within the family, we need to be able to join with them by accepting the realities of their developmental stage. Rather than challenge these, we need to understand them. By understanding them, we enable the young person themselves to work through the challenges that they inevitably confront.

> **There are several approaches to helping the young person with relationship issues**

In helping the young person to address relationship problems within the family we can use the following approaches:

- family counselling
- individual counselling for the young person
- subgroup counselling for the young person and a sibling or siblings
- subgroup counselling for the young person and parent/s.

Family Counselling

Sometimes relationship problems within the family involving a young person can be resolved through a family counselling process which includes the whole family, as explained in Chapters 8 and 9. As a consequence of such a process, a young person may be able to openly express the relationship issues that are troubling for them. This can then lead to a dialogue between members of the family about the issues and decisions will be made which will resolve a relationship problem. Unfortunately, this is not always the case. Some young people are reluctant to participate openly in a family counselling session. There are a number of reasons for this, including the following:

- they may feel disempowered by other family members
- their experience in the family might be that whenever they try to express their point of view they are attacked by other members of the family
- they may not want to cooperate with the family counselling process because they want to separate from the family and not be part of it
- they may not be prepared to trust the family counselling process.

Where a counsellor recognizes that the young person has a relationship issue but is not able to talk about it within the family system, the young person can be offered individual counselling, or counselling within a subgroup.

Individual Counselling

We believe that when helping young people with relationship problems it is necessary to use a proactive approach such as that described in our book *Counselling Adolescents: The Proactive Approach* (Geldard and Geldard, 2004), and outlined in Chapter 15. In order to join with the young person and to maintain their interest and cooperation in the counselling process we can make use of symbolic, creative, cognitive behavioural, and psycho-educational strategies. To address the relationship issues of the young person in the family we use:

- symbolical or projective approaches
- creative experiential approaches.

Symbolic and projective approaches

Sometimes young people find it very difficult to talk directly within the family about the relationship issues that are affecting them. They may be embarrassed to talk about them or believe that the counsellor would be judgemental if they were to talk about them.

In this case, it can be useful to work indirectly with the young person using symbols or miniature animals, as described when working with children in Part Three. These can be used with young people to help them to:

- get in touch with troubling feelings, ideas, or beliefs
- identify particular aspects of a relationship that trouble them
- make decisions.

> **Symbolic and projective methods can enable a young person to address troubling relationship issues**

Sometimes in a counselling situation a young person will have trouble identifying or talking about their feelings, ideas, or beliefs. For example, the counsellor might ask: *'What is the most troubling relationship issue for you in the family?'*, and the young person may respond: *'I don't know'*. The counsellor may then invite the young person to sit quietly, think about their family, and see what thoughts or feelings come into their awareness. The young person can then be invited to choose a symbol or symbols from the objects available to represent their current feelings or thoughts (see Chapter 12 regarding types of symbol).

Once the symbol or symbols are chosen, the counsellor might ask: *'I'm not going to ask you what the symbols represent, although you can tell me if you want, but if you can, I'd like you to tell me about those symbols?'* It is likely that the young person will respond by describing the properties of the symbol, for example its shape, size, and perhaps its use in a metaphorical way.

The counsellor can invite the client to hold each symbol and to say what it is like and what they would like to do with it. Through this symbolic exercise the young person may be able to get in touch with, and possibly express, their feelings and thoughts. Alternatively, they may be able to process these privately without disclosing them directly to the counsellor. This approach provides the young person with safety as they need only disclose what they feel ready to share.

Similarly, symbols can be selected to represent things that the young person would like to change in a relationship.

Where the young person is able to directly talk about the relationship issues, the counsellor can invite them to explore options. These options might include talking to the other family member with whom the young person has an issue, or deciding to behave differently in response to the other person. In looking at the options available, the consequences of each option can be explored. For example, the counsellor might ask: *'If you decided to talk to your brother about the issue, how would you do that?'*, *'What would you say?'* and *'What do you think the likely outcome would be?'*

A creative experiential approach

A very useful experiential approach for helping young people work through relationship issues is role-playing, as in psychodrama or Gestalt therapy. Initially, a client may be reluctant to participate in such an exercise so it is useful to begin an experiential technique by bridging the gap between what the client expects and what the counsellor has in mind. It often helps to formulate an experiential exercise as a novel experience by saying something like: *'I wonder if it would be useful to explore this problem by doing something different? How would it be if we tried something new to try to understand this a little better?'* Labelling the newness of the process can help the client to overcome any beginning awkwardness or self-consciousness (Leveton, 1984).

> **Creative experiential approaches can have a powerful influence on the young person's relationships**

During experiential techniques in counselling the client relies on their experiences to discover and learn more about the issue that is being explored. The counsellor adopts a facilitating role, and if the exercise is to have positive outcomes for the client the counsellor must be willing and able to become active themselves, to guide the client from one part of the activity to another, to demonstrate if necessary, or help by being a model (Leveton, 1984).

In order to carry out the role-play described below the counsellor begins with a pile of cushions of various sizes, colours, patterns, and shapes.

Consider the following example where role-playing might be useful. In this example, a young person named Rob is having trouble with his sister Maureen. The counsellor might start by asking the Rob to choose a cushion to represent himself. After the cushion has been selected the counsellor might ask, *'What is that cushion like?'* and, after the initial answer, follow up with, *'Can you tell me more?'* and *'Is there anything else you can tell me about that cushion?'* This process helps the client to identify the characteristics of themselves that are represented by the cushion. For example, the young person may describe the cushion as soft and pliable with a shabby fringe around the edge. The counsellor might then say, *'You chose that cushion to represent yourself. Are you like that cushion in some ways?'* Often this will help the client recognize their attributes and these may be positively connoted by the counsellor. Next, the counsellor can ask the client to choose a cushion for Maureen, and ask similar questions about that cushion in order to help the young person verbalize their perceptions of, beliefs about, and feelings towards Maureen.

Having chosen the two cushions, the counsellor can ask the young person to place them about two paces apart on the floor in the centre of the room. The young person can then be invited to stand beside the cushion which represents themselves and face the cushion which represents Maureen. They can then be asked, *'What would you like to say to Maureen?'* The young person can be invited to imagine that Maureen is actually standing where the cushion that represents her has been placed, and to talk directly to her using 'I' statements.

The young person might say, '*Maureen, I don't like it when you go to Dad and tell him that I haven't done the work I was supposed to have done'.* The counsellor might recognize that the young person is really furious with Maureen but in the role-play is not expressing anger. In order to help the young person express their anger more fully so that there is some cathartic release the counsellor might use the alter ego approach.

The alter ego approach

The words 'alter ego' literally mean a substitute or alternative personality (Weiner et al., 2003). In counselling, when using the alter ego approach the counsellor acts out what the counsellor believes the client would say if they were uninhibited and spoke without censoring.

In the example given of Rob and Maureen, the counsellor might stand beside, or slightly behind Rob, and after Rob's statement, say in a loud voice using an angry expression, '*Maureen, I'm not furious with you because you go to Dad and tell him that I haven't done what I'm supposed to have done.'* By doing this the counsellor gives the young person permission to openly express their feelings and vent the associated anger.

Before using the alter ego approach the counsellor needs to explain the process to the client. The counsellor might do this by saying, *'I'm going to stand beside you and act as another part of you. I might say some of the things that I think you might be thinking or feeling but not saying. When I do this you don't have to agree with what I say. Remember I can only guess at what might be going on inside you. So if I'm on the wrong track, let me know, or if you feel like it, you can argue with me.'*

The example continued

After Rob has been able to tell Maureen in the role-play what he wants, the counsellor will invite Rob to stand behind the cushion which represents Maureen facing his own cushion. The young person is then invited to imagine he is Maureen and respond to what he has previously said as though he were Maureen using 'I' statements. As Maureen, he might say, '*I don't care what you think. I'm going to tell Dad anyway.'*

The exercise can continue with the counsellor inviting the young person to move from being Maureen to being himself and back again so that the dialoguing continues. During this 'discussion' it might emerge that Maureen believes that when Rob doesn't do what he is supposed to do, she has to do more work herself.

Through the dialoguing Rob may be able to release emotions and also start to recognize what it might be like to be Maureen and perhaps to understand something of her point of view. Additionally, the dialoguing can be useful in helping Rob to rehearse what he might say to Maureen in the future. Through this rehearsal, he might be coached in choosing words that would allow for negotiation rather than inflaming the situation further.

Once the dialoguing has reached a natural conclusion, the counsellor can invite Rob to talk about what the dialoguing process was like for him, and to share anything that Rob has learnt from the process that might be useful.

It might emerge from the dialoguing that Rob has unrealistic expectations of his sister. In this case, it could be useful for the counsellor to use a cognitive behavioural strategy to help Rob to replace this unrealistic expectation with a more helpful one.

Cognitive behavioural strategies

Ideas from rational emotive behaviour therapy (REBT), originated by Albert Ellis (2001), and Reality Therapy, originated by William Glasser (2001), can be useful in helping young people to address relationships. Albert Ellis drew attention to the need for counsellors to challenge what he described as clients' 'irrational beliefs'. Readers who would like to make significant use of rational emotive behaviour therapy may wish to read Dryden and Neenan's *The Rational Emotive Behavioural Approach to Therapeutic Change* (2004).

> **Cognitive behavioural strategies suit an adolescent's exploration of new constructs**

In the example given above, Rob might have the expectation that Maureen should always be helpful, reliable, and trustworthy, whereas it might have emerged in the dialogue that over a long period of time Rob has not found Maureen to have consistently demonstrated these attributes. It would therefore be appropriate for the counsellor to draw attention to the difference between Rob's experience of Maureen and Rob's expectations of Maureen. By relinquishing this expectation and replacing it by a more realistic expectation Rob might make a different decision about how to respond to Maureen, and hopefully this will have positive consequences for their relationship.

In this example, it might also be useful to incorporate ideas from reality therapy, where there is a focus on the individual's ability to make choices and to take responsibility for the consequences of the decisions made. Rob could decide to continue to strive to change Maureen. But when considering this he might recognize that the most likely consequence would be that Maureen would become even more uncooperative. Alternatively, he could decide to deliberately cooperate in some ways with Maureen with the possible consequence that his relationship with her might be less conflictual.

Psycho-educational strategies

Sometimes it can be helpful for a counsellor to provide educational material for a young person, particularly as young people do not have the life experience of adults. In the

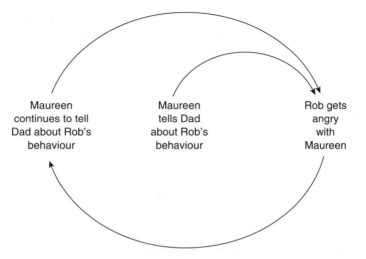

FIGURE 16.1(a)   *Circular process with negative outcome*

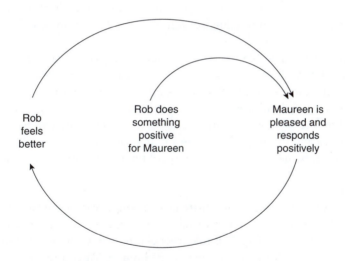

FIGURE 16.1(b)   *Circular process with positive outcome*

example used above, the counsellor might want to encourage Rob to draw on a white-board a variety of circular processes that might occur in the interaction between Rob and Maureen. Figure 16.1(a) and (b) shows two alternative circular processes. By looking at these and other alternative processes, Rob might decide to make decisions about how to behave in the future. Another psycho–educational strategy of use to young people is transactional analysis (Berne, 1964) as discussed in Chapter 18.

When using psycho-educational models there is a risk that a young person may uncritically accept a complete model and try to fit themselves into that model. It is more important that they be encouraged to examine critically and modify the model so that it suits them personally.

Young Person–Sibling Subgroup Counselling

When considering subgroup counselling for a young person with a sibling or siblings we need to consider two different situations:

1. Subgroup counselling involving two adolescents
2. Subgroup counselling involving an adolescent and a younger sibling or siblings.

Subgroup counselling involving two adolescents

In our experience, when engaged in relationship counselling with more than one adolescent it needs to be recognized that many young people tend to be less able to control their emotional responses than most adults. Consequently, it is important for a counsellor to manage the counselling session in a way that ensures some containment to promote a safe environment.

Many young people are able to work through issues with their siblings in a counselling environment. As discussed in Chapter 8, circular questions can be used to engage the participants in conversation so that they can each share their point of view. During this conversation it is helpful if excessive discussion of unsatisfactory past events which have impacted on the relationship can be minimized. Instead, the emphasis is placed on looking at options and finding solutions in the here and now.

Sometimes it can be helpful to use role reversal for a short time during such a session.

Role reversal

In role reversal two young people are invited to exchange seats and imagine that they are the other person. They are then invited to talk to each other from their reversed roles about the issues that are causing conflict. This role reversal can often result in successful outcomes, particularly if the counsellor is able to encourage humour. After a reasonably brief interchange in the reversed roles, invite the participants to change seats again and return to being themselves. Once they do this the counsellor can process the experience by asking them how they felt when they were in each other's roles, and whether they had discovered anything new about themselves, the other person, or the issue being discussed.

> **Role reversal can influence the young person's understanding of others**

Subgroup counselling involving an adolescent and a younger sibling or siblings

Where there is a relationship problem between a child and an adolescent sibling an evaluation needs to be made as to whether a satisfactory counselling process can be achieved without the presence of a parent. If a parent is present, they can ensure that any resolution of conflicting issues is consistent with their wishes and the family rules.

Sometimes it will be possible for a younger child to talk to an older sibling in a counselling session, particularly where the older sibling is sensitive to the needs of their younger brother or sister. Where a child is involved in the counselling process it is usually advantageous to make use of some media or activity which can be used to engage both parties. For example, it may be possible for the clients to reconstruct situations where relationship problems arise by using figurines in the sand tray, miniature animals or symbols. While the activity is in progress, the counsellor can observe the interactions and give feedback which may be helpful in enabling the participants to alter the way they interact.

Young Person–Parent Subgroup Counselling

Although it can sometimes be difficult when helping a young person and parent to resolve relationship issues, counsellors need to pay careful attention to avoid giving the impression that they are biased towards one party. If either the parent or the young person gain the impression that the counsellor is taking sides, the counselling process is likely to be compromised.

When helping a young person and parent work through their relationship issues a similar process can be used to that used when helping two adolescent siblings. The major differences between these subgroups are likely to be related to power and intimacy. The young person is likely to be thinking and behaving in ways that will enhance their individuation. Consequently, rather than wanting intimacy with their parent in the way they experienced closeness as a child, they are likely to want more separation. With regard to power, it is almost inevitable that most parents will find it difficult to relinquish, or ease up on, their level of control of the young person, while at the same time the young person will be struggling to be in control of their own life by striving for autonomy and freedom from parental control. A psycho-educational strategy can be useful in helping to address this issue. The situation can be normalized by explaining the inevitability of the struggle between a parent and adolescent.

> **Power and intimacy are often important issues affecting parent–adolescent relationships**

Commonly, when counselling a parent and young person, there will be difficulties with regard to the sharing of airtime in any conversation. Additionally, the parties may have difficulty in hearing what each other has to say. In this situation, it may be helpful to address basic communication behaviours based on the need to listen and validate what each other is saying.

Encouraging listening and validation

Where a parent and adolescent son or daughter both talk at the same time, interrupt each other, fail to listen to each other and validate what is being said, the counsellor can interrupt the conversation by saying: '*It seems to me that both of you are very good debaters. That's good. However, it does create some problems for you when you communicate with each other. I wonder if you would like to take part in an exercise so that we can explore your communication?*'

The counsellor can then use a whiteboard marker, or another similar object, and explain to the clients that whichever of them has the marker can talk while the other remains silent. They can then be asked whether they think they are capable of doing the task. The counsellor might say, '*I think it might be very hard to stay quiet when the other person is saying things that you find annoying. Do you think you will be able to do it?*' This effectively challenges them to succeed in remaining quiet while the other talks.

After one person has held the marker and said what they want to say, they can be invited to hand the marker over to the other person. Before the other person starts to talk the counsellor can ask them to validate what they have heard by summarizing what they have been told. Sometimes when a person has talked for a long time it is difficult for the respondent to accurately validate what has been said because too much information has been included. The counsellor can point this out and encourage both parties to make short statements which only deal with one issue at a time.

We recommend that the use of the marker should be confined to not more than two or three statements by each client otherwise the process becomes tiresome. However, it is useful in drawing attention to the value of listening and validating.

Clients often find it useful to be invited to feed back to their conversational partner what they like about the new way of communicating. This feedback paves the way for moving the focus from excessively exploring unsatisfactory past events to looking for solutions which are likely to enhance the relationship.

Integration into Whole Family Counselling

As explained in Chapter 10, after individual or subgroup counselling it is often important for relevant information arising from such counselling sessions to be shared in some way with other members of the family. This is not always necessary as sometimes changes in relationships achieved through individual subgroup counselling will positively influence the family climate. In such a case, all that is necessary is for a follow-up family counselling session to confirm that positive changes have been achieved.

KEY POINTS

- Counsellors need a sound theoretical understanding of the adolescent development stage.
- A young person's relationships in the family can be addressed through family counselling, individual counselling and subgroup counselling.
- Sometimes young people are not able to talk openly about their issues in the presence of the family.
- Symbolic, projective, creative and psycho-educational approaches are particularly useful when working individually on relationship problems with young people.
- The alter ego approach can assist a young person to be more fully in touch with their emotional feelings and thoughts with regard to relationships.
- Cognitive behavioural strategies appeal to young people as they challenge their constructs.
- Psycho-educational strategies are useful when helping young people with relationship issues as they provide information which the young person may not have obtained through life experience.
- Role reversal is a helpful strategy when two young people are exploring their relationship in a subgroup.
- Media and activity are often needed when counselling an adolescent and their younger sibling in a subgroup.
- Intimacy and power are common issues affecting relationships between young people and their parents.
- Encouraging listening and validation is important in the promotion of good relationships.

QUESTIONS FOR GROUP DISCUSSION OR STUDENT ASSIGNMENTS

1. Discuss the most important issues that you believe affected your relationships either positively or negatively within your family. Explain how you would help a young person to deal with similar issues.
2. Discuss what you believe are the most important moral issues that challenge young people today and affect their relationships within the family. Explain how you would work in counselling to help a young person who was troubled by such issues.

17

Focusing on the Young Person's Relationships with Peers

Positive relationships within a young person's family can provide them with security and support. This can enable them to seek a level of individuation, and to work on establishing their personal identity, while experimenting with and learning from relationships in the wider environment. During adolescence young people are certain to encounter new relationship experiences with their peers. Negative experiences can be very damaging for their self-esteem. However, a supportive family can help a young person discover their strengths and promote resilience so that they can learn how to deal with relationship difficulties and disappointments. Unfortunately, some young people do not have families that can provide the necessary support during this turbulent period of their life. Parents typically struggle with a young person's desire to individuate, and where relationships are compromised within the family a young person may feel isolated unless they have a supportive peer network.

Generally, peer support systems themselves are vulnerable to change and, consequently, may be unreliable with regard to providing support as each member of a peer group seeks to eventually find an individual personal identity. This is particularly true for younger adolescents (Geldard, 2006). A young person's process of socialization is based on the balance between individuation with the formation of personal identity, on the one hand, and integration with society on the other (Adams and Marshall, 1996). Unless this balance is achieved, there are likely to be personal crises for the young person as they get older. For example, older adolescents focus on identity formation which relies on integrating personal constructs with self–identity and their views about who they would like to become in the future (Geldard, 2006). If a young person seeks a very high degree of individuation, the consequence may be that relationships with peers are compromised. This may result in the young person becoming marginalized. In this situation, young people sometimes seek the company of other marginalized peers. Even so, there are likely to be consequences as the young person's sense of being valued by others may be reduced (Schlossberg, 1989).

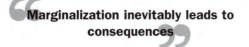

"Marginalization inevitably leads to consequences"

If, as counsellors, we are to help young people successfully manage their peer relationships, we need to have an understanding of the challenges which these relationships inevitably present. These challenges include:

- building and maintaining relationships
- the influence of peer pressure
- dealing with sexuality issues.

Building and Maintaining Relationships

As a young person matures it is inevitable that they will from time to time be confronted by the need to build new relationships and changing relationships. Within the family, relationships with parents, siblings and other relatives will undergo change. The young person is no longer a child and will strive to be treated differently. During this process it is likely that relationships will at times be conflictual, particularly with their parents.

As the young person's relationships within the family changes there will be a natural tendency for them to want to join with peers. For some young people this process is relatively easy as they have personality traits which make them attractive to other young people, and they are able to develop the necessary social skills. For example, Pizzamiglio (2003) suggests that popularity acts as a buffer between the young person being socially competent and anxiety. However, for many young people this process is a difficult one, in which they may feel rejection as a result of changing relationships. Because of the individuation process young people are continually experimenting with their relationships and many tend to be fickle and changeable with regard to their friendships. Consequently, many young people will face rejection from time to time and this can negatively affect their self-esteem. If they are to succeed socially, they need to join with their peers and, as a consequence, are susceptible to the influence of peer pressure.

The Influence of Peer Pressure

Young people in peer groups are generally subjected to strong social pressures to conform to group behaviours. This is particularly true of younger adolescents who navigate the individuation process by first establishing their social identity in the peer group. Younger adolescents are more likely to respond to events and interactions for reasons of social desirability among their peers (Geldard, 2006). Unfortunately, where these behaviours are self-destructive or anti-social they are likely to be negative consequences for the young person. However, we do need to acknowledge that it is inevitable that young people will exert pressure on each other. This is often most noticeable in the way in which they present themselves with regard to their appearance. Often this can be disconcerting for parents, who become anxious when their adolescent offspring make changes to their personal appearance in ways which are not easily acceptable to them. For example, they may have tattoos and piercings. However, what is seen by an adult as mutilative or destructive may, from a young person's point of view, be decorative (Martin, 1997). The way young people present themselves is subject to fashion and group membership. It is important to recognize that such changes in personal appearance, although due to the influence of peer pressure and the need for acceptance by peers, are also consistent with the young person's search for individuation and social identity. For many adults, it seems paradoxical that this behaviour is directed towards the achievement of both individuation and peer group affiliation.

> **Young people can strive for individuality by joining a peer group!**

Risk-taking behaviour

Adolescence is a time of experimentation and trying out new behaviours in response to new situations. This is risky. Unfortunately, young people are inherently susceptible to engaging in excessive and unchecked risk-taking because they often have the egocentric belief that they almost indestructible (Elkind, 1967). This tendency to take risks is often exacerbated by the influence of peers, who may encourage such behaviour by demonstrating their own ability to take risks, or through a desire to obtain vicarious pleasure from observing another young person's risk-taking behaviour. Additionally, young people in groups tend to compete for status and attention. Consequently, there is likely to be strong pressure to participate in life-threatening and risk-taking behaviours.

Dealing with Sexuality Issues

Young people are at a stage in life where there are likely to be romantic attachments involving sexual attraction, most generally in opposite-sex relationships and sometimes with same-sex relationships. These relationships may well be temporary, unstable and vulnerable to change. As most adolescents experience powerful feelings of romantic love they may suffer in self-esteem when rejected by the person they love. Alternatively, they may feel confused if their feelings change and they become attracted to someone else. However, the often transitional nature of adolescent relationships is consistent with the adolescent development stage of exploration and experimentation, and consequently presents a challenges for most young people. In addition, there are those young people who, because of personality or poorly developed social skills, are unable to experience a relationship with someone they find attractive. This can have a negative effect on their self-esteem and may lead to depression (Carr, 2009).

Sexual issues

There are wide differences between cultures with regard to what are considered to be acceptable sexual behaviours of young people (Dusek, 1996). At one extreme, there are cultures where young people are expected to refrain from engaging in sexual activity until marriage and adulthood. At the other end of the continuum, there are societies where sexual behaviour develops more gradually and may be allowed or even encouraged in young people with few restrictions. In contemporary Western society, there are clearly wide individual differences in attitudes and behaviours, both culturally and because of belief systems. Young people may therefore be faced with difficult choices. Decisions need to be made on the basis of information from a variety of sources, which offer differing opinions about what is appropriate. Consequently, when helping young people address such issues, as counsellors we need to be aware of the way in which young people are continually reviewing their constructs. We need to recognize that young people may change their point of view frequently. What is important is that we facilitate their exploration of the issues in a way which allows them freedom to make decisions that will have the best outcomes for them and enable them to express themselves openly. This involves helping them to explore the consequences of their behaviour in response to their thoughts and beliefs with regard to their relationships with other young people.

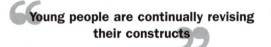

Young people are continually revising their constructs

   It has been suggested that young people who have sexually active friends, or believe their friends are sexually active, are more likely to be sexually active themselves. These factors are stronger for older rather than younger adolescents and also for females rather than males (Philliber et al., 2002). Clearly, sexual issues, beliefs, attitudes, and behaviours have an important impact on peer relationships.

Individual Counselling

During individual counselling of a young person who has relationship problems with their peers, a counsellor can use a range of strategies, including symbolic, creative, cognitive behavioural and psycho-educational strategies. These strategies can be used in

similar ways to those described in Chapter 16 for working with a young person individually with regard to family relationships. However, when addressing relationship
problems with peers, the differences between family relationships and peer relationships
must be recognized. In most families there is an assumption by the young person and
other family members that, regardless of what transpires within the family, the young
person will remain a member of the family. This is clearly not the case in peer relationships. Relationships among young people are commonly temporary, fickle, and
lacking in long-term commitment because in adolescence young people are navigating
through a process of identity formation which necessitates frequent changes with regard
to social relationships.

   One of the most useful strategies for helping a young person with peer relationships
is the use of role-playing, together with ideas from cognitive behavioural therapy. These
strategies are described in Chapter 16. Additionally, it can sometimes be helpful to use
the 'circle concept' (Champagne and Walker-Hirsch, 1982) to help young people recognize how they can adjust their relationships with others with regard to closeness and
distance. The circle concept is a useful strategy as it invites the young person to consider using behaviours which will hopefully enable them to meet their own personal
needs while remaining a member of their peer group.

> **Role-playing and cognitive behavioural therapy
> can help young people achieve more
> satisfactory relationships**

The circle concept

Managing and maintaining friendships, and also allowing friendships to change, requires
considerable skill, and much of this skill is learnt during adolescence. Often, young
people have problems in discriminating between what they perceive as and what may
actually be rejection by others. Rejection by others, or the perception of rejection, is a
consequence of others setting boundaries that are important for those people. If an
adolescent is able to understand the nature of boundaries, then they will be better able
to set their own boundaries and accept rejection when it occurs, as it inevitably will.

   To help adolescents to understand the concept of boundaries, a modified version of
the circle concept suggested by Champagne and Walker-Hirsch (1982) can be used. We
will call this the circle model. Figure 17.1 shows the circle model, which can be drawn
on a large sheet of paper using felt pens, or on a white board. The circles, in order of
size, represent the following:

The central circle.   This circle is described as the young person's own personal space,
which does not have to be shared with anyone else unless they decide to invite someone

to do so. The young person can be invited to write their name in this circle. If another person is allowed into this circle, intimate behaviour will occur. This might involve the sharing of very private and personal information and/or touching. Sexual behaviour, which might include sexual intercourse, may also occur if that is what is mutually desired.

The touching circle.   This circle is one in which the adolescent might engage in some non-sexual physical contact, such as hugging. Special friends may be invited into this circle.

The good friends circle.   This circle is for people with whom there are, warm, positive and mutual feelings. Personal and intimate information might be shared with them. However, for many young people, there will be little or no touching or hugging.

The OK people circle.   This circle includes people who are in the young person's social system. Relationships with these people are comfortable, but they are not close friends. The young person may not particularly either like or dislike them. These people are part of the group to which they belong. For a person to move from this 'OK people circle' to the 'good friends circle' they would need to spend more time with the young person, share more about themselves and participate more fully in common interests.

The other people circle.   This circle includes all of those people whom the young person might meet but who don't belong within the smaller circles. Thus, the people in this circle are familiar faces, such as shop keepers and bus drivers, and other people who are recognized but with whom there are not generally conversations.

Outside the outer circle is the space occupied by strangers.

When using the circle model, the young person is invited to describe the kinds of people who might be invited into each circle, and to write their descriptions or names within the correct circle. In addition, using a different coloured marker pen, behaviours which are appropriate for each circle are discussed and written in the relevant circle. Thus, the circle model is used to teach behaviours that are connected with the development of appropriate boundaries and relationships with others. In particular, the young person may learn the following:

1. It is appropriate for young people to have boundaries, which they set themselves, which set limits to the closeness of relationships with other people. On the circle model, no one has the right to move into a circle closer to the centre without mutual agreement.
2. Other people have their own boundaries, which can similarly be represented by sets of circles, and have the right to decide who may enter a particular circle. Consequently, young people will not be able to control where someone else will place them. Just as they control how close they will allow others to be, so other people will similarly set limits.

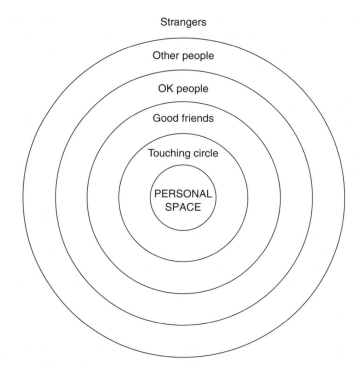

FIGURE 17.1   *The circle model*

3. Relationships are not fixed; they are dynamic. If the young person wishes, they can, on their circle model, allow other people to move from one circle to another. They have the right to be in control of whether or not they allow a person to move from a larger circle to a smaller one. When inviting someone to move into a smaller circle, they need to respect the other person's wishes. Also, it may be that the other person will not wish to move in closer.

4. While young people have control over allowing others to move from one circle to another in their own model, they will not have control over whether they themselves are allowed to move from one circle to a smaller one in somebody else's set of circles.

5. There are different kinds of behaviours that are appropriate for relationships within each of the circles. If the young person wishes someone to move from a larger circle to a smaller circle, then they will need to display behaviours that are inviting and create a climate which encourages the other person to want to move. Equally, if the adolescent wishes to move from an outer circle to an inner circle, or from an inner circle to an outer circle in somebody else's model, they will need to develop behaviours that are appropriate for achieving this, subject to the other person's cooperation.

6. Behaviours must be developed which will give other people clear messages about where they belong, so that consistent relationships will be developed without unnecessary

misunderstanding occurring. These behaviours will involve social skills such as friend-ship-formation skills, assertive skills, negotiation skills and conflict-resolution skills. The ability to have some level of flexibility is also useful, provided that boundaries are not inappropriately transgressed.

7. Boundaries need to be respected and violations addressed. The young person needs to respect other people's rights to set their boundaries. Additionally, the adolescent needs to learn assertive behaviours to let other people know when their own boundaries are being infringed. For example, if someone who is not in the touching circle touches them, they need to be able to say clearly that this is not okay. In this regard, the coun-sellor may need to role-play situations so that the young person can learn appropriate responses.

Group Counselling

It can sometimes be useful to help young people who have relationship problems with their peers by including them in a group with other young people who have similar prob-lems. Group work with young people has a number of advantages over individual work. It enables them to learn from one another and to establish friendships and connections within the group (Sharry, 2004). A counsellor facilitating such a group can help the par-ticipants to learn experientially from the group process as they relate to each other.

Counsellors running groups for young people who have relationship problems are sensible if they obtain group consensus about the rules that should apply within the group, and the consequences for infringement of these rules. It is advantageous to have clear limits to behaviour in the group, incorporating rules relating to abuse of any kind, including emotional and verbal abuse. It is to be expected that, because of the adoles-cent developmental stage, some group members will test the limits of the rules as they attempt to assert their own individuality. What is desirable is to respond to such testing in ways which will promote positive learning about relationships. For example, when unhelpful behaviours occur which might compromise relationships within the group, the counsellor can use circular questions to explore the effect of the behaviour on those involved and also on other group members. The group can be encouraged to suggest alternative, more helpful behaviours so that group membership becomes a learning experience for the participants.

Group work provides an opportunity for a young person to gain information not only about relationships but also about other issues that influence relationships, such as sexual activity, drugs, alcohol, and other risk-taking behaviours.

> **Confidentiality is a major issue when working with young people in groups**

Confidentiality is an important issue when running groups for young people because they are likely to be extremely sensitive to the possibility that information they have shared within the group might be disclosed to others outside group. Clearly, in the early stages of a group, agreement needs to be reached between group members with regard to confidentiality.

If young people are to be actively engaged in a group, the group programme needs to be varied so that group members are interested in what they are doing and enjoy participating. Thus, a group might spend times in discussion, times when educational information is being shared, when they are playing a game, when they are involved in physical activity, and when they are involved in a creative activity of some sort.

A creative activity might involve members of the group role-playing a scenario which one of them has experienced where a relationship problem developed. Alternative behaviours to those used when the relationship problem developed can be role-played to check whether these might have led to different outcomes.

KEY POINTS

- Relationship counselling for a young person needs to include building and maintaining relationships, the influence of peer pressure, and sexuality issues.
- Young people are simultaneously searching for individuation, personal identity, and acceptance by peers.
- Risk-taking behaviour is often exacerbated by the influence of peers.
- There are wide differences about what is considered to be acceptable sexual behaviour for young people.
- Individual counselling for a young person having relationship problems with peers can include strategies from symbolic, creative, cognitive behavioural, and psycho-educational strategies.
- The circle model can be useful in helping young people understand the nature of relationships.
- Group counselling of young people for relationship problems enables them to learn experientially from, and through conversation with, each other.

QUESTIONS FOR GROUP DISCUSSION OR STUDENT ASSIGNMENTS

1. Identify and discuss the most difficult issues that arose for you in your relationships with peers during adolescence. Explain how, as a counsellor, you would attempt to address similar issues expressed by young people.

2. Discuss the challenges young people confront with regard to relationships with peers and sexuality. Include in your discussion the influence of cultural and spiritual issues. Explain how you would help a young person to explore their constructs regarding relationships and sexuality while being congruent and also careful not to impose your own views.

18

Addressing a Young Person's Relationships with Teachers, Employers and Other Adults

A major challenge for young people as they move through adolescence is their need to find their place in society and to gain a sense of how best to relate to adults, including those in positions of authority. This is a process of socialization involving integration with adult society. The socialization process and the search for personal identity in adolescence are strongly interrelated and interdependent (Geldard, 2006). Socialization enhances the sense of personal identity, and the development of personal identity helps the young person to deal with society's expectations.

Adult society, and in particular teachers and employers, have expectations regarding young people. These expectations are based on the assumption that a young person is now becoming capable of behaving more responsibly, and this assumption is certainly not one that can be relied upon. As explained in Chapters is 15, 16, and 17, during adolescence the young person is experimenting with and learning new behaviours, so it is unrealistic to expect that they will behave responsibly at all times. For a young person, this expectation will clearly be pressuring at times. However, society's expectations are of value in helping young people to progress along the path to adulthood. Interestingly, it has been shown that in communities where adults express consistent values and expectations, young people tend to develop a positive sense of self (Ianni, 1989).

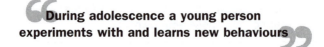

During adolescence a young person experiments with and learns new behaviours

It is self-evident that a young person can only construct a personal identity in the context of relationships with others. Having comfortable relationships with others unquestionably involves respecting and responding appropriately to their expectations. Adults in general have expectations about how adolescents should behave and these will often conflict with a young person's expectations. A young person's need to achieve individuation provides a conflictual challenge as they explore new ways of fitting into society. As a consequence, there is likely to be marked ambivalence in many young people with regard to expressing their attitudinal and behavioural changes while maintaining social relationships (Archer, 1997).

Expectations of Teachers and Employers

Generally, as a result of training and experience, teachers tend to be fairly realistic regarding their expectations of adolescent students. However, because teachers have the task of educating young people, they will inevitably have an expectation that at some level their students will be motivated to learn and to be conscientious in carrying out the tasks assigned to them. In addition, by recognizing that they inevitably fulfil a role as models for their students, they will try to promote responsible behaviour through demonstrating such behaviour and encouraging it. It is certain that at times most teachers' expectations will not be fulfilled because of the characteristics of the developmental stage of adolescence, and this may lead to relationship problems between them and the young people they teach.

Many young people leave school to go into full-time employment, while others continue to attend school, and go on to college or university. Many of those who continue to study will engage in part-time employment. In employment environments, adult behaviours are generally expected. Consequently, adjusting to life in the workplace is likely to impact on a young person's developmental processes.

In the workplace, young people learn to take responsibility for the completion of tasks assigned by supervisors and often experience some level of autonomy. They also have to deal with conformity issues regarding workplace expectations and are subjected to a variety of relationship issues (Safyer et al., 1995). In the workplace, they are generally in relationships with peers who work alongside them, with adults, and with those in authority, and they are in an environment which has structure and expectations.

Clearly, such a situation presents a range of relationship issues which will challenge the young person.

> **Most young people have difficulty reconciling the need for autonomy with conformity**

As young people grow older, they start to look and behave in more adult ways and are able to communicate with some level of maturity and more effectively than they did as children. As a consequence, many adults expect that their behaviour will reflect the norms of adult behaviour. However, the expectation that young people will be responsible and work conscientiously, and proactively set out to meet the developmental tasks challenging them, is not necessarily realistic. The young person is in a process of growth and is dealing with new and previously unmet challenges, so is unlikely to stay focused on particular tasks and is sure to make mistakes. It is therefore inevitable that at times employers and other adults in supervisory positions will become frustrated by the behaviours, attitudes and performance of their young employees, resulting in conflict. Counselling a young person to enable them to satisfactorily respond to relationship challenges from adults in authority positions can therefore be useful. It can help them to develop a positive personal identity and to use behaviours that will support them in the future.

Counselling Strategies

Individual counselling for a young person can be helpful in enabling them to address relationship issues with teachers, employers, and other adults. Counselling skills and strategies described in previous chapters in this part of this book can be helpful. In addition, there are some particular approaches that are especially useful in helping young people to address issues arising in such relationships. These include:

- transactional analysis
- cognitive behaviour therapy
- psychodrama.

Transactional Analysis

Transactional analysis was originated by Berne (1964) and developed by Harris (1973). Ideas from transactional analysis are particularly useful for helping young people improve their relationships as it enables them to understand the principles of effective

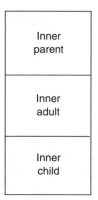

The critical parent: powerful, dominating, rigid, controlling, coercive and restrictive.
The nurturing parent: caring, permissive, protective and with a high level of responsibility for self and others.

The adult: able to choose responses, self-directed, reality-based and logical. Respectful of others, seeks information before making decisions, independent and self-sufficient. Flexible and able to change in response to new information.

The child: dependent, childlike, helpless, submissive or rebellious. Responds without thought to emotional feelings. Easily takes the victim role, experiences high levels of emotion and is prone to tantrum.

FIGURE 18.1   *The transactional analysis model of personality*

and respectful communication. Transactional analysis concepts appeal to many young people because they provide easy-to-follow explanations of relationship behaviours.

Transactional analysis communication processes can be represented by pictorial drawings on a whiteboard or poster paper. These drawings provide an anchor for the ideas which are being presented and allow the young person to participate by modifying the drawings to suit their own situation.

In the transactional analysis model proposed by Berne (1964), there are three inner components identified within each individual. These are:

1. *Inner parent:* The inner parent can be either a critical parent or a nurturing parent. The critical parent is powerful, dominating, rigid and controlling, whereas the nurturing parent is warm, protective and caring. The parental role has a high level of responsibility, including responsibility not only for self, but also for others.
2. *Inner adult:* The inner adult is:

   - reality-based and logical
   - is respectful of others rather than seeking to control others
   - seeks information before making decisions, rather than being governed by emotional responses
   - is not submissive but independent and self-sufficient
   - is flexible and able to change in response to new information.

3. *Inner child:* The inner child is childlike and helpless. It may be submissive or rebellious. It is dependent, responds reactively and without thought to emotional feelings, easily takes the victim role, may experience high levels of emotion and is prone to tantrum.

In using this model of personality with a young person, a diagram such as that shown in Figure 18.1 can be used. As this diagram is being drawn, it can be useful to invite the young person to suggest the characteristics they believe apply to an inner critical parent, an inner nurturing parent, an inner adult and an inner child. By doing this, they will inevitably become involved in an exploration of parts of themself.

The adolescent can then be invited to explore the ways in which relationships are influenced by communications which come from differing parts of the inner self and which are directed to various parts of the inner self of the other person, as shown in Figures 18.2 and 18.3. These figures include examples of communication patterns, some of which are unhelpful and unsatisfactory because the communication lines cross each other. Many patterns such as these are described by Harris (1973). Parallel communications, as shown in Figures 18.2(d) and 18.3(b), (c) and (d), tend to be more satisfactory than crossed communications, although they may still cause problems. For example, the communication pattern between a person who is behaving like an angry critical parent and another person responding as a dissatisfied child is certain to be uncomfortable (Figure 18.3(b)).

Generally, people are more satisfied if the communication lines are both parallel and horizontal, as shown in Figures 18.2(d) and 18.3(c) and (d). Parent-to-parent and child-to-child communications can be quite enjoyable and satisfying at times. However, there may sometimes be disastrous consequences from these communications because both parties might collude to engage in undesirable behaviour. The communication pattern shown in Figure 18.3(d) has this potential. The optimum mode of communication is that between inner adult and inner adult, as shown in Figure 18.3(c).

> ❝ **Adult-to-adult communication is generally the most effective** ❞

Clearly, every person has choice about which inner part of themselves they use in communicating with others. This choice is certain to influence the outcome of communication and also to impact on the relationship. By teaching young people the transactional analysis model, they can be assisted to understand more about the ways in which they communicate with other people and may become more aware of the likely consequences of their style of communication on relationships with adults, particularly those in positions of power. Readers who wish to learn more about transactional analysis may wish to read Berne, Steines and Dusay (1996).

CBT

Albert Ellis, the originator of rational emotive behaviour therapy (REBT), suggested that counsellors need to challenge what he described as client's irrational beliefs. Although we support Ellis's ideas, we prefer to use the term self-destructive beliefs

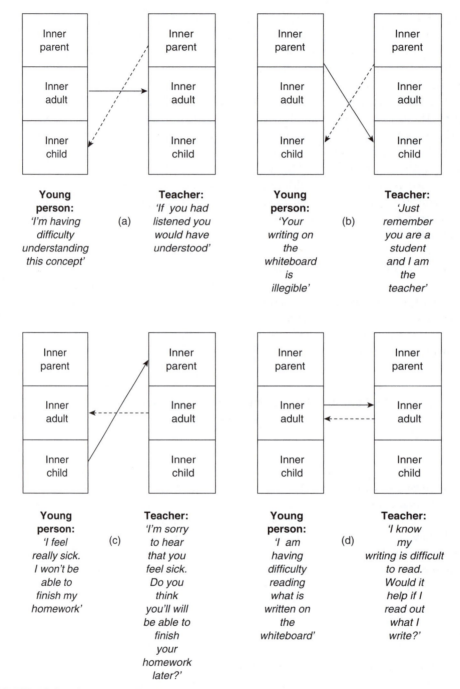

FIGURE 18.2   *Communication between a young person and a teacher*
The solid arrows represent the first message and the broken arrows the response.

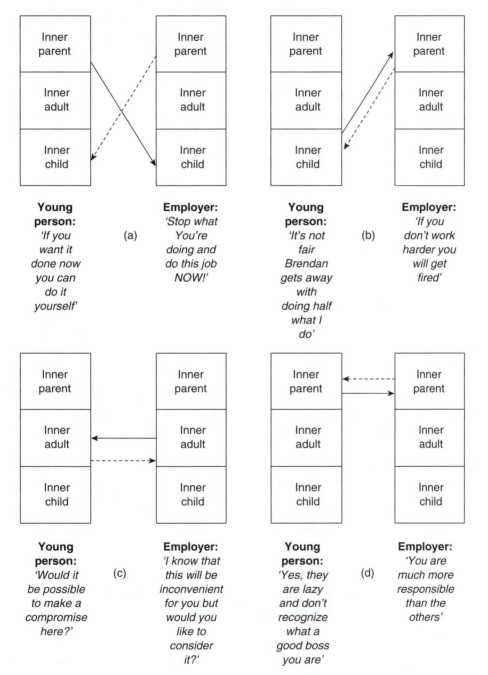

FIGURE 18.3   *Commuication between a young person and an employer*
The solid arrows represent the first message and the broken arrows the response.

rather than the irrational beliefs because some beliefs that are self-destructive may not be irrational. Readers who would like to make significant use of rational emotive behaviour therapy may wish to read Dryden and Neenan (2004).

REBT is particularly useful when working with young people who have relationship difficulties because they commonly hold beliefs which lead them to behave, or think, in ways that are unhelpful to their relationships. Table 18.1 compares a list of self-destructive beliefs, which are likely to impact negatively on a young person's relationships, with more helpful beliefs. Self-destructive beliefs which are likely to affect a young person's relationships generally fit into one or more of the following categories:

- should, must, ought-to and have-to beliefs
- catastrophizing beliefs
- 'always' and 'never' beliefs
- blaming beliefs
- negative self-perception beliefs.

Challenging self-destructive beliefs

When challenging a young person's self-destructive beliefs it is advantageous if counsellors recognize that adolescents are different from adults. They are in a process of moving out of childhood, where they have naturally and inevitably absorbed beliefs that may now need to be changed. As a consequence, counsellors need to be careful not to alienate a young person when disputing their self-destructive beliefs, as some of those beliefs may have been held throughout childhood. We therefore recommend that when counselling young people, challenging self-destructive beliefs should involve two stages:

1. In the first stage, the young person can be complemented for the existing beliefs. These can be validated as having been useful in the past, particularly during childhood.
2. In the second stage, self-destructive beliefs can be challenged as needing to change as a consequence of the young person's movement from childhood into adulthood. The young person no longer needs to be constrained by self-destructive beliefs, but can reject them.

> ❝ **Challenging is best done using an adolescent debating style of conversation** ❞

The challenging needs to be done by debating the issues in a way which parallels the way in which young people debate with each other, and may involve a level of self-disclosure. For example, the counsellor might say, *'I have some difficulty when people tell me*

TABLE 18.1   *Self-destructive beliefs compared with more helpful beliefs*

Self-Destructive Beliefs	More Helpful Beliefs
Should, must, ought-to and have-to beliefs	
Adults *should* live up to my expectations of them.	Adults may not live up to my expectations, and that is the way it is.
At school and work I *must* conform to my peers.	I can be an individual and do my own thing.
I *ought to* do whatever the boss asks at all times.	When necessary I will be politely assertive about my own needs so that I feel okay.
I *must* win.	According to the law of averages, most people only win 50 per cent of the time. I don't need to win to feel okay.
Catastrophizing beliefs	
I messed up at work so it would be too embarrassing for me to go back there.	Everybody makes mistakes at times, so I'm normal and proud to be me. I'm going back!
Nobody will ever respect me at school again.	I don't need other people's respect to feel good about myself. I am okay.
It's all too much. I just can't cope any more.	I can cope. I always have in the past, and I will now.
I might as well stop work on this college project altogether because it is a total failure.	I've done really well to take on such a hard project. It's not a total failure. I can still get some positives out of it.
Always and never beliefs	
I *never* succeed in anything I do at work.	Sometimes I succeed and sometimes I fail. I'm human and I'm okay.
Everybody *always* criticizes me.	People sometimes criticize me, but that's okay because it's impossible to please everybody all the time.
I'm not going to ask my teacher because she *always* says 'no'.	I am going to ask my mother because she might say 'yes'.
I should never make mistakes.	Everybody makes mistakes. The only way to avoid making mistakes is to do nothing, and that's not me.
Blaming beliefs	
If Bob stopped annoying me I wouldn't get into trouble with the boss.	I can choose other ways to deal with Bob's annoying behaviour so that I don't get into trouble.

(Continued)

TABLE 18.1

I am always late back at work because they are so slow in the canteen.	I will take responsibility for being late because I don't go straight to the canteen at the start of my break and know that the canteen gets crowded and the staff are slow.

Negative self-perception beliefs

I'm a victim.	I'm powerful.
I'm a loser.	I'm a winner.
I'm no good.	I'm okay.
I'm worthless.	I'm worthwhile.
I'm helpless.	I'm resourceful
I'm a bad person.	I'm a good person
I'm incapable.	I'm capable.
I'm stupid.	I'm smart.
I'm unlovable.	I'm lovable.

that I should do things. I prefer to do things I choose to do rather than necessarily doing things other people believe I should do.' By making a statement such as this, the counsellor discloses their own need for individuation, and their desire to take responsibility for their own decisions without being excessively influenced by other people 's expectations. The counsellor's goal is not to replace the young person's beliefs immediately with a new set of beliefs. Rather, it is to leave the young person feeling freer to think about alternative beliefs and with an openness and readiness to explore and change those beliefs which are self-destructive.

In helping a young person improve their relationships with adults in their life, the counsellor can usefully explore those self-destructive beliefs which may be acting negatively on the young person's relationships.

Psychodrama

Psychodrama originated in the work of Moreno in the 1940s (Vondracek and Corneal, 1995). An approach taken from psychodrama using cushions can be very helpful in enabling a young person to express their feelings regarding relationships with an adult, to resolve these, and to discover new ways of thinking and behaving. This creative experiential approach is described in Chapter 16 in the example where a young person called Rob is having trouble with his sister Maureen. As when working with a sibling, in this approach, the young person is invited to choose from a pile of assorted cushions of various colours and styles. They are invited to choose a cushion to represent themselves and another cushion to represent the adult with whom they are having a relationship issue. The cushions are placed apart on the floor and, as described in Chapter 16, the young person is invited to alternate between standing by the cushion which represents themselves and saying what they would like to say to their adult proponent, and standing by the proponent's cushion and responding. Thus dialogue is created between themselves and the role played adult.

> **The alter ego process is useful in helping to bring out the feelings**

In the process described, the alter ego approach can be used (see Chapter 16) to help the young person to be kept fully in touch with their feelings and to express them.

Once the dialoguing has reached a natural conclusion, the counsellor can invite the young person to talk about what the process was like for them, and to share anything that they may have learned from the process that might be useful. For example, it may be that as a result of a role-play the young person will recognize the difficulties confronting an employer and their problems in managing the work situation.

KEY POINTS

- A challenge for young people is to discover their place in society and how to relate to adults in positions of authority.
- Adult expectations of a young person will often conflict with the young person's expectations.
- Young people have to deal with new and previously unmet challenges so are certain to make mistakes at times.
- Counselling strategies suitable for helping a young person deal with relationship problems with an adult include transactional analysis, cognitive behavioural therapy, and psychodrama.
- Transactional analysis highlights the way in which communication can come from, and be directed to, the inner parent, adult, or child.
- Self-destructive beliefs often interfere with a young person's ability to have satisfactory relationships with adults. Consequently, challenging these beliefs as in cognitive behavioural therapy can be helpful.
- Psychodramatic dialoguing using cushions can enable a young person to get in touch with and release their feelings and gain a fuller understanding of the relationship issue.

QUESTIONS FOR GROUP DISCUSSION OR STUDENT ASSIGNMENTS

1. Identify situations in the workplace where young people inevitably face challenges as a consequence of their developmental stage in life. Explain how, as a counsellor, you would help a young person to deal with their relationship issues in these situations.
2. Using an actual conflict situation which you have either experienced yourself or have observed, use the transactional analysis model to describe what happened in the communication and the outcome. Explain how transactional analysis could be used to help the people involved to communicate differently and achieve a more satisfactory outcome.

Part 5

Relationship Counselling for Parents

When counselling families it is quite common to discover that the parental relationship or parenting issues are compromising family functioning. In such cases, when using the CACHO model of relationship counselling, a counsellor can invite the parents to address these issues in separate counselling sessions.

We recognize that there are special issues for parents in blended families so we have included a separate chapter to address these issues.

19

Helping Parents Address their Relationship Issues

When we, as counsellors, endeavour to help parents address issues relating to their relationship as a couple, it is important for us to continually respect and be aware that the parental relationship does not exist in isolation but exists within the context of:

- influences from each partner's family of origin
- the developmental stage of the relationship
- the family system
- the partners' notions of an intimate relationship.

All of the above can tend to constrain the couple's relationship and will inevitably influence the way it is expressed.

Influences from each partner's family of origin

For each of us, our expectations of family life derive from information gleaned from our experiences gained in our families of origin. Because each family is unique and has its own way of functioning, it is frequently the case that partners will have different ideas from each other about how they expect their family to function.

For example, as explained in Chapter 5, power and intimacy issues vary from family to family. Consequently, a parent who has grown up in a family where the power was shared among family members is likely to confront difficulties if their partner is a person whose family of origin was dominated by one individual who exercised most of the power. This is because they will have different expectations about how a family should operate with regard to these dimensions. Similarly, a parent may have expectations that parenting will be carried out in a particular way because that was their experience in their family of origin. Difficulties between couples are likely to occur with regard to parenting where there have been differences between the parenting style in each partner's family of origin. This will be discussed further in Chapter 20.

Developmental stages of couple relationships

Couple relationships are not static but inevitably change as a consequence of the developmental stage of the relationship. Some important stages that occur in many couple relationships include:

- the initial development of the relationship
- learning to live together
- getting married
- the birth of the first child
- the birth of other children
- the first child going to school
- subsequent children going to school
- children moving into adolescence
- sons and daughters moving out of home
- sons and daughters becoming partners/marrying
- the arrival of grandchildren.

> ❝Couple relationships inevitably need to respond to developmental changes❞

In each of these stages partners will be faced with new challenges which necessitate changes in behaviours. Additionally, the couple must show some ability to change their rules for relating to each other as their relationship develops, while maintaining some rules in order to sustain a level of stability in their relationship (Goldenberg and Goldenberg, 1990). It is clear that establishing an understanding of the issues faced at different stages in the life cycle helps in identifying the changes that might be needed in a relationship (Bubenzer and West, 1993).

Influences of the family system

Because of the developmental stages described above, roles within a partnership have to be adaptable if they are to fit social and family changes as they occur. As a result of changes, behaviour that was previously enjoyed may be perceived to be unacceptable (Butler and Joyce, 1998). Moreover, because the couple is a subsystem of the wider family system, the parental relationship will inevitably be influenced by the behaviours of other members of the family.

Notions of an intimate relationship

Freedman and Combs (2002) point out that there are powerful discourses that shape people's understanding about what an intimate relationship should look like. These discourses influence couple relationships regarding issues such as appropriate intimacy, length of relationship, ways of communicating, degree of romance, and many other practicalities. Clearly, problems will arise when the discourses of partners are significantly different from each other's.

The Counselling Process

There are differences of opinion among relationship counsellors about the most helpful way to address relationship issues. Some counsellors insist that convening conjoint sessions involving both partners is the most helpful. Certainly, research has demonstrated that there is a greater chance of positive outcomes with relationship difficulties when both partners are involved in therapy conjointly than when only an individual is seen (Street, 2006). However, a distinctive feature of contemporary couple counselling is to work conjointly with the couple and also to have individual sessions with each partner (Bennun, 1991). This is consistent with the counselling model recommended in Part One of this book.

"Couple counsellors need to be proactively involved"

We support the contention of Kessler (1996) that couples counselling requires the counsellor to be active and engaged. This is necessary because many couples who seek counselling will have acquired destructive patterns of interaction and inevitably they will repeat these patterns in the counselling process. Kessler (1996) suggests that just as a movie director has to be 'up close and personal' in order to guide the actors' performances, a counsellor has a parallel task. By being actively involved, the counsellor engages in activities that are helpful in enabling the clients to learn new interactive skills, how to de-escalate arguments, how to give and take information about each other, how to switch off the blame game, and to discover new ways of relating. Active involvement by the counsellor requires the appropriate use of behavioural management skills, such as is required when one or both partners stop listening, fail to work at understanding one another, and instead fall into accustomed and problematic patterns of interaction (Bubenzer and West, 1993).

The presenting problem

By the time couples make a decision to come to relationship counselling they are usually frustrated by their inability to resolve their problems, have exhausted all their usual coping strategies, and feel vulnerable and powerless to do more. Butler and Joyce (1998) suggest that the client's position is analogous to being lost in the middle of a forest where there are numerous paths to try but some are entirely unsuitable for one or both of the clients. The counsellor's role is to enable them to find a viable path which is acceptable to them both.

Initially, clients will usually present the counsellor with what they perceive as their major problem. This might range from money, issues related to sex, in-laws, children, or jobs. However, behind any particular conflict situation there is often a larger issue, such as power and control, commitment, or self-esteem, and behind the larger issue lurks basic concerns, such as attachment versus loss, and trust versus insecurity (Hendrick, 1995).

Bubenzer and West (1993) suggest that typically presenting problems relate to areas such as:

1. Economic issues
2. Companionship–intimacy (including sexual activity)
3. Work and recreation
4. Parenting
5. Household chores
6. Relationships with extended family
7. Religion
8. Friends
9. Substance abuse
10. Communication.

Underlying issues – changing core needs

We believe that issues underlying the presenting problem invariably relate to each individual partner's core needs. Unless each partner's core needs are met, there will inevitably be tension in the relationship. Although joined together in a relationship, the ability of each partner to appreciate the other's needs with regard to individuality or separateness is important. For most couples, if each partner is to have their core needs fulfilled, respect for both togetherness and independence should be present. This may appear to be paradoxical, but couples do need to maintain some individual boundaries within the relationship in order to pursue and develop individual interests (Bubenzer and West, 1993).

Counselling Skills and Strategies

When counselling couples using the CACHO model of change, as described in Chapter 2, we believe that working in accordance with the sequence described below can often be useful:

1. Joining
2. Facilitating effective communication
3. Raising awareness
4. Discovering the origin of issues
5. Identifying core needs
6. Exploring solutions
7. Experimenting during counselling and at home.

Joining

As discussed in Chapter 4, for counselling to be maximally effective the counsellor must create an appropriate relationship of trust with clients. This is particularly important when counselling couples because unless the counsellor is careful to be, and to appear to be, even-handed, one of the partners may start to believe that the counsellor is biased towards the other partner. This potential problem may be exacerbated by gender issues. For example, where a couple is being counselled by a female counsellor, the male partner may believe that the female counsellor is more understanding of his female partner's position than his own. However, an alternative problem may arise where a female client becomes jealous of a perceived relationship between a female counsellor and the client's male partner.

> **Perceptions of bias towards one partner can arise**

In order to deal with the above problems counsellors must be careful to ensure that the messages they give to the couple appear to be even handed and unbiased. In some situations, it may be useful for a counsellor to openly address the issue of possible bias. For example, the counsellor might say, *'I want to be careful to hear both your points of view and to respect them. If at any time during the counselling process you believe that I am giving preferential treatment to one of you, or being biased in any way, I would like you to tell me. I hope that you will feel able to do that?'*

Perceptions of bias can also be minimized by being careful to attend to each partner equally when confronting particular behaviours. For example, it may be that one partner dominates the conversation while the other sits quietly. Rather than criticizing the partner who dominates the conversation, the counsellor might say, *'I'm interested in the way that you talk with each other. I have noticed that one of you talks very freely while the other is very quiet.'* By giving this feedback the counsellor can then help the couple to explore what it is like for each of them when they behave in this way, and through raised awareness of the communication pattern they may be able to change their communication behaviours if they choose.

It is also helpful to the joining process if the counsellor can address each partner equally when facilitating the counselling process, so that each partner has an opportunity to express themselves fully.

Initially, in a couple counselling session it can be useful to use circular questions, as described in Chapter 4. For example, when counselling a couple, Susan and Michael, the counsellor might ask Susan, 'How do think Michael feels about coming to counselling?' or, 'What you think is Michael's biggest concern about your relationship?' After hearing Susan's response and inviting Michael to put forward his point of view, the counsellor might then similarly ask Michael circular questions about Susan.

Encouraging direct communication between partners

As the counselling session proceeds, it can be helpful to ask the client's to talk directly to each other, whenever possible and appropriate, rather than to address comments to the counsellor.

> ## Encouraging the clients to talk directly to each other is helpful

If the counsellor is able to encourage the couple to communicate openly with each other, useful progress in raising the clients' awareness of their 'here and now' relationship can be made. First, they have an opportunity to talk about difficult issues in a safe situation, where the counsellor will do what is possible to contain the situation if unhelpful behaviour occurs. Secondly, the counsellor can observe the couple's communication patterns and can give them feedback about these in order to raise their awareness and hopefully enable them to experiment with alternative, more helpful patterns. Thirdly, by communicating with each other directly, the couple may discover their own strengths with regard to finding solutions to their problems.

Facilitating effective communication

Some couples who come to counselling have well-developed and effective communication skills. They give each other equal air time, listen to what each other says, and validate what their partner has said before responding. However, many couples have difficulty communicating in this way, particularly when discussing issues that evoke strong emotions. Where this is the case it can be useful for the counsellor to spend some time helping a couple to learn to communicate more effectively.

To help a couple learn to communicate more effectively it may be necessary for the counsellor to interrupt an unhelpful communication pattern. For example, the counsellor might say, 'I notice that you are both getting frustrated as you try to explain your *situations to each other. I get the impression that neither of you feels properly heard and under-stood by the other. This is quite understandable because the issues that you are talking about are very important to you both.'* This feedback statement avoids blaming either partner and normalizes the situation so that they can feel okay rather than feeling criticized or inadequate.

Next, the counsellor can invite the couple to participate in an experiment to try to discover whether they can succeed in helping each other to understand the individual points of view.

The communication experiment

This experiment was explained in Chapter 16 with regard to helping a young person and parent communicate. However, we think that it is important to also discuss the method in detail in this chapter as it can be an important strategy to use when coun-selling couples. When working with a couple we recommend the following process.

In introducing the communication experiment, the counsellor picks up an object, such as a whiteboard marker, and explains the rules:

1. A person can only talk when they are holding the whiteboard marker.
2. Once one person has finished talking they must hand the whiteboard marker to the other person.
3. On receiving the marker, the other person should try to repeat back to the first person a short summary of what the first person has said.
4. If possible, they should continue by saying something to indicate that they understand the first person's point of view.
5. If this summary is accepted by the first person as being correct, the second person can respond, otherwise the whiteboard marker is returned to the first person.
6. The counsellor can speak at any time without holding the marker.

In this process, the counsellor directs and controls the movement of the marker from person to person until the participants can do this satisfactorily without guidance. As the process continues, the counsellor might make suggestions regarding ways to enhance communication. For example, the counsellor might:

- Point out that short statements which encompass just one issue are generally more effec-tive than long ones in getting a message across.
- Give feedback to identify unhelpful communication processes, such as responses which deflect away from the topic under discussion. A common way of deflecting is to bring up other past, present, or possible future issues. Another way is to bring up a different issue altogether, resulting in attack and counter-attack (Weeks and Treat, 1992).
- Suggest that it is not helpful to continue trying to convince someone else to accept your point of view when they strongly disagree. Instead, it may be more helpful to acknowl-edge and recognize that it is okay to think differently from each other.

We recommend that the exercise should not continue over a long period of time as it becomes tedious and may lead to stilted conversation. However, using the exercise for long enough to give each partner an opportunity to make a few statements and responses can be a good learning process for a couple.

The focus of this exercise is on the process of communication. It is likely that, as an outcome of taking part in this experiment, solutions to difficulties will be discovered. It can be tempting for the counsellor to become involved in the conversation concerning the issue under discussion. However, by carefully and deliberately focusing on the communication process, the individuals concerned are likely to see the counsellor as being a facilitator rather than attempting to influence decisions or solutions discovered.

Raising awareness

As discussed in Chapter 2, a central component of the theory of change underpinning the CACHO model is the raising of awareness. When working with couples on their relationships, a number of strategies can be used to help raise awareness of what is in the 'here and now'. These strategies include the use of:

- circular questions
- observation and feedback of communication processes
- instructions
- role reversal
- the alter ego process
- psycho-educational methods
- cognitive behavioural methods.

Circular questions

While all of the relationship counselling skills described in Chapter 4 are useful when counselling couples, other-oriented circular questions are particularly useful. Examples of these questions that might be used in a couple counselling session with clients Sandra and Jason are:

'Sandra, if you had a guess, how do you think Jason felt when you said … ?'
'Jason, what do you believe is troubling Sandra most?'
'Jason, how do you think Sandra interprets your silence?'
'Sandra, how does Jason let you know that he cares about you?'

After responding to a circular question the couple can be encouraged to talk directly to each other. In this way, they can be invited to start looking through each other's lenses, raising their awareness, and enabling them to appreciate each other's point of view.

Observation and feedback of communication processes

As discussed earlier in this chapter, it can be useful for a counsellor to encourage the clients to talk with each other directly and to observe the communication processes. By feeding back these processes, and possibly encouraging adaptive communication by using the communication experiment, the couple's awareness of the way they communicate is raised with the possibility of change occurring.

Instructions

As explained earlier when counselling couples, it is important for the counsellor to be active and to facilitate the process which raises awareness in a variety of ways while also encouraging their clients to talk directly with each other. In facilitating the process, the counsellor can usefully give instructions, such as the following:

'It might be helpful if, instead of talking to me, you generally talk to each other about what is troubling you.'

'Jason, I think it would be helpful if you were to say that directly to Sandra now.'

'I'd like us to stop here.', or *'I wonder if you might stop here.'* (Sometimes it is necessary for a counsellor to interrupt an unhelpful communication process rather than allowing it to continue. The counsellor can then give feedback about the process that was occurring and ask the participants how it felt for them.)

'I think it would be helpful if you swapped seats and role-play each other.' (The counsellor might then check whether the clients were willing to do this.)

Role reversal

As explained in Chapter 16 when counselling a young person in the family, the counsellor might invite the couple to change chairs and to reverse their roles – to assume the body posture, mannerisms, and attitudes of their partner. The counsellor might then ask the couple to talk to each other for a short while about a troubling issue as though they were the other person. After this, they can be invited to change back to their original seats and you can ask them to comment on the experience of role reversal. Alternatively, when the partners are in the role-reversed position, they can be interviewed by the counsellor to discover what they understand their partner to be thinking or feeling (Bubenzer and West, 1993).

> " **Role reversal can help partners understand each other's points of view** "

The alter ego process

The alter ego process described in Chapter 16 can be used either during role reversal or during general communication between the two partners. This process is particularly useful where one partner is reluctant to openly express their feelings for some reason. For example, Jason may remain silent instead of responding to a statement made by Sandra. The counsellor, acting as alter ego, can stand beside Jason and say on his behalf, *'I can't tell you what I would like to say because I'm frightened of the consequences if I do.'*

When using the alter ego process the couple need to be made aware in advance of the way that the process might be used and their agreement sought to use this process as explained in Chapter 16.

Psycho-educational methods

As explained in Chapter 6, a couple's awareness of the circular processes that occur between them can be raised by drawing diagrams on a whiteboard such as those shown in Figure 19.1 and in Figure 19.2 on page 235.

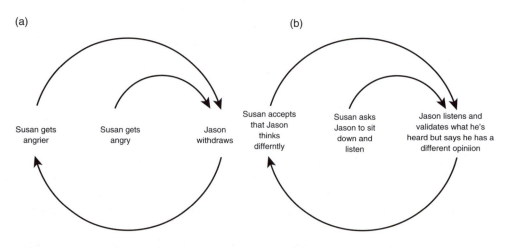

FIGURE 19.1   *Circular processes between Sandra and Jason*

Cognitive behavioural methods

Partners often have unrealistic expectations of each other. Awareness of their unrealistic expectations can be raised by using a cognitive behaviour strategy, as explained in Chapter 18 and illustrated in Table 18.1. Additionally, a cognitive behavioural approach can be used to challenge commonly encountered myths, identified by Kessler and Thaler Singer (1996), such as the 'fix my mate' myth and gender-related myths.

The 'fix my mate' myth is encountered when one partner believes that the relationship problem is entirely the responsibility of the other person and they themselves do not need to make any changes. For example, a person may say that their partner is entirely to blame, or that their partner has emotional or psychiatric problems and that if these were addressed the relationship would be fine. As counsellors, if we accept cybernetic theory and its relevance to family systems, we must assume that any relationship problem involves whoever is involved in the system. Perhaps the best way to address the 'fix my mate' myth is to identify one or more circular processes that may be occurring and to draw these on a whiteboard for discussion. In this way, both partners' awareness of the circular processes can be raised with the possibility of change occurring.

We need to stress the importance of developing the clients' trust before challenging unhelpful beliefs (Butler and Joyce, 1998).

Discovering the origin of issues

Many issues experienced by couples have their origin in the families in which the partners were raised – their families of origin. In order to raise awareness of these issues, it can be helpful to use a genogram (as explained in Chapter 9). A genogram can be drawn on a whiteboard in collaboration with the clients and they can then each be asked to talk about their families of origin with particular reference to issues which might be pertinent. For example, it might have emerged in the counselling process that Sandra gets angry because when she wants to talk about a problem Jason becomes silent. When exploring information about Sandra and Jason's families of origin it might be recognized by both of them that in Sandra's family of origin issues which might be conflictual were brought out into the open and talked about, whereas in Jason's family of origin conversation relating to troubling issues was avoided. Having discovered this information, the counsellor could then normalize what might be happening between Sandra and Jason. The counsellor might say, *'Now that I know about the way problems were dealt with in the families you grew up in, I think it's inevitable that you Sandra would want to talk things out, whereas you Jason would want to avoid doing this.'* The counsellor could continue by explaining that we are all influenced by our families of origin but we don't need to be controlled by the behaviours and rules that applied in those families. We can, if we choose, decide on new behaviours and rules that will work better for us.

Identifying core needs

Identifying each individual's core needs is central to couple counselling. As explained previously, if these needs are not met, there is certain to be tension in the relationship. The strategies explained earlier in this chapter are designed to raise the couple's awareness by encouraging respectful and effective communication between them. As they communicate openly with each other in the counselling process each partner's core needs will inevitably become apparent.

Every person has their own individual core needs and these will be personal and may not be similar to other people's core needs. Commonly experienced core needs include the need for:

- effective communication
- sharing of duties
- quality time as a couple
- sexual satisfaction
- independent space.

> **Having each partner's core needs met is essential in a good couple relationship**

Effective communication
Communication is a process that takes time. Couples need to discover that effective communication requires not just their energy, commitment, and understanding, but also time (Weeks and Treat, 1992). Consequently, couples need to be encouraged to deliberately put aside time to communicate with each other. This may mean setting aside a regular designated time and place when the couple can talk privately and separately from the rest of the family.

Sharing of duties
When one partner feels as though they are not being supported in performing the many tasks associated with family life the relationship is certain to be uncomfortable.

Quality time as a couple
Many couples who have children become overwhelmed by the many demands on their time either in caring for the children, performing household chores, or with regard to paid work. As a consequence, it is common for couples to have little or no time in which to enjoy quality time together as a couple. Spending time together is very important because in addition to the need for partners to be supportive of one another, being friends can contribute greatly to relationship success (Hendrick, 1995).

Sexual satisfaction
Although sometimes a couple will attend counselling with the primary role of addressing sexual satisfaction issues, it is more common for couples to avoid talking about such issues. This is not surprising because for many people it is embarrassing to talk about sexual issues, particularly with a stranger such as a counsellor. It is therefore sensible for a counsellor to be confident that a good relationship has been established with the clients before raising sexual issues, if these have not already been mentioned by the clients. However, where it appears to the counsellor that intimacy issues may be of concern, we

believe that it is appropriate for the counsellor to ask the couple whether they would like to explore these issues within the context of the counselling process. Clearly, this needs to be done sensitively and respectfully so that the clients do not feel as though the counsellor is unnecessarily prying into their personal lives.

Independent space

Some couples enjoy having a very close relationship with only limited independence whereas for others such a relationship would be claustrophobic. It often happens that one or both partners, while being committed to their relationship, would like more freedom to explore interests of their own. It is therefore very appropriate that in counselling the issue of independent space should be explored, and that the partners should be clear about their needs and also clear about their attitude to each other seeking independent space.

Exploring solutions

As repeatedly stressed in this book, central to the change process in the CACHO model is the need to raise the clients' awareness. This can be done using the strategies described earlier in this chapter. As the process develops, it is most likely that a variety of solutions to problems will spontaneously emerge. The counsellor's role is to work collaboratively with the couple in the exploration of possible solutions and their likely consequences.

Experimenting during counselling and at home

When a couple decide to adopt new behaviours it can be helpful to remind them that they are, in effect, doing an experiment. The results of the experiment will let them know whether the new behaviours are helpful or not. As a result of the experiment, they may discover new solutions which they have not previously considered. By reminding the couple that they are 'doing an experiment', if a change in behaviour doesn't have positive consequences, the couple will not feel that they have failed but instead may realize that they have learned from the experiment. What they planned to do was not effective so they can look for and test out an alternative solution.

> **Labelling a new behaviour as an experiment guards against feelings of failure**

Violent Relationships

Differences of opinion exist in society and among counsellors concerning the most effective way to intervene in relationships where there is domestic violence (Hanks, 1996). Many counsellors strongly oppose the use of couples counselling where there is, or has been, violence. This stance is supported by evidence that women who have suffered from violence in the home can be exposed to further abuse if the relationship is allowed to continue on the basis that couple counselling is occurring. There is a strong case for recommending that before couple counselling is considered, the violent partner should satisfactorily engage in, and complete, a series of group sessions specifically designed for perpetrators of violence.

While we believe that the most appropriate way to deal with violence is through the use of group work in the first instance, we also recognize that at times it can be useful to work conjointly with some couples where violence has occurred in the past, particularly where both partners are determined to seek counselling. Additionally, in many cases when working with couples, the issue of violence is not raised until a trusting relationship between a counsellor and couple has been established. At this point, it is clearly appropriate to engage in education for both partners about the nature of violence in the home and to strongly encourage the perpetrator to attend a group.

The cycle of violence diagram shown in Figure 19.2 can be used by counsellors to draw attention to the escalating nature of the cycle. First, a strong emphasis is required to make it clear that the use of any kind of abuse – verbal, emotional, financial, and especially physical abuse – is NOT okay under ANY circumstances. It needs to be made clear that provocation is unacceptable behaviour, and it must be stressed that provocation is no justification for abuse and cannot excuse such behaviour.

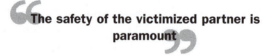

When working with a couple where violence has ceased, a counsellor needs to be vigilant in monitoring the situation with regard to safety and in addressing other forms of abuse.

In discussing the cycle of violence with a couple where violence has ceased, it cannot be assumed that it will not resume. Consequently, a full discussion of the cycle of violence is required. The couple might be asked if they would like to discuss and modify the stages in the standard cycle of violence model shown in Figure 19.2 to fit in with their own experiences. A strong message is required with regard to the way in which, over time, if the cycle of violence is allowed to continue, it tends to shorten. This is shown by the dotted line running from 'explosion' to 'build-up' in Figure 19.2. Later the dotted line is likely to move from 'explosion' to 'ready to burst'. Such a situation is highly dangerous and can lead not only to serious injury but also to death.

Clearly, counsellors need to be vigilant in ensuring the safety of their clients. Whenever a counsellor discovers during the course of counselling that violence has

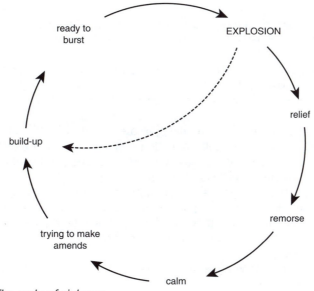

FIGURE 19.2   *The cycle of violence*

occurred, it is sensible for them to consult with their supervisor to make decisions to ensure that any ongoing counselling contact is ethically sound and directed towards promoting the safety of the abused partner.

Where violence has occurred in the home it is inevitable that children in the family will have been traumatized. We recommend that, wherever possible, children from violent families should be included in a group with similar children. A programme for working with children from homes where domestic violence has, or is, occurring is described in our book *Working with Children in Groups: A Handbook for Counsellors, Educators and Community Workers* (Geldard and Geldard, 2001). We have used this programme on many occasions ourselves and found it to be beneficial for the children who have participated.

KEY POINTS

- Couple relationships are affected by influences from each partner's family of origin.
- Couple relationships need to change as each stage in the family's development is reached.
- Couple counselling sessions, together with individual counselling sessions, can be effective.

- For a good relationship each partner's core needs must be met.
- Perceptions of counsellor bias towards one partner need to be addressed if they arise.
- Encouraging direct communication between partners is a useful strategy in couple counselling.
- The facilitation of effective communication is required early in a couple counselling session.
- Significant change results from raising awareness through the use of a variety of strategies, including circular questions, observation and feedback, giving instructions, role reversal, the alter ego process, and psycho-educational and cognitive behavioural methods.
- Discovering family-of-origin issues can remove restraint to change.
- Identifying core needs of each partner is central to couple counselling.
- Effective communication, sharing of duties, quality time as a couple, sexual satisfaction, and appropriate independent space are common to many people's core needs.
- Labelling decisions to change behaviours as 'experiments' minimizes perceptions of failure.
- Abuse is not okay under any circumstances and provocation is no excuse for abuse.
- Counsellors must be vigilant in promoting the safety of the victimized partner when violence in relationships has been identified.

QUESTIONS FOR GROUP DISCUSSION OR STUDENT ASSIGNMENTS

1. Discuss a particular developmental stage in a couple relationship. Describe how the demands of this stage will impact on the relationship, explain what changes might be needed to enable the relationship to function effectively, and describe how as a counsellor you would help a couple negotiate this developmental stage.
2. Discuss specific examples to illustrate how family-of-origin issues can impact on couple relationships. Explain how, as a counsellor, you would help a couple to deal with such issues.

20

Enabling Parents to Address Parenting Problems and Differences

As experienced relationship counsellors, we recognize that couple relationships in families are sometimes compromised as a consequence of the couple experiencing difficulties with regard to parenting their children. Although the problems of parenting in blended families may be more complicated, as explained in Chapter 21, parenting problems also commonly create relationship difficulties between parents in intact families.

Factors Contributing to Parenting Problems

Parenting problems arise from a variety of factors, including:

- the influence of families of origin
- systemic imbalance in the family
- inadequate parenting education.

Unfortunately, many parents are reluctant to openly discuss their parenting problems because they may feel to some extent guilty or embarrassed, and do not know how to parent more effectively. They assume that they are to blame. However, in our experience, most parents are doing the best they can, and are limited by their lack of knowledge and experience through no fault of their own.

The influence of families of origin

As discussed in Chapter 19, ideas about how to parent are generally learnt from our own experience as children in our families of origin. For some people what they have learnt is extremely useful, but for those who grew up in families which were less adaptively functional these learnings may be unhelpful and set them up to repeat ineffective or inappropriate parenting behaviours modelled by their own parents.

As stressed throughout this book, all families are unique and different from each other. As a result, we frequently find that partners who are experiencing difficulty in parenting their children have grown up in families where ways of relating and parenting styles differed. It is inevitable in such situations that, unless the couple are able to openly discuss their differences, a level of tension will arise between the partners as they each struggle to parent in their own way. Unfortunately, in such situations it is likely that one parent may either inadvertently or intentionally undermine the parenting of the other.

> ❝ **A person's parenting style is likely to be influenced by their parents' parenting style** ❞

In some cases, a parent may have strong negative feelings about the way in which they were parented as a child with the consequence that they are determined to parent differently. Some parents may manage to do this with success and positive outcomes. However, others will fail because they have not experienced parenting in a different way from the way in which they were reared. Consequently, they will make mistakes. Sometimes they will be able to learn from these mistakes, but at other times they may become disillusioned and disheartened, and uncertain about how they should be parenting.

Systemic imbalance in the family

It is not uncommon for inappropriate parenting to become established as a consequence of systemic imbalance in a family. Consider an example where the parental relationship is dysfunctional but rather than address this relationship problem the mother forms a coalition with one of the children and this coalition is directed against the father. The structural change to the family system helps maintain homeostasis or balance in the family and enables the parents to deflect away from addressing the tension in their relationship. However, in this situation, the father may become angry with both the mother and child, and may become excessively punitive with the child while the mother may become overly protective of the child. It is not surprising that in situations such as this a child's behaviour will become problematic. Taking note of cybernetic theory, it is to be expected that as these behaviours become entrenched they may also become more extreme, causing major problems in the family system and resulting in extremely unhelpful parenting strategies.

> ❝ **Inappropriate parenting may occur where there is systemic dysfunction** ❞

Inadequate parenting education

As explained in Chapter 19, couple relationships naturally move through many developmental stages. One of the stages involves the transition into the parenting role, and for many people this can be an overwhelming experience (Johnson, 1996). This problem is exacerbated in Western society where families are commonly required to move away from the place where the parents grew up in order to gain employment. As a consequence, many parents do not have the support of an extended family when they are raising their children. Additionally, there is generally a lack of adequate education of young people in preparation for parenting. This raises the question of how do new parents learn their parenting skills? For many, it is a case of learning through trial and error, and this can be emotionally costly for the parents individually, for their relationship, and for the well-being of their children.

Addressing Parenting Problems

In addressing parenting problems it can be helpful if counsellors take into account the influence of families of origin, the possibility of systemic imbalance and/or that parenting education may have been inadequate. There are a number of ways of addressing these issues, including:

- using strategies to raise awareness
- videotaping parent–child interactions
- providing options for parenting education.

Using strategies to raise awareness

As discussed throughout this book, the CACHO model of relationship counselling relies on Gestalt therapy's theory of change process of raised awareness. With regard to parenting problems, awareness-raising is required with regard to:

- parenting differences and their origins
- systemic problems affecting parenting
- the need for parenting education.

Parenting differences and their origins

The first step in addressing parenting differences is to raise awareness of the origins of these differences. In order to do this, the counsellor can invite each of the partners to describe what it was like growing up in their family of origin and to explain their style of parenting and the involvement of each of their parents in parenting. As each partner listens to the other's descriptions of their family of origin they will become more aware of the reasons why the partner parents in the way they do. Consequently, this exploration will encourage the partners to start talking about their different styles and to begin exploring new ways of behaving. The counsellor can make it clear that the way that families function tends to be passed from generation to generation, but that this is not necessarily inevitable. The couple can change their parenting styles from those of their parents and decide on a style that suits them best as a couple.

Sometimes a parent will explain that they have rejected their own parents' style of parenting because they didn't like it when they were a child and would like their own children to experience something different. Even so, it is helpful to recognize that the style of parenting that they are using is a response to the one they experienced. Parents can be helped to understand that they do not need to be constrained by their desire to be different from their parents, but if they wish, they can adapt their style to a new way of parenting which may be more acceptable to their partner.

Systemic problems affecting parenting

When parenting problems become apparent in a counselling session it is useful to provide the couple with the opportunity to describe and fully explore the way in which they carry out their parenting. By raising their awareness of their parenting behaviour and its consequences, any systemic problems which influence the parenting will inevitably be discovered. These can be addressed by using strategies discussed in previous chapters, and particularly in Chapter 19.

The need for parenting education

As discussed earlier in this chapter, many parents are not prepared for the developmental stages in their relationship as they have children and as these children grow older. Not only do they need to learn how to parent young children, they also need to learn how to adapt their parenting style as their children grow older.

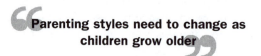

Parenting styles need to change as children grow older

It is unfortunate that many parents come to counselling believing that they should already know how to be good parents and how to parent effectively. In raising their awareness of their need for parenting education, it is important for the counsellor to be sensitive so that the parents do not feel as though they are being labelled as incompetent. Instead, they need to be positively connoted for the way in which they have succeeded in raising their children up to this point. Normalizing their experience with regard to 'trial-and-error' parenting when raising children can be affirming. It can be made clear that whenever we engage in a new task we have to experiment with what works and what doesn't, and that it can be helpful to receive information from others about what might work.

Options with regard to parenting education are provided later in this chapter.

Videotaping parent–child interactions

Particularly when working with young children, it can be useful to offer parents an opportunity to be videotaped as they interact with one or more of their offspring. When making this offer, the counsellor can make it clear that they are interested in seeing how the child/ren respond to the parenting methods used. By explaining the task this way, the parent is less likely to feel as though they are being judged with regard to their parenting style.

When parents agree to be videotaped we will fully explain to them the procedure that we intend to use and obtain their consent in writing for the process.

We set up our play therapy room with materials for particular activities which the parents and child/ren might find interesting. While videotaping, we observe the process from an observation room connected to the play therapy room by a one-way mirror. An integrated audio system allows us to hear what is being said. We also have an inter-com phone system between the observation room and the play therapy room so that we can give the parent/s instructions from time to time.

During the process we will at times use the intercom (which has a handset so that the child/ren can't hear what is being said) to suggest to the parent that they interrupt an activity which the child is enjoying to move on to something else. We do this to observe how the parent/s manage this process and how the child responds to this transition.

After the parent/s and child/ren have interacted for a sufficient time to provide useful parenting information, we will finish the session and join with the parent/s to debrief them and give them feedback. We will ask them about the session and invite them to discover alternative strategies that they might have used instead of those they used in the situations where managing their child's behaviour was problematic. In collaboration with the parents, it can often be helpful to arrange another session to playback parts of the videotape. During playback the parents are invited to take control and pause the tape at various points where they notice a situation in which they responded in ways which were not helpful in their view. This process allows parents to examine their parenting strategies and raises the parents' awareness of the effects of their parenting style.

> **Most parents are doing the best they can and need to be praised for this**

This process of self-reflection by the parent enables the counsellor to positively con-note their parenting while providing an opportunity to suggest alternative strategies which could be trialled to test their effectiveness.

Providing options for parenting education

Counsellors who have training and experience with regard to parenting education may use the counselling situation to provide information to their clients that can be helpful regarding parenting. For example, a counsellor might provide information about parent mediation of sibling conflict, or might suggest that it could be useful for parents to participate in a parent training course.

Parenting mediation

Where partners have marked differences in their parenting styles it can be helpful to encourage them to work together so that they can agree on a united and consistent approach to managing specific situations. Working together has been found to be successful, particularly when dealing with issues related to managing conflict between children (Smith and Ross, 2007). Parents often identify sibling conflict as the most prevalent behavioural problem in families (Brody and Stoneman, 1987; Prochaska and Prochaska, 1985).

The challenge for parents is how to bring about more constructive conflict resolution between their children. Smith and Ross (2007) found that helping parents to use formal mediation procedures in sibling disputes resulted in their children subsequently using more constructive conflict resolution strategies themselves, and being better able to compromise and control the outcomes of conflict situations.

Counsellors can help parents learn the four steps of mediation which are supported by the work of Deutsch (1973), Kressel (2000) and Shantz and Hartup (1992):

Step 1: parents are encouraged to set ground rules with regard to particular situations in the family. For example, a rule might be that each child's room is private and off-limits to their siblings.

Step 2: when conflict arises, the issues are immediately identified. Using the example above, it might be that a brother has 'trespassed' into his sister's room to borrow a particular object when his sister is not there. Recognizing the issues is central as it helps to identify what the children are fighting about.

Step 3: involves the parents talking separately with each child in the other's presence with the goal of helping each child to understand the circumstances in which the event occurred. In the earlier example, the brother may have lost his only eraser and was urgently completing a homework assignment which needed correcting. The issue for his sister may have been that she prized her only eraser as it was given to her by a close friend. It is believed that such understanding makes reaching an acceptable resolution easier.

Step 4: parents are encouraged to help their children suggest and adopt solutions. As an outcome in the example above, it may be that the sister allows her eraser to be used, but that it is to be returned to her at a time agreed upon by both parties. For her brother, this may mean that he needs to complete his assignment within a specific time frame. By suggesting solutions, attention is focused on the future, rather than past negative behaviours. It is important that each child is satisfied with the solution.

Parenting programmes

There are many parenting programmes available throughout the world. A programme which has been researched internationally is the Positive Parenting Program, commonly known as 'The Triple P Programme', which was devised by Professor Matt Saunders. Details of this programme are available from the website: www.triplep.net.

KEY POINTS

- Factors influencing parenting problems include the influence of families of origin, systemic dysfunction, and inadequate parenting education.
- Differences in partners' parenting styles may have their origins in the partners' families of origin.
- Systemic dysfunction can result in inappropriate parenting.
- Many parents lack adequate parenting education.
- Videotaping and observation of parent–child interactions can help parents discover new ways of parenting.
- Parenting programmes are useful in providing parenting education.

QUESTIONS FOR GROUP DISCUSSION OR STUDENT ASSIGNMENTS

1. Give an example (other than the one described in this chapter) of a situation where systemic dysfunction might have an adverse effect on parenting. Explain what this effect might be and describe how you would work as a counsellor to help the parents improve their parenting.
2. With reference to your own family of origin, explore the parenting behaviours of your parents and discuss how these may have been influenced by accepted beliefs and values within your family. Discuss how you would decide which of your parents' behaviours you would use yourself as a parent. Explain what alternative strategies you would use and what you would expect the effect of these to be.

21

Addressing Parenting Issues in the Blended Family

There are many different types of blended family, but in all of these families one of the adult partners is the biological parent of one or more of the children while the other partner does not have a biological relationship with these children (Connolly, 1983). In some blended families both partners will have children from previous relationships and the couple may also have a child or children resulting from their own relationship. In some cases, the children from previous relationships will live for most of the time in the blended family whereas in other cases they will usually live with a previous partner and only join the blended family for visits.

Difficulties Specific to Blended Families

As discussed by Bearsley-Smith (2007), there are number of unique challenges for step-families. When working with partners in a blended family it can be useful for counsellors to consider these challenges and use the skills and strategies outlined in Chapters 19 and 20. Important among these challenges are:

- the establishment of a blended family
- differences in family cultures
- competing individual and family needs
- environmental pressures
- parenting issues.

The establishment of a blended family

One of the most demanding issues for a couple, where one or both partners have children from a previous marriage, is integrating the individuals concerned into a new blended family system. Consider a situation where both partners bring one or more of their children from previous relationships into the blended family. Before joining the blended family, the adults concerned will have established relationships with their own children. These relationships may include particular alliances and coalitions. When joining the blended family there is likely to be a strong tendency for individuals to try to retain the characteristics of the family relationships they previously experienced. However, in the context of the blended family, it is most likely that these relationships will need to change in order for the family to function adaptively.

> **Creating a blended family usually requires changes in family relationships**

Consider an example where Fred, who is father to Peter, joins with Jasmine, who is mother to Arthur and Rachel, to create a new blended family. Prior to joining the blended family, Peter may have had a very close relationship with his father Fred. When joining the blended family he may become distressed when his father starts to pay attention to Arthur and Rachel, and Fred may be confused about how he should respond to the situation. Clearly, establishing a blended family is a stressful time for the individuals concerned as they readjust to their inclusion in the new family system.

An additional problem with regard to establishing a blended family is often created by members of the extended families of the partners. While in first marriages extended family members are generally supportive and respectful of the relationship of the couple, it often happens that divided loyalties of extended family members creates disharmony and friction when a new relationship is established.

Differences in family cultures

During the establishment of a blended family the couple have to cope with their lack of history as a couple, and while they are still discovering and exploring ways of relating together they also are adjusting to their role as step-parents. This can be complicated by uncertainty and/or conflict regarding family norms, structure, boundaries, ways of relating, the nature of step-relationships, the role of relationships with ex-partners, and co-parenting arrangements.

Often it is only after the establishment of a blended family that partners discover major differences in their expectations with regard to the way in which their new family should operate. Unless these are clearly negotiated conflict is likely to arise. It is clear that whenever a blended family is established there will be confusion unless there is some clarity about the structure of the new family, expected boundaries within the family, and the nature of step relationships. Additionally, problems can be created by ex-partners, as it is inevitable that there will be contact with ex-partners where co-parenting arrangements occurs.

Competing individual and family needs

The organization and management of a blended family is likely to be more complicated than that of an intact nuclear family. Because of family demands, privacy and time together for the parental couple may be limited and in some cases non-existent. This is in contrast to first marriages where often there is a period of time before children arrive which gives the couple an opportunity to develop their relationship, and deal with relationship issues between them before having to also address relationship issues concerning children.

> ❝The quality of the couple relationship is central
> to blended family functioning❞

We believe that the most vulnerable part of a blended family system is the couple relationship. A primary goal of counselling must be to enable the partners to consolidate their relationship in such a way that family stability and security is ensured. In order to establish a sound couple relationship it is essential for each partner's core needs to be met, and in some blended families this may be problematic.

For a partner who has not previously experienced a live-in couple relationship, joining a partner who has children can quite possibly result in conflictual family situations which will divert energy away from the consolidation of the couple relationship.

Environmental pressures

Frequently, partners who join a blended family have constraints imposed on them by their previous relationships, particularly if these relationships have ended in the recent past. The partners may be stressed by changes to their social relationships and with their management of previous social relationships, especially when ex-partners were previously included in their social circle. There may be legal and financial issues, particularly if one of the partners has been married and is seeking a divorce. Again, these issues are likely to increase the emotional stress experienced by the couple. In addition, suitable accommodation is required for a blended family and obtaining this may be compromised by financial issues resulting from past relationships.

Parenting issues

A very significant issue affecting the adaptive functioning of blended families relates to parenting. This issue is more complex than issues faced by parents in an intact nuclear family because before joining a blended family parents will have experienced a particular style of parenting to which their own children have become accustomed. If a couple joins together in a blended family and they have quite different styles of parenting, they may find it difficult or be reluctant to adjust. This is likely to have unhelpful consequences for their relationship and the effective management of the children.

The problem of parenting is further complicated by the reality that one partner is not the biological parent of a child or children. In some cases, biological parents may become protective of their own children and may undermine their partner's attempts to join in the parenting process. Similarly, it is not uncommon for children to resent being parented by a step-parent, and attempt to undermine the couple relationship in response to this.

> **Parenting by a step-parent may raise issues for the natural parent**

Further, it would be unrealistic to expect that the parenting skills of a partner who has not previously had experience of parenting a child or children will be the same as the parenting skills of partner who has experience in parenting children. A partner who has not previously parented children may also have unrealistic expectations of children's behaviours.

Implications for counselling

In discussing the difficulties specific to blended families we have only covered common major difficulties that tend to arise in these families. However, every blended family is unique, so what is difficult for one family may not trouble another. We believe that there is no one best way in which a blended family should operate. What is important is that the partners explore and discover ways of operating that are effective and suit their particular family. Additionally, for a positive couple relationship to be achieved, it is essential that each partner adapt their behaviours so that the other's core needs are met.

Counselling Strategies to Address Parenting in a Blended Family

In this chapter we have first taken time to discuss difficulties which are specific to blended families. We have done this because we believe that it is helpful if a counsellor is familiar with these issues when working with parents in blended families to help them to discover and choose effective ways of addressing parenting problems. Parenting strategies will inevitably have an influence on the quality of family life in a blended family. If children in the family discover that the partners are not working together harmoniously with regard to parenting, there will almost certainly be consequences for relationships within the system. The children are likely to feel uncertain, insecure, and worried about expectations regarding their relationships and behaviours. However, if the partners are clear and united in their parenting approach, the children are more likely to be able to feel secure and to adapt to the family environment.

In order to address parenting issues within the blended family using the CACHO model, awareness needs to be raised with regard to the following:

- the couple's communication processes
- the couple's relationship
- the family system
- parenting roles
- parenting styles
- family communication processes.

The couple's communication processes

As with any couple in any family, unless the couple are able to communicate effectively they will not be able to address and resolve day-to-day problems arising in the family, and in particular they will not be able to resolve any parenting problems that arise. Where it emerges in the counselling process that the partners' communication styles are unhelpful, the strategies described in Chapter 19 for helping a couple to become more aware of the way they communicate and to enable them to develop more helpful and effective communication processes can be used.

The couple's relationship

We must recognize that children in blended families have previously experienced a breakdown in the relationship between their natural parents. Consequently, if they are to feel secure in a blended family they need to have confidence that the parental couple have a stable and comfortable relationship. It can therefore be useful to spend time in the counselling process in helping the couple to become aware of the importance of the way in which their couple relationship contributes to the well-being of the family as a whole. Where there are relationship problems, the strategies described in Chapter 19 can be used.

Perhaps because the day-to-day tasks involved in being a parent in a blended family can be onerous, and sometimes overwhelming, it is not unusual for the partners to fail to allocate sufficient time and attention to their couple relationship. Unless they do this, their relationship will be compromised, and the children are likely to perceive this with subsequent effects on their behaviours.

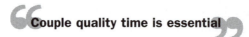
Couple quality time is essential

It is therefore appropriate that when counselling a couple with regard to parenting problems in a blended family that issues relating to their own relationship are addressed.

The counsellor may explore with them what strategies they can use to ensure that they have quality time together and are able to communicate privately with each other on a regular basis.

The family system

Understanding the family system is very important when parenting issues arise. Consequently, in counselling it may be helpful to draw a genogram, as shown in Figure 21.1. This genogram shows in dotted lines possible boundaries which might exist within the family. For example, in one blended family there may be a boundary around the mother and her natural daughter and son, a boundary around her and her partner, and a boundary around the complete family. However, in another blended family the boundaries may not be constructed in this way. For example, there could be a strong boundary around the father in the genogram and the mother's natural son, particularly if they have a common interest and, as a consequence, spend a lot of time together (Figure 21.2). As explained in Chapter 1, Minuchin believed that the most functional families had a strong boundary around the parental dyad (Minuchin, 1974). However, all families are unique and some blended families operate differently from others. Certainly, parenting issues are likely to arise if the parental couple are not adequately joined together and do not have a dyadic boundary of some type.

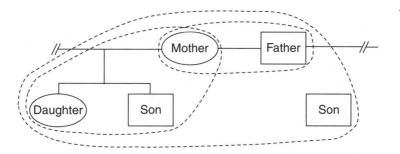

FIGURE 21.1   *Possible boundaries in a blended family*

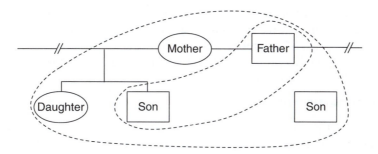

FIGURE 21.2   *Possible boundaries in a blended family*

Raising the couple's awareness by drawing a genogram on a whiteboard and asking them to draw in the boundaries they believe exist in their family can be useful in raising their awareness of the way their family functions so that they are able to make changes if they wish.

Parenting roles

In blended families there are frequently misunderstandings and/or confusion about parenting roles. These need to be explored by the counsellor so that the partners become fully aware of the way in which they are trying to carry out their roles and become clear about what their partner expects of them. It is not uncommon for one partner to give the other mixed messages about how they expect them to carry out their parenting role. Some partners are very clear in believing that it is not appropriate for their partner, who is not the natural parent, to manage the behaviour of their child or children. Also, it is common for older children to resent attempts by a step-parent to attempt to manage their behaviour.

Parenting roles need to be clear and agreed

If the partners are to carry out their parenting roles effectively they need to be clear about their expectations of each other, and to agree with regard to the way in which they carry out their parenting role. Additionally, it is usually sensible if the parents clearly communicate with the children about the way in which each of them will exercise their parenting role. Consequently, a counsellor can be helpful to a couple by raising their awareness of the issues, enabling them to talk through these, and to seek solutions which fit for them.

Parenting styles

In a blended family a partner's parenting style is likely to be influenced by their past experiences both as a child and as a parent in a previous relationship. Once again, the counsellor can help the couple to discuss their parenting styles with each other so that their awareness is raised of any differences. As a consequence of this, they may then look for new ways in which to parent which will be more satisfactory for them both.

Family communication processes

In all families, and particularly in blended families, it is helpful if all members of the family are clear about the way in which the family will operate, and also have an opportunity to express their opinions with regard to this. In counselling, it can therefore be helpful for a counsellor to draw parents' attention to the advantages of having free and open communication so that their own children and step-children are clear with regard to the way the family functions and also have an opportunity to express their own needs within the family.

KEY POINTS

- Creating a blended family necessarily involves changes in relationships within the joining families.
- The quality of the couple relationship will inevitably influence the functioning of the blended family.
- Environmental pressures, such as legal, financial, social, and practical issues, can cause partner stress in a blended family.
- To address parenting issues within a blended family, awareness can be raised with regard to the couple's communication processes and relationship, the family system, parenting roles and styles, and family communication processes.

QUESTIONS FOR GROUP DISCUSSION OR STUDENT ASSIGNMENTS

1. Discuss the role of the step-parent and any ethical issues which are involved in carrying out this role.
2. Discuss the issues which might arise for a child when one of their natural parents decides to join with a new partner in a blended family.

References

Adams, G.R. and Marshall, S.K. (1996) A developmental social psychology of identity: understanding the person-in-context. *Journal of Adolescence*, 19: 429–42.

Andreozzi, L.L. (1996) *Child-centered Family Therapy*. New York: Wiley.

Archer, R.P. (1997) *MMPI–A: Assessing Adolescent Psychopathology* (2nd edn). Hillsdale, NJ: Lawrence Erlbaum Associates.

Bailey, C.E. and Sori, C.E.F. (2005) Involving parents in children therapy. In C.E. Bailey (ed.), *Children in Therapy: Using the Family as a Resource*. New York: W.W. Norton. pp. 475–502.

Barker, P. (1986) *Basic Family Therapy* (2nd edn). London: Collins.

Barnhill, L. (1979) Healthy family systems. *Family Coordinator*, 28: 94–100.

Bateson, G. (1972) *Steps to an Ecology of Mind: Collected Essays in Anthropology, Psychiatry, Evolution, and Epistemology*. Lanham, MD: Jason Aronson.

Bateson, G., Jackson, D.D., Haley, J. and Weakland, J. (1956) Toward a theory of schizophrenia. *Behavioral Sciences,* 1: 251–64.

Bearsley-Smith, C. (2007) Adapting family therapy for step-families. *InPsych*, 29: 17.

Bennun, I. (1991) Working with the individual from the couple. In D. Hooper and W. Dryden (eds), *Couple Therapy: A Handbook*. Milton Keynes and Philadelphia, PA: Open University Press. pp. 110–24.

Berne, E. (1964) *Games People Play*. New York: Grove.

Berne, E., Steiner, C.M. and Dusay, J.M. (1996) Transactional analysis. In J.E. Groves (ed.), *Essential Papers in Short-term Dynamic Psychotherapy*. New York: New York University Press. pp. 149–70.

Bertolino, B. (1999) *Therapy with Troubled Teenagers: Rewriting Young Lives in Progress*. New York: Wiley.

Bowen, M. (1978) *Family Therapy in Clinical Practice*. New York: Jason Aronson.

Bowlby, J. (1964) *Maternal Care and Mental Health: A Report Prepared on Behalf of the World Health Organization as a Contribution to the United Nations Programme for the Welfare of Homeless Children*. Geneva: World Health Organization.

Brody, G.H. and Stoneman, Z. (1987) Sibling conflict: contributions of the siblings themselves, the parent–sibling relationship, and the broader family system. *Journal of Children in Contemporary Society,* 19: 39–54.

Bubenzer, D.L. and West, J.D. (1993) *Counselling Couples*. London: Sage.

Buhrmester, D. and Prager, K. (1995) Patterns and functions of self-disclosure. In K.J. Rotenberg (ed.), *Disclosure Processes in Children and Adolescents*. Cambridge: Cambridge University Press. pp. 10–56.

Butler, C. and Joyce, V. (1998) *Counselling Couples in Relationships: An Introduction to the Relate Approach*. Chichester: John Wiley.

Carr, A. (2009) Combating depression. In K. Geldard (ed.), *Practical Interventions for Young People at Risk*. London: Sage.

Champagne, M.P. and Walker–Hirsch, L.W. (1982) Circles: a self-organisation system for teaching appropriate social/sexual behaviour to mentally retarded/developmentally disabled persons. *Sexuality and Disability*, 5: 172–4.

Connolly, J. (1983) *Step-families: Towards a Clearer Understanding*. Condell Park, NSW: Corgi.

Dacey, J. and Kenny, M. (1997) *Adolescent Development*. Chicago, IL: Brown & Benchmark.

Dattilio, F.R. (ed.) (1998) *Case Studies in Couple and Family Therapy: Systemic and Cognitive Perspectives*. New York: Guilford.

de Shazer, S. (1985) *Keys to Solution in Brief Therapy*. New York: W.W. Norton.

de Shazer, S. (1991) *Putting Difference to Work*. New York: W.W. Norton.

Deutsch, M. (1973) *The Resolution of Conflict: Constructive and Destructive Processes*. New Haven, CT: Yale University Press.

Dryden, W. and Neenan, M. (2004) *The Rational Emotive Behavioural Approach to Therapeutic Change*. London: Sage.

Dusek, J.B. (1996) *Adolescent Development and Behavior*. Englewood Cliffs, NJ: Prentice-Hall.

Eisenberg, N., Guthrie, I.K., Murphy, B.C., Shepherd, S.A., Cumberland, A. and Carlo, G. (1999) Consistency and development of prosocial dispositions: a longitudinal study. *Child Development,* 70(6): 1360–72.

Elkind, D. (1967) Egocentrism in adolescence. *Child Development*, 38: 1025–34.

Ellis, A. (2001) *Overcoming Destructive Beliefs, Feelings, and Behaviours: New Directions for Rational Emotive Behaviour Therapy*. Amherst, NY: Prometheus.

Eltz, M.J., Shirk, S.R. and Sarlin, N. (1995) Alliance formation and treatment outcome among maltreated adolescents. *Child Abuse and Neglect*, 19: 419–31.

Epstein, M., Bishop, D. and Levin, S. (1978) The McMaster model of family functioning. *Journal of Marriage and Family Counselling*, 4: 19–31.

Etzioni, A. (1993) *The Spirit of Community: Rights, the Reinvention of American Society*. New York: Simon & Schuster.

Fransella, F. and Dalton, P. (1990) *Personal Construct Counselling in Action*. London: Sage.

Freedman, J. and Combs, G. (2002) *Narrative Therapy with Couples… and a Whole Lot More!* Adelaide: Dulwich Centre Publications.

Friedman, S. (1997) *Time-effective Psychotherapy*. Boston, MA: Allyn & Bacon.

Gajewski, N. and Mayo, P. (1989) *Social Skills Strategies*. New York: Thinking Publications.

Geldard, K. (2006) Adolescent peer counselling. Unpublished doctoral dissertation. Queensland University of Technology, Brisbane, Queensland, Australia.

Geldard, K. and Geldard, D. (2001) *Working with Children in Groups: A Handbook for Counsellors, Educators and Community Workers*. Basingstoke: Palgrave Macmillan.

Geldard, K. and Geldard, D. (2004) *Counselling Adolescents: The Proactive Approach*. London: Sage.

Geldard, K, and Geldard, D. (2005a) *Basic Personal Counselling: A Training Manual for Counsellors*. Sydney: Pearson.

Geldard, K. and Geldard, D. (2005b) *Practical Counselling Skills: An Integrative Approach*. Basingstoke: Palgrave Macmillan.

Geldard, K. and Geldard, D. (2008a) *Counselling Children: A Practical Introduction* (3rd edn). London: Sage.

Geldard, K. and Geldard, D. (2008b) *Personal Counseling Skills: An Integrative Approach*. Springfield, IL: Thomas.

Gergen, K. (2000) *An Invitation to Social Construction*. London: Sage.

Glasser, W. (2001) *Counselling with Choice Therapy*. New York: Quill.

Glasser, W. and Wubbolding, R. (1995) Reality therapy. In R. Corisini and D. Wedding (eds), *Current Psychotherapies* (5th edn). Itasca, IL: Peacock. pp. 293–321.

Goldenberg, I. and Goldenberg, H. (1990) *Counselling Today's Families*. Pacific Grove, CA: Brooks/Cole.

Hanks, S.E. (1996) Domestic violence. In H. Kessler (ed.), *Treating Couples*. San Francisco, CA: Jossey-Bass. pp. 189–227.

Harris, T.A. (1973) *I'm OK – You're OK*. London: Pan.

Heidemann, S. and Hewitt, D. (1992) *Pathways to Play*. Minneapolis, MN: Redleaf Press.

Hendrick, S.S. (1995) *Close Relationships: What Couple Therapists Can Learn*. Pacific Grove, CA: Brooks/Cole.

Ianni, F.A.J. (1989) *The Search for Structure: A Report on American Youth Today*. New York: Free Press.

Jackson, D.D. (1959) Family interaction, family homoeostasis, and some implications for conjoint family therapy. In J. Masserman (ed.), *Individual and Family Dynamics*. New York: Grune & Stratton. pp. 35–52.

Johnson, V.A. (1996) The parenting couple. In H. Kessler (ed.), *Treating Couples*. San Francisco, CA: Jossey-Bass. pp. 229–55.

Kendall, P.C. and Southam-Gerow, M.A. (1996) Long-term follow-up of cognitive behavioural therapy for anxiety disordered youth. *Journal of Consulting and Clinical Psychology*, 64: 724–30.

Kessler, H. (1996) Basics of couple therapy. In H. Kessler (ed.), *Treating Couples*. San Francisco, CA: Jossey-Bass. pp. 2–34.

Kessler, H. and Thaler Singer, M. (1996) Myths in couples therapy. In H. Kessler (ed.), *Treating Couples*. San Francisco, CA: Jossey-Bass. pp. 35–60.

Kressel, K. (2000) Mediation. In M. Deutsch and P.T. Coleman (eds), *The Handbook of Conflict Resolution: Theory and Practice*. San Francisco, CA: Jossey-Bass. pp. 522–45.

Lee, C.C, and Richardson, B.L. (1991) *Multicultural Issues in Counseling: New Approaches to Diversity*. Alexandria, VA: AACD.

Leveton, E. (1984) *Adolescent Crisis: Family Counseling Approaches*. New York: Springer.

Linzey, G. (1959) On the classification of projective techniques. *Psychological Bulletin*, 56: 158–68.

Lowe, R. (2004) *Family Therapy: A Constructive Framework*. London: Sage.

Lowe, R. and Guy, G. (1999) From group to peer supervision: a reflecting team process. *Psychotherapy in Australia*, 6(1): 36–41.

Mabey, J. and Sorensen, B. (1995) *Counselling for Young People*. Buckingham: Open University Press.

Martin, A. (1997) On teenagers and tattoos. *Journal of the American Academy of Child and Adolescent Psychiatry*, 36: 860–1.

Mayer, J.D. and Salovey, P. (1997) What is emotional intelligence? In P. Salovey and D. Sluyter (eds), *Emotional Development and Emotional Intelligence: Educational Implications*. New York: Basic Books. pp. 3–31.

Melnick, J. (2000) Power and intimacy. Paper presented at the 2nd International Gestalt Therapy Conference, Brisbane, Australia, August.

Mercer, J. (2006) *Understanding Attachment*. Westport, CT: Praeger.

Minuchin, S. (1974) *Families and Family Therapy*. Cambridge, MA: Harvard University Press.

Nichols, M.P. and Schwartz, R.C. (2007) *The Essentials of Family Therapy* (3rd edn). Boston, MA: Pearson.

Oaklander, V. (1988) *Windows to Our Children*. New York: Center for Gestalt Development.

O'Hanlon, B. and Wilk, J. (1987) *Shifting Contexts: The Generation of Effective Psychotherapy*. New York: Guilford Press.

Olson, D.H., Russell, C. and Sprenkle, D.H. (1983) Circumplex model of marital and family systems: VI. Theoretical update. *Family Process*, 22: 69–83.

O'Rourke, K. and Worzbyt, J.C. (1996) *Support Groups for Children*. Philadelphia, PA: Taylor & Francis.

Parry, A. and Doan, R. (1994) *Story Re-Visions: Narrative Therapy in the Postmodern World*. New York: Guilford Press.

Philliber, S., Kaye, J.W., Herrling, S. and West, E. (2002) Preventing pregnancy and improving health care access among teenagers: an evaluation of the Children's Aid Society–Carrera Program. *Perspectives on Sexual Reproductive Health*, 34: 244–51.

Piaget, J. (1948/1966) *Psychology of Intelligence*. New York: Harcourt Brace Jovanovich.

Pizzamiglio, M.T. (2003) Variability in perceived social competence as a predictor of emotional reactivity in early adolescence. *Dissertation Abstracts International*, 63(10) 4966B. (UMI No. AAINQ73351).

Prochaska, J.M. and Prochaska, J.O. (1985) Children's views of the causes and 'cures' of sibling rivalry. *Child Welfare*, LXIV: 427–33.

Reis, I.L. and Lee, G.R. (1988) *Family Systems in America* (4th edn). New York: Holt, Rinehart & Winston.

Resnick, R. (1995). Gestalt therapy: principles, prisms and perspectives. *British Gestalt Journal*, 4(1): 3–13.

Reynolds, C. (2005) Gestalt therapy with children. In A.L. Woldt and S.M. Toman (eds), *Gestalt Therapy: History, Theory, and Practice*. Thousand Oak, CA: Sage. pp. 153–78.

Rose, S.D. and Edleson, J.L. (1987) *Working with Children and Adolescents in Groups: A Multi-method Approach*. San Francisco, CA: Jossey-Bass.

Ruckert, J. (2000) A creative approach to Gestalt Therapy. Paper presented at the 2nd International Gestalt Therapy Conference, Brisbane, Australia, August.

Ryce-Menuhin, J. (1992) *Jungian Sand Play: The Wonderful Therapy*. New York: Routledge.

Safyer, A.W., Leahy, B.H. and Colan, N.B. (1995) The impact of work on adolescent development. *Families in Society*. January, 76: 38–45.

Satir, V.M. and Baldwin, M. (1983) *Satir Step by Step: A Guide to Creating Change in Families*. Palo Alto, CA: Science and Behavior Books.

Satir, V.M. and Bitter, J.R. (2000) The therapist and family therapy. In A.M. Horne (ed.), *Family Counseling and Therapy* (3rd edn). Itasca, IL: Peacock. pp. 62–101.

Schlossberg, N.K. (1989) Marginality and mattering: key issues in building community. *New Directions for Children Services*, 48: 5–15.

Selvini Palazzoli, M., Boscolo, L., Cecchin, G. and Prata, G. (1980) Hypothesising–circularity–neutrality: the guidelines for the conductor of the session. *Family Process,* 19: 3–12.

Shantz, C.U. and Hartup, W.W. (1992) Conflict and development: an introduction. In C.U. Shantz and W.W. Hartup (eds), *Conflict in Child and Adolescent Development.* New York: Cambridge University Press. pp. 1–14.

Sharry, J. (2004) *Counselling Children, Adolescents and Families.* London: Sage.

Shave, D. and Shave, B. (1989) *Early Adolescence and the Search for Self: A Developmental Perspective.* New York: Praeger.

Shirk, R.S. and Kaver, M. (2003) Prediction of treatment outcome from relationship variables in child and adolescent psychotherapy: a meta-analytic review. *Journal of Consulting and Clinical Psychology,* 71: 452–64.

Singer, D.G. and Revenson, T.A. (1996) *A Piaget Primer: How a Child Thinks* (2nd edn). New York: Penguin.

Smith, J. and Ross, H. (2007) Training parents to mediate sibling disputes affects children's negotiation and conflict understanding. *Child Development,* 78: 790–805.

Spinelli, E. (1996) The existential–phenomenological paradigm. In R. Woolfe and W. Dryden (eds), *Handbook of Counselling Psychology.* London: Sage. pp. 180–200.

Steinhauer, P.D., Santa-Barbara, J. and Skinner, H. (1984) The process model of family functioning. *Canadian Journal of Psychiatry,* 29: 77–88.

Street, E. (2006) Family and systemic therapy. In C. Feltham and I. Horton (eds), *The Sage Handbook of Counselling and Psychotherapy.* London: Sage. pp. 523–7.

Tseng, W.S. and McDermott, J.F. (1979) Triaxial family classification. *Journal of the American Academy of Child Psychiatry,* 18, 22–43.

Vondracek, F.W. and Corneal, S. (1995) Psychodrama. In F. Vondracek and S. Corneal, *Strategies for Resolving Individual and Family Problems.* Pacific Grove, CA: Brooks/Cole. pp. 282–92.

Waiswol, N. (1995) Projective techniques as psychotherapy. *American Journal of Psychotherapy,* 49(2): 244–59.

Weeks, G. and L'Abate, L. (1982) *Paradoxical Psychotherapy: Theory and Practice with Individuals, Couples, and Families.* New York: Brunner/Mazel.

Weeks, G.R. and Treat, S. (1992) *Couples in Treatment: Techniques and Approaches for Effective Practice.* New York: Brunner/Mazel.

Weiner, I., Stricker, G. and Widiger, T.A. (eds) (2003) *Handbook of Psychology.* Chichester: John Wiley & Sons.

Wetchler, J.L. (1996) Social constructionist family therapies. In F. Piercy and D. Sprenckle (eds), *Family Therapy Source Book.* New York: Guilford Press. pp. 129–52.

Whitaker, C.A. (1976) The hindrance of theory in clinical work. In P.J. Guerin (ed.), *Family Therapy: Theory and Practice.* New York: Gardner Press. pp. 182–92.

White, M. and Epston, D. (1990) *Narrative Means to Therapeutic Ends.* New York: W.W. Norton.

Winter, D.A. (1996) The constructivist paradigm. In R. Woolfe and W. Dryden (eds), *Handbook of Counselling Psychology.* London: Sage. pp. 241–60.

Yontef, G. (1993) Gestalt therapy. In C.E. Watkins (ed.), *Handbook of Psychotherapy Supervision.* New York: John Wiley. pp. 147–63.

Yontef, G.M. (2005) Gestalt therapy theory of change. In A.L. Woldt and S.M. Toman (eds), *Gestalt Therapy: History, Theory, and Practice*. Thousand Oak, CA: Sage. pp. 81–100.

Zinker, J. (1978) *Creative Processes in Gestalt Therapy*. New York: Random House.

Index

Research Methods Books
from SAGE

Action Research
in the Classroom

Vivienne Baumfield, Elaine Hall & Kate Wall

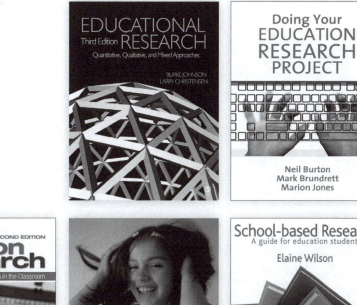

EDUCATIONAL
Third Edition RESEARCH
Quantitative, Qualitative, and Mixed Approaches

BURKE JOHNSON
LARRY CHRISTENSEN

Doing Your
EDUCATION
RESEARCH
PROJECT

Neil Burton
Mark Brundrett
Marion Jones

SECOND EDITION
Action
Research
Teachers as Researchers in the Classroom

Craig A. Mertler

Researching
with Children &
Young People

Research,
Design Methods
and Analysis

Kay Tisdall, John Davis
& Michael Gallagher

School-based Research
A guide for education students

Elaine Wilson

www.sagepub.co.uk/education

SSAGE

The Qualitative Research Kit

Edited by Uwe Flick

Read sample chapters online now!

Michael Angrosino — Doing Ethnographic and Observational Research
The SAGE Qualitative Research Kit — Edited by Uwe Flick

Marcus Banks — Using Visual Data in Qualitative Research
The SAGE Qualitative Research Kit — Edited by Uwe Flick

Rosaline Barbour — Doing Focus Groups
The SAGE Qualitative Research Kit — Edited by Uwe Flick

Uwe Flick — Designing Qualitative Research
The SAGE Qualitative Research Kit — Edited by Uwe Flick

Uwe Flick — Managing Quality in Qualitative Research
The SAGE Qualitative Research Kit — Edited by Uwe Flick

Graham Gibbs — Analyzing Qualitative Data
The SAGE Qualitative Research Kit — Edited by Uwe Flick

Steinar Kvale — Doing Interviews
The SAGE Qualitative Research Kit — Edited by Uwe Flick

Tim Rapley — Doing Conversation, Discourse and Document Analysis
The SAGE Qualitative Research Kit — Edited by Uwe Flick

www.sagepub.co.uk